Charles Chesnutt Reappraised

Charles Chesnutt Reappraised

Essays on the First Major
African American Fiction Writer

Edited by
DAVID GARRETT IZZO *and*
MARIA ORBAN

McFarland & Company, Inc., Publishers
Jefferson, North Carolina, and London

ALSO OF INTEREST AND FROM MCFARLAND

The Influence of Mysticism on 20th Century British and American Literature, by David Garrett Izzo (2009)

Christopher Isherwood Encyclopedia, by David Garrett Izzo (2005)

W.H. Auden Encyclopedia, by David Garrett Izzo (2004)

The Writings of Richard Stern: The Education of an Intellectual Everyman, by David Garrett Izzo (2002)

Huxley's Brave New World*: Essays,* edited by David Garrett Izzo and Kim Kirkpatrick (2008)

Henry James Against the Aesthetic Movement: Essays on the Middle and Late Fiction, edited by David Garrett Izzo and Daniel T. O'Hara (2006)

Stephen Vincent Benét: Essays on His Life and Work, edited by David Garrett Izzo and Lincoln Konkle (2003)

The essay "'Those Folks Downstairs Don't Believe in Ghosts': The Eradication of Folklore in the Literature of Charles W. Chesnutt" originally appeared in *CLA Journal* 49:2 (2005): 184–204 and is used by permission of The College Language Association.

LIBRARY OF CONGRESS CATALOGUING-IN-PUBLICATION DATA

Charles Chesnutt reappraised : essays on the first major African American fiction writer / edited by David Garrett Izzo and Maria Orban.
    p.   cm.
Includes bibliographical references and index.

ISBN 978-0-7864-4111-2
softcover : 50# alkaline paper ∞

1. Chesnutt, Charles W. (Charles Waddell), 1858–1932 — Criticism and interpretation.   2. African Americans in literature.   I. Izzo, David Garrett.   II. Orban, Maria.
PS1292.C6Z64   2009
813'.4 — dc22   2009004647

British Library cataloguing data are available

On the cover: Charles Waddell Chesnutt at the age of 40, Cleveland Public Library Image Collection; background ©2009 Shutterstock

Manufactured in the United States of America

McFarland & Company, Inc., Publishers
  Box 611, Jefferson, North Carolina 28640
  www.mcfarlandpub.com

To Carol Ann Corrody, David Powell, and Paul Robeson
— David Garrett Izzo

In loving memory of my mother
— Maria Orban

Table of Contents

Introduction

by *Maria Orban*

"I will live down the prejudice, I will crush it out. I will show to the world that a man may spring from a race of slaves, and yet far excel many of the boasted ruling race."
— Charles W. Chesnutt

In a speech given to the Normal Literary Society in Fayetteville, N.C., on March 10, 1882, Chesnutt argued "the class of men in whose lives we feel the most intense interest, is that class who are commonly known as 'self-made men,' men who, with few opportunities, few adventitious advantages, have exhibited the development of mind under what seemed insurmountable difficulties" (McElrath, 34). Chesnutt himself more than amply demonstrated this more sophisticated variation of the cultural myth of masculine success and individualism, "the development of mind," by not only developing his own mind, a feat which under the historical circumstances of his life would have been quite an accomplishment in itself, but also by developing the minds of his contemporaries and of many generations to come. As for the "insurmountable difficulties" he had to overcome, they were many.

Born in Ohio in 1858 to free black parents from Fayetteville, N.C., Chesnutt grew up in the small town in the South during the Reconstruction era, experiencing racial discrimination. He attended the Howard School, a well-funded, progressive, public institution with better standards of education at the time than the white schools. Improving himself as a human being and his prospects in the world through learning was one of his lifelong goals and he pursued it passionately. He clearly crossed the color line, winning the help and esteem of a bookstore owner and of his Jewish German teacher, who contributed to his education in spite of the racial divide. His aim was to beat the system through education.

1

He first secured a job as an assistant teacher in Charlotte and later rose to the top of his profession when he was appointed at age 22 principal of the State Colored Normal School in Fayetteville. But this ambitious young man had big plans. He took every opportunity to improve his education in spite of the meager possibilities available to him and he proved worthy of every opportunity. At the same time he was painfully aware of the limits imposed on his success by an unfair system. He made several attempts to relocate North and escape racial discrimination. Eventually, he resigned his position at the school and moved first to New York and then to Cleveland in search of better career opportunities. He became a successful businessman and well-established member of the middle class. But it was a literary career that had a special allure for him. He wrote in his journal: "Every time I read a good novel, I want to write one. It is the dream of my life — to be an author! It is not so much the *monstrari digito*, though that has something to do with my aspirations. It is not altogether the money. It is a mixture of motives. I want fame; I want money" (Brodhead, 154).

And an author he was. The first major African American writer, Charles Waddell Chesnutt scored his first literary success with the publication of the conjure stories in the late 1880s and followed up with his first novel, *The House Behind the Cedars*, in 1900. He is the author of more than fifty stories published in newspapers and magazines, two collections of short stories, three novels published during his lifetime and three more posthumously, two plays, over twenty essays, poems, letters, journals, speeches, and a biography of Frederick Douglass. Controversial then and now, he acquired a national reputation through his protest literature and as an integrationist. In doing so he managed to cross the color line and be published in prestigious periodicals, winning the appreciation of a racially diverse audience. Although his popularity peaked during his lifetime and then declined, since the 1960s there has been a notable interest in his works, which have been frequently reprinted. The literary conventions of the nineteenth century, the novel of passing, and the drama of the mulatto have lost much of their appeal to twentieth and twenty-first century audiences, but Chesnutt's reputation as a writer and an equal rights activist has continued to grow, against all odds. The expansion of the academic canon and the emergence of African American studies have played a part in the regenerated interest for his works. The Chesnutt scholarship has kept expanding to keep up with this interest. For too long, he was overlooked at best and misinterpreted at worst, at times by great critics. Nevertheless, there has been a resurgence of articles studying his work published in periodicals and books, albeit few and far between.

This collection of critical essays reevaluates the Chesnutt legacy from the perspective of the twenty-first century, introducing new scholarship reflective of the many facets of his fiction, his sophisticated narrative strategies, and the dominant themes and particular political and social issues raised by his construction of race. The essays provide historical and cultural contexts that frame a new epistemological reality for his narrative of redemption. In a way, to follow Chesnutt's line of reasoning, they "illustrate the process by which such men [self-made men, Chesnutt specifically] rise to eminence" (35).

Linda Belau and Ed Cameron compare the perspectives of two main African American literary sources on the Wilmington riot in "Charles W. Chesnutt, Jack Thorne and the African American Literary Response to the 1898 Wilmington Race Riot." The political implications of the rhetorical choices become evident when they reconstruct the details of the event using various contemporary sources to underscore the role aesthetics can play in destabilizing epistemological unity and in amending history. They take a psychoanalytical approach to violence in discussing the mechanisms by which Chesnutt contributed the African American perspective immediately following the event, bringing a scrutiny that would change public perception. They also highlight Chesnutt's role in reconfiguring its historical and cultural legacy.

"'The Fruit of My Own Imagination': Charles W. Chesnutt's *The Marrow of Tradition* in the Age of Realism," **Willie J. Harrell, Jr.'s** essay, explores the part representation and aesthetic choices play in configuring the perspective of the events classified as the Wilmington riot, while tracing the constitutive elements of Chesnutt's invention of identity, including race identity.

Christopher Bundrick's essay, "'I Shall Leave the Realm of Fiction': Conjure, Genre, and Passing in the Fiction of Charles W. Chesnutt," re-evaluates Chesnutt's legacy for the late nineteenth and early twentieth century African American literary tradition and the way in which questions of race surface at the intersection of literary and cultural traditions. The essay examines how Chesnutt's texts resist the structures of racism by subverting genre conventions in order to undermine the cultural conventions they represent and expose the values they are rooted in. Chesnutt's narrative techniques distort the predictable norms in order to call into question the process that constructs the norm and the deviation from the norm, and ultimately the cultural traditions supporting a racist hierarchy that shape generic expectations.

Wiley Cash in "'Those folks downstairs believe in ghosts': The Eradication of Folklore in the Novels of Charles W. Chesnutt" examines the character of Uncle Julius in *The Conjure Tales*, with whom Chesnutt wished to enchant America's white readership by entertaining them with the palatable and much loved plantation lore of the kindhearted slave while simultaneously chipping away at the very prejudice and stereotypes that fostered and propagated the same image.

Maria Orban's "The Fiction of Race: Folklore to Classical Literature" analyzes Chesnutt's choice of literary sources and the significance of his shift from folklore to classical literature in *The House Behind the Cedars*, underscoring Chesnutt's ambivalent position of being caught between two worlds; an authorial position that makes him a representative and an outsider at the same time for both the white and black cultures. The question the essay raises is: if race is a cultural construct, what is the significance of identifying with a particular literary model, the romance in this case, in reading Rena's body as a text?

Coleman C. Myron's essay "Charles W. Chesnutt's *The House Behind the Cedars:* An Outlaw(ed) Reading" analyzes Rena Walden by placing her within the American tradition of the outlaw, the countercultural hero that goes against the norms of the society, one in a line of cultural heroes such as Huck Finn. She breaks with her predictable evolution in the novel triggered by the choices available to her, choices that highlight the all-enveloping cycle of race and class prejudice that is pervasive and annihilates opposition. She wants to step outside the system in a heroic attempt to forge a parallel universe ruled by her own values.

Kim Kirkpatrick provides an analysis of the double narrative structure and the layers of readings and readers provided by Chesnutt's *The Conjure Woman* in "Reading the Transgressive Body: Phenomenology in the Stories of Charles W. Chesnutt." The multiplicity of readers and readings is also provided by "reading" the bodies as texts allowing multiple levels of interpretation.

"'Your People Will Never Rise in the World:' Chesnutt's Message to a Black Readership," by Tyrie J. Smith, investigates the intriguing implications of the assumption that Chesnutt might have written not with a white audience in mind, the traditional critical approach, but instead a black audience. The essay explores what effect this supposition of reversed perspective would trigger in evaluating Chesnutt's message and to what extent it would affect our understanding of his views on race and the plight of the new, liberated black individual.

The fight for authority over American historical memory and the way Chesnutt's philosophy of history plays into it is the topic of Zoe Trodd's essay, "Vanished Past and Vanishing Point: Charles W. Chesnutt's Short Stories and the Problem of American Historical Memory." She examines how Chesnutt's tales of metamorphoses that employ embedded stories and framing layered narratives create a space where possible worlds, incommensurable spaces, and multiple voices co-exist, and how this newly created space undermines the dominant monolithic authorial voice model.

Gregory E. Rutledge further pursues Chesnutt's aesthetic response to the legal and cultural justifications of racism during the post–Civil War period in "All Green with Epic Potential: Chesnutt Goes to the *Marrow of Tradition* to Re-Construct America's Epic Body." He argues that many critics considered Chesnutt's use of melodrama and sentimentality in *The Marrow of Tradition* a failure and proposes a new reading instead, using the figure of the epic trickster and "an African-American epic aesthetic" Chesnutt created. Rutledge provides a historical view of the aesthetic category of the epic, of its Western and African variants, in order to establish its genesis and function in the novel. Against the background of epic traditions, Chesnutt critiques the ethical instability of the myth of superiority at the center of the body politic and turns the policies of the status quo into satire.

In "'The Wife of His Youth': A Trickster Tale," **Cynthia Wachtell** advances an alternative reading of Chesnutt's tale, a trickster reading, and argues that so far the story has been "under-understood." Her argument shows how the social satire of the color line has been ignored. She also provides a feminist take on Liza Jane using *The Odyssey* as a point of comparison, and investigates the racial and gender dynamics at play in Chesnutt's story. The subversive upset in the balance of power, Wachtell argues, makes this tale a tale of conquest, the triumph of the empowered underdog.

Tiel Lundy looks into a little discussed aspect of Chesnutt's legacy, namely the influence of African socio-religious traditions. His essay, "With Myriad Subtleties: Recognizing an Africanist Presence in Charles W. Chesnutt's *The Conjure Woman*," invites a reading of the tales reflective of a cultural identity that incorporates African thinking leading to an alternative moral order.

Julie Iromuanya's essay "Passing for What? *The Marrow of Tradition's* Minstrel Critique of the Unlawfulness of Law" analyzes the use of the passing trope and minstrelsy, humor and the grotesque to underscore competing discourses of racial classification and racial loyalty. The tension generated by a complex pattern of parallels and oppositions along racial and social lines points to the incongruent nature of values and laws that allow for a racial construction of suffering and sacrifice. The radically shifting definitions of race underscore Chesnutt's views of ethnicity and race as invention and social performance.

Michelle Taylor reevaluates Chesnutt's role in the Harlem Renaissance era by analyzing the importance of the memories of the slave past to forging a representative male identity and securing the place of black people in the future in "Geographies of Freedom: Race, Mobility, and Uplift in Charles Chesnutt's Northern Writing." She traces the ideological complexities of his model of modern black manhood emerging from competing historical narratives. This model, she argues, promoted a masculine ideal that shows continuity between Chesnutt and the political discourse of the Harlem Renaissance writers.

In "Motherhood, Martyrdom and Cultural Dichotomy in Charles W. Chesnutt's *The House Behind the Cedars*," **B. Omega Moore** analyzes what is arguably the most complex of all human relationships — the one between a mother and her children — as depicted in *The House Behind the Cedars*.

In the Epilogue, Michelle Taylor considers the new interest in evaluating Chesnutt's body of work.

The immediate value of this collection of literary criticism is that it provides fresh perspectives in reinterpreting Chesnutt's works, foregrounding his modernity, and proposes a necessary reassessment of his position within the American and African American literary traditions. It is definitely not the ultimate evaluation of his work, but, nevertheless, it writes a new chapter in the expanding body of criticism on the work of Charles Chesnutt.

WORKS CITED

Brodhead, Richard M. *The Journals of Charles W. Chesnutt*. Ed. Richard M. Brodhead. Durham: Duke University Press, 1993.

McElrath, Joseph R. "Superstitions and the Folklore of the South." In *Charles W. Chesnutt: Essays and Speeches*. Eds. Joseph R. McElrath, Jr., Robert C. Leitz, III and Jesse S. Crisler. Stanford, CA: Stanford University Press, 2000.

CHAPTER 1

Charles W. Chesnutt, Jack Thorne and the African American Literary Response to the 1898 Wilmington Race Riot

Linda Belau and *Ed Cameron*

In the establishment of the super-ego we have before us, as it were, an example of the way in which the present is changed into the past.

— Sigmund Freud

Despite recent publication of a draft of the Wilmington Commission Report, it is a little-known fact that a violent race riot raged in southern North Carolina in 1898, well after the political upheavals of Reconstruction. Supplementing this historical oversight, however, a number of fictional treatments of the event have been instrumental in bringing this important incident to a wider public audience, and have also taken their turn at representing the event in order to determine its cultural legacy and public reception. In this sense, the only two novels that were written by African American authors shortly after the event (Charles Chesnutt's *The Marrow of Tradition*, written in 1901 and Jack Thorne's *Hanover*, written in 1900) have attempted, each in its own way, to represent the African American perspective.

These fictional literary works reconfigure and recontextualize the journalistic and historical accounts of the event, which are not necessarily intentionally untruthful, but are, for the most part, plagued by a certain blindness in regard to their investment in the racializing of the historical account. Almost every single newspaper report, for example, characterized the Wilmington incident as an uprising by insurgent blacks led by white Republicans who had over-identified with black radicals and desired what was called "Negro dom-ination" in the South. The rhetoric of white supremacy, which was rampant in the popular press at the time, supported the notion that patriotic white Democrats saved the day by protecting the town from marauding and mur-derous blacks. On the cover of *Collier's Weekly*, a New York newspaper that covered the riot and interviewed one of its main instigators, a white man named Alfred Waddell, the artistic rendering of the event shows an unruly mob of black men firing pistols. In fact, just five days after the racial mas-sacre — the so-called "riot" — a *Wilmington Messenger* article entitled "Let Us Have Peace" praises whites for their inborn heroism and sense of justice. Both of these publications, however, gave a skewed and inaccurate representation of what actually occurred.

Because of the rhetoric of white supremacy and the fact that whites con-trolled all mediums for representing the event to the greater public, every news account depicted things in this manner. There was absolutely no rep-resentation of the event from the black perspective, which would have (more accurately) shown angry mobs of whites shooting at unarmed black men and burning black businesses to the ground. This absence of black perspective is not surprising, however, given the fact that the riot initially organized itself around the burning of *The Daily Record*, a black-owned and managed daily newspaper. Immediate justification for the riot was a demand for complete destruction of *The Daily Record* press and the exile of its editor, Alex Man-ley, a prominent and educated African American. Using his newspaper to counter some of the white supremacy rhetoric that pervaded recent elections in the city and throughout the state, Manley's newspaper was the only pub-lic forum that dared present the black perspective. With the destruction of *The Daily Record* and no newspaper to represent the black experience of the riot, the racist white rhetoric that accompanied every report was disseminated unchecked, and no newspaper account ever considered the event from the per-spective of the African American victim.

It is interesting to note how the racist rhetoric that frames the event — both as the condition of its advent as well as the vehicle that legitimated it — still persists in the way we characterize it, even today, as a "race riot." For, in truth, what took place in Wilmington on November 10, 1898, (and the months preceding) was more of an illegal seizure of a duly elected government and the unprovoked slaying of a peaceful citizenry than it was a riot. In this sense, "massacre" or "coup d'etat" is a more accurate characterization of the events. According to William Gleason, the "white democratic interpretation of the riot stood unchallenged by American historians until the 1951 publication of Helen G. Edmund's *The Negro and Fusion Politics in North Carolina, 1894–1901*" (23–24). No one had presumed until that time that "race riot" might refer to the illegal and unruly practices of the whites who controlled all the mediums for disseminating information to the public. To refer to the chain of events and their aftermath as a riot, in fact, plays directly into the racist rhetoric of the Southern Democratic Party, which was entirely responsible for the massacre and the subsequent disenfranchisement of the African American population. It was, after all, the Southern Democrat who first used the rhetoric of "race riot" and the fear of racial insurgency to impose a clearly demarcated color line and a successful campaign of white supremacy, which were both so elemental in this massacre.

W.E.B. Du Bois wrote that "the problem of the twentieth century is the problem of the color line" (23). From the perspective of race relations in the nineteenth century, Du Bois's statement is optimistic in its very essence, especially since the "color line," as such, really did not exist during the era of slavery. Because African Americans were completely powerless, because they had absolutely no political or cultural currency, race was hardly a "problem" in the political sphere. The establishment of a clearly demarcated color line within the horizon of political concerns is, in fact, a product of the emancipation of the slave and the establishment of a social order that included the freedman in the universe of the political, albeit in the most restricted way possible. As the American South moved beyond slavery and through Reconstruction toward the turn of the century, the color line, so sharply drawn at the close of slavery, began to show signs of blurring, at least in southern North Carolina. By the mid–1890s, in fact, it might have begun to appear to some that a new era of racial equality was dawning. This, at least, is how things appeared in Wilmington in 1897 and early 1898.

Given its majority of African American citizens and the burgeoning economic prosperity of its black citizenry, the Wilmington of 1898 was just the place for this new beginning. Considering the era, Wilmington was a fairly integrated city and the two races lived harmoniously, side-by-side, in what was then the largest municipality in the state. According to Leon Prather, "Wilmington was one of the best cities for blacks in the American South" in the late nineteenth century (16). Conditions steadily improved for Wilmington's African American population toward the close of the century, especially since the state political campaigns of 1894 had succeeded in unseating, almost universally, the conservative Southern Democratic Party, a defeat that led the way to more political and economic power for the black community. Because the Southern Democratic Party in North Carolina had been slowly losing its voting base — particularly white farmers who defected to the Populist Party after economic troubles had been largely ignored by the ruling Democrats — the progressive, largely African American, Republican Party was able to merge with the working class, largely white, Populist Party and sweep the state elections in 1894, winning control of both houses of the General Assembly. This initially appeared to be a great boon for the social, economic, and political advancement of the black man in North Carolina. According to Prather, however, in the alliance of working-class whites with the Republicans and the subsequent political defeat of the racist Democrats, who had run things "their way" for decades, "lay the wellspring of the racial massacre of 1898" (Brodhead, 18).

Much to the chagrin of the Southern Democrat and "mainly due to black voting, the Fusionist cause won every statewide race in North Carolina" in 1896 (19). As class interests were placed above racial solidarity in this interracial "Fusion" ticket, the new governor of the state, white Republican Daniel L. Russell of Wilmington, set out to dismantle the racist Democratic Party's hold on Wilmington's local governance. With its strong contingent of African American voters, the 1894 Fusionist legislature first established an election law to restore local self-government and autonomy that also "abolished the Democrat's policy of appointment of local offices, making them subject to popular election" (19). This gave the Republican Party a marked political advantage in Wilmington since African Americans constituted the majority of the city's population. After the spring elections of 1897 in Wilmington, a number of key political positions had gone to the Fusionists. Democrats found themselves out in the cold as the mayor and the majority of the city's ten aldermen, including two African Americans, claimed Fusionist alliance.

Completely panicked by the turn of events, white Democrats set their sights on Wilmington's fall elections of 1898. Democrats vowed that they would take the elections, whatever the cost, and embarked on an aggressive campaign of white supremacy that was supported by the demand for "home rule." "Negro domination" must end, they maintained, if what they called "permanent good government by the party of the White Man" was to emerge victorious (Cecelski and Tyson, 8). This response to the Fusionist landslide was not restricted to Wilmington, however. All across the state, Democrats embraced the cause of white supremacy in response to their massive defeat at the spring polls. According to Prather, this white supremacy campaign, "unparalleled in American history," was the condition of possibility for the Wilmington massacre (Prather 20). White supremacy rhetoric played directly into the fantasies of Wilmington's poor white population, which was already disgruntled about the growing black middle class and had been growing increasingly resentful about the higher standard of living their African American neighbors were beginning to enjoy. While the rhetoric of white supremacy and "Negro domination" certainly caught the attention of whites across the state, however, it was not enough to decisively reverse the blurring of the color line that had become the norm in Wilmington during the 1890s. In order to re-establish a clearly demarcated color line that would ensure blacks had no political or economic power, the Democrats needed an issue that would transcend party lines. So naturally they chose the issue of feminine sexuality — white woman's purity — and the fear of miscegenation.

Months before the massacre at Wilmington, white, Democratic newspapers jumped on board the party wagon and began to disseminate embellished stories of "Negro atrocities" on a daily basis. According to Glenda Gilmore, Democrats "would use a rape scare to pull white apostates back into the Democratic Party ... Headlines screamed 'An Incubus Must Be Removed'...." The Democrats charged that as the white man slumbered, allowing African Americans to take political power, the incubus of black power had visited their beds as well" (74). Gilmore believes that it was the sexualization of the political conflict that ultimately allowed regular men to become cold-blooded killers on the streets of Wilmington in November 1898. The rhetoric of rape and "home protection" gave the white man's political and economic discontent "a powerful psychosexual charge" (76–77). It was this particular form of rhetoric and the libidinal crisis attached to it that gave rise to the intensity of the event. "To be remade into killers," Gilmore writes, "white men had to connect gender and race; they had to believe that one duty — the exercise of patriarchy — prevailed over all other commandments, including the biblical injunction against murder" (77).

Timothy Tyson and David Cecelski agree: "If white supremacy provided the fuel for the conflagration of 1898, Democrats used the rough side of sexual politics to strike the match" (7). Just two days before the Wilmington massacre, in fact, *The Wilmington Messenger*, Wilmington's white-owned newspaper, ran the lyrics to a favorite song of the white supremacy campaign:

Rise, ye sons of Carolina!
Proud Caucasians, one and all;
Be not deaf to Love's appealing —
Hear your wives and daughters call,
See their blanched and anxious faces,
Note their frail, but lovely forms;
Rise, defend their spotless virtue
With your strong and manly arms [1].

This particular publication was likely a response to an earlier exchange in the newspapers concerning the purity of white women and the threat the black man posed to her virtue. In August 1898, a year-old speech delivered by Rebecca Latimer Felton of Georgia was published in the *Wilmington Record*, a white-owned newspaper that supported the Democratic cause. Felton's argument concerned the laxity of white men in protecting their women in the countryside against marauding black rapists. The situation had gotten so bad,

Felton claimed, that desperate measures were needed: "If it takes lynching to protect woman's dearest possession from drunken, ravening human beasts," she exclaimed, "then I say lynch a thousand a week" (quoted in Chesnutt, 411).

Attempting to counter the rape scare that had become so prevalent in the media with his own newspaper, *The Daily Record*, Manly published an editorial responding to Felton's incitement to violence. Manly countered her argument by pointing out that many white women cried rape to save their reputations after an illicit affair with a black man had been exposed. Furthermore, he claimed, black women have been at the mercy of white men's rapacious sexual appetites for generations, and the threat of rape applies more to them than to white women. Finally, he argued, it is not entirely unreasonable that a white woman might desire a black man or that a black man might be sufficiently attractive to draw a white woman's affections. "Tell your men that it is no worse for a black man to be intimate with a white woman than for a white man to be intimate with a colored woman," Manley wrote (quoted in Chesnutt 408). Not surprisingly, Manley's editorial created an explosive backlash. What emerged as the greatest impudence, the most egregious insult, was, interestingly enough, Manley's claim that a white woman might actually prefer a black man as an object of desire. White Democrats seized the editorial and published it piecemeal to support their campaign of white supremacy and home protection. Using the article as an excuse, white Democrats began a well-organized campaign of intimidation on the streets of Wilmington. For months prior to the massacre, African Americans were not allowed to purchase guns or ammunition while white citizens spent over $30,000 on weapons, including a whopping $1,200 on a Gatling gun that was kept in plain view. To make matters worse, huge bands of unemployed white criminals — organized in a gang of nightriders called the Red Shirts — patrolled the streets, striking fear into the hearts of law-abiding citizens.

Although Manley's article appeared in August, it supposedly provided the provocation for the riot more than two months later on November 10, since the destruction of the printing offices of *The Daily Record* and the expulsion of Manley from Wilmington was the initial aim of the mob of armed white men who marched up Market Street around 8:30 that morning. In fact, in order to ensure that Manley's editorial provided "the atmosphere within which violence and destruction were acceptable to preserve virginal white women," *The Wilmington Messenger* printed the most inflammatory parts of Manley's article along with editorial responses to it "in every issue from August 23 to November 8, excluding Sundays" (Kirshenbaum, 81, 44).

Fueled by the rhetoric of feminine purity, the fall elections became the coveted prize of the white supremacy campaign; the Democrats won by a landslide. On November 8 — election day — no African American and very few Fusionists showed up to vote, probably because armed Red Shirts patrolled the polls and the Gatling gun was parked nearby. The word had been spread: any colored person who dared exercise his right to vote would be shot on sight. In a well-attended speech delivered to the citizens of Wilmington the night before the election, Waddell told a crowd of cheering Democrats: "Go to the polls tomorrow, and if you find the Negro out voting, tell him to leave the polls, and if he refuses, kill him. We will never surrender to a ragged raffle of Negroes, even if we have to choke the current of the Cape Fear with carcasses." Consequently, the Democrats won the elections. On November 9, an air of relief swept the city. It appeared that the storm had passed. The riot broke out the next morning, however, after a group of Wilmington Democrats — called the Secret Nine — drew up a "Wilmington Declaration of Independence," which called for the permanent expulsion of all black men from local government. Interracial politics must never again be imposed on the dignity of the white man. The declaration also called for the expulsion of Manley and the destruction of his press. The Secret Nine asked Waddell to read the resolution aloud and sent it to the leading black citizens of the city. They were instructed to respond by 7 the next morning or Manley would be expelled by force.

Completely intimidated by the declaration and fearing for their lives, the black leaders of Wilmington sent a written response indicating that they would comply with all the stipulations of the document and see to Manley's departure, but the message never made it to Waddell's house. According to the official record, an attorney who was charged with the duty of delivering the message did not deliver the reply to Waddell personally but instead left it in his mailbox. This avoidance probably had something to do with the fact that this lawyer already knew his name was included on a list of citizens marked for banishment or lynching by the Secret Nine. By 8:30 a huge mob of armed white men had gathered and was waiting for the response, which never came. Waddell took charge of the mob and led them to the offices of *The Daily Record*. As the newspaper building burned to the ground, the mob swelled to over 2,000 men. Word of the riot spread quickly around Wilmington, reaching the predominantly black neighborhood of Brooklyn, and blacks began to flee, though a few met in the streets to defend themselves. On the corner of 4th and Hartnett Streets, a group of about twenty-five mostly unarmed black men gathered. Suspecting trouble, a gang of whites gathered on the other side of the street. No one knows what happened between those two groups or how the shooting started, but a shot rang out. According to *The Wilmington Messenger*, a black man incited the shooting and wounded a white man. Regardless, a volley of gunfire followed as the whites opened their weapons on the group of black men. Six men fell, two died instantly, and the rest fled down Hartnett Street. In response to this street skirmish, a massive army consisting of the Red Shirts gang, the Rough Riders, the Wilmington Light Infantry, two mounted cannons and the Gatling gun descended on Brooklyn.

The riot lasted well into the night and when the shooting settled down, at least 14 blacks had been killed, though most historians maintain this as too conservative an estimate. (There were fourteen coroner's inquiries, but there were undoubtedly a number of victims who did not receive a coroner's investigation). Hundreds of black citizens fled the city and hid out in the swamps on the outskirts of town, and some may have died of exposure. In the weeks and months that followed, thousands of African Americans left Wilmington. According to Prather, "The black entrepreneurial and professional class departed the port city in droves.... By 1900 whites represented a small majority that was destined to grow steadily. Wilmington's black heyday had ended" (Prather, 37–38). With this white majority came a systematic forgetting of the events of 1898. Because the white press represented the affair as a "race riot" to justify the illegal takeover of the local government, the event was never recorded as a massacre that violated the civil rights of the black citizens of Wilmington. It would take a century for the historical record to be amended and for the city of Wilmington to officially recognize the "race riot" as a massacre and publicly acknowledge the atrocities that were committed that day in the name of white supremacy.

Awareness of two omissions emerged from the centennial of the race riot in Wilmington. The first omission, pointed out during many of the Wilmington 1898 Foundation's reconciliation events, was the utter repression of the horrific, racist nature of the 1898 riot. In fact, as of the centennial date, the lack of any monument or memorial to the victims of the racial massacre is symptomatic of the general ignorance about the truth of the historical event. Most of the prominent white citizens of 1890s Wilmington who were behind the massacre became, as far as the standard record and history textbooks were concerned, heroes who stood up for justice and democracy. Many public parks, buildings, and streets bear the names of those who benefited politically and financially from the forced exile of the majority of the 1898 black population in the wake of the riot. This repression, many argue, has hurt race relations and has prevented the economic and political development of the Wilmington African American community.

The second omission, which has been primarily recognized by historians of postbellum Southern culture, is a lack of research specifically examining the white supremacy ideology behind the Wilmington political coup d'etat of 1898. As Timothy Tyson and David Cecelski point out, "While scholarship for seventy years after the 'race riot' tended to characterize the white supremacist leaders as heroes who saved the state from 'Negro rule,' more recent scholarship may have gone too far the other way, caricaturizing the white vigilantes in such a way that we cannot see them as human enough for their actions to cast light on the more general roots of racial violence" (12). This lack of scholarship prevents many from seeing the top-down character of the white supremacy race riot.

In the contemporary city of Wilmington, groundwork for a new memorial has begun at the corner of 3rd Street and Red Cross — a few blocks from where the riot began — to commemorate the victims of the event and to re-inform those who have been misguided. This monument, along with the other community work of the Remembering 1898 committee, should begin the process of compensating for the first omission as the racist legacy of this historical event is acknowledged. Acknowledging racism, however, does not necessarily address it in a significant or transformative manner. While such memorialization merely marks an event as past, no longer in the present, it does not address the very foundations of the racist legacy — a legacy that, despite the altruistic call for memorialization, still persists in the present. This leads us to the second omission, cited above, which, it seems, can only be corrected by those who follow the call for further research into the nature of the white supremacy ideology that provoked this racial event and its initial representation in both the contemporary journalistic treatments and in the historical record of the city of Wilmington.

Some of this work, however, has already been completed through literary supplements to the historical register. Literature has a way of integrating that which is deemed too metaphysical by more quantitatively inclined mediums like journalism, history, and sociology. Following political or social crises, literary writers have often composed fictional works to, paradoxically enough, correct the sometimes all-too-fictive nature of the journalistic public record. This was the case with the Wilmington massacre. Since the representation of the event was limited to the actual perspective of the white supremacy campaign and disseminated solely through white newspapers, no black perspective was ever published. At least not in the newspapers. There were, however, two literary accounts of the massacre, which were published shortly after the riot (in 1900 and 1901), that gave a different version of the events. Written by Charles Chesnutt and Jack Thorne (a pseudonym of David Bryant Fulton), these two fictional narratives presented the turmoil that erupted in Wilmington from the black perspective.

Several critics have correctly noted how both authors, in their own way, attempted to supplement the historical register by showing the events from a perspective that would provide a more realistic and truthful account. Marjorie George and Richard Pressman, for instance, have claimed that Chesnutt's motivation for writing fiction was always to "improve the lot of his people" (287). Through *The Marrow of Tradition* he corrects the "enormous historical imbalance" in the accounts of the Wilmington riot by "making American society more hospitable to the poor blacks' struggle" (291). Bryan Wagner has also argued that Chesnutt "decided to set the record straight" with his literary account of the riot. By creating an "alternate account," Wagner argues, Chesnutt was able to "expose the collective hysteria" that not only fueled the riot but also fueled the blatant misrepresentation of the event by the media of the time. He further claims that the open-ended conclusion of Chesnutt's narrative "aggressively counters the accounts of the riot in the national press" (330). Other critics have focused on both Chesnutt and Thorne together as writers who have intervened in setting the record straight. William Gleason, for example, has argued that even though Chesnutt's and Thorne's representations are "ideologically polar," they both present their own "truer versions of history" (28). While Chesnutt's account "occupies a more subtle and shifting middle ground," which takes place in the context of a number of arguments between his level-headed protagonist Dr. Miller and his vengefully combative character Josh Green, Thorne's stance, according to Gleason, is "more consistently militant" (22, 23). While Gleason characterizes Chesnutt's symbolic and psychological novel as a literary attempt to counter established stereotypes and Thorne's more polemical novel as a radical defense of the black race, both writers' works functioned as a "voice of protest" to the racist rhetoric surrounding the Wilmington riot (22). And, while Richard Yarborough's critical analysis of both novels focuses on each writer's dilemma over the possibility of creating a novel form of black heroism, he maintains that both Chesnutt and Fulton "sought to intervene in the controversy by creating fictional narratives designed to dramatize the events from the perspective of the African American community" (230). In the "war over images," fiction, it would seem, was the most effective means for African Americans at the time to "depict Wilmington blacks sympathetically" and "to shape the popular conception of the African American" (226). According to Yarborough, these authors possessed a "fictive drive" to write a novel that corrected the misinformation that was being publicly propagated about the event. Their stories also functioned to paint a more faithful picture of the massacre and the African American community, a picture that was not so invested in justifying the illegal acts of the riot organizers.

So, even though the critics have aptly illustrated how both Chesnutt and Thorne, through their literary depictions of the riot, have helped to set forth what has been repressed by the misrepresentation of the actual events, little has been written about how these literary accounts also offer an examination of the white supremacist ideology that instigated the events surrounding the riot. While Wagner's reading begins to move in that direction, his analysis never really gets to an examination of how Chesnutt's novel explores the psychical logic of racist ideology. Even though Wagner has argued that Chesnutt's novel "exposes the ideological subtext that structures white responses" to the growing middle-class black population in 1890s Wilmington, he limits his analysis to a simple economic determinism. He claims, for example, that the growth of a black middle class in Wilmington before the riot created an epistemological crisis, a radical destabilization of the traditional Southern white perception of itself. By closely analyzing how the disintegrating, elite white characters in Chesnutt's novel tend to estimate the value of black characters of the servant — and, therefore, traditional — class, Wagner illustrates how the white characters' denial of the all-too-present existence of the black middle class keeps their own image intact, since this identity is based on white economic superiority. But because the growing presence of the black middle class can only be denied for so long in the novel — as in the reality of 1890s Wilmington — the racial violence that is propagated by the whites is represented as an "attempt to repair the dangers of this epistemological crisis" (312). In Wagner's argument, then, the riot amounts to a violent rearrangement of the field of perception to the pre–Reconstruction era parameters when whites were seen as those who prospered. Even though Wagner claims that racial violence is not simply a matter of economic self-interest, but rather is the prerequisite for what he calls the "very possibility of white identity," he still equates white identity with economic self-interest, thereby diminishing the epistemological crisis on which the riot was supposed to be based. For Wagner, the epistemological crisis is really just an economic crisis that concerns the growing perception by whites that they have to share wealth and prosperity with the emerging black middle class.

What remains to be explored, however, is how these two novels, both written by African American authors, expose the true psychological motivation behind the white supremacy ideology that spawned the riot. To this end, we might consider Yarborough's reading more closely, since his choice of the term "drive" might actually be more telling than he himself allows. According to Freud, drive satisfaction can take one of two forms. First, it can manifest itself through repression in the form of a symptom. This symptom can be read into the Wilmington affair as the disintegration of race relations and the chronic suppression of African American political and economic power brought on by the repression of the truth. But drive satisfaction doesn't always rely on repression; it can be produced through sublimation. Contrary to popular belief, sublimation is not about making the explicitly sexual implicit; it is where, in art (literature included), the aesthetic touches the ethical. In the 7th Seminar, Jacques Lacan claims that sublimation is ethical because "it creates socially recognizable values" (107). But, as Alenka Zupancic has pointed out, sublimation does not simply adhere to already existing values; it creates new values (73). In other words, if we understand what Freud called the reality principle as the current supreme ideology, works of sublimation challenge the reality principle's criterion and attempt to formulate a different one. Sublimation, according to Zupancic, is ethical precisely because it is not subordinated to the reality principle, to any notion of the common good. It is ethical because it creates an awareness of that which has no space within the given reality principle; it, in a sense, makes noticeable what is not noticeable within the confines of the reality principle. This is precisely how these two novels by Chesnutt and Thorne should be viewed: they make noticeable what is not noticeable within the written public account of the events of November 1898 in Wilmington. Rather than merely adding to existing accounts to give a more complete picture or to correct its misrepresentations, *The Marrow of Tradition* and *Hanover* actually change the very coordinates from which the Wilmington riot must be seen.

We can therefore only support Tyson and Cecelski's claim that little work has been done to "examine the white supremacy movement and their ideology" in relation to the Wilmington race riot, if we ignore the sublimatory potential of Chesnutt's and Thorne's novels. Both novels, through their own more or less truthful depiction of the actual historical events, accurately display the underlining mechanism of the Democratic revolt against democracy in Wilmington.

Surrounding the 1898 events is the long-standing debate amongst historians over whether the violent eruption that led to the murder of at least fourteen African Americans was the result of a sort of carnivalesque outburst by the primarily working class Red Shirts, or whether the violence was carefully orchestrated by the landed white interests of the city. Even though the post-reconstruction South can be characterized by its "troubled relationship between law and lawlessness," Chesnutt's and Thorne's Wilmington riot novels illustrate precisely how the lawless violence during the coup d'etat was less opposed to the law than it was the seamy underside of the law itself.

In a psychoanalytic understanding, violence usually evolves from one of three motives, articulated around the classificatory principles of the ego, id, and superego. Ego-violence usually springs from self-interest or greed, where personal principles seem to stand in as universal principles. One reading of the 1898 coup d'etat sees selfishness as a prime motivation. Many whites simply joined in the rioting in order to get a slice of the pie that was at the time held by the ever-growing black middle class. Many of the Red Shirts were in fact promised the manufacturing and stevedore jobs that would become vacant after blacks had been forced out of the city. Also, many of the city's previous white political leaders who had recently been voted out of office by the strong Fusionist campaigns simply concocted the riot as a means of illegitimately reacquiring the lost political power on which their individual wealth depended. Not entirely distinct from ego-violence, id-violence is a form of violence usually associated with xenophobia. Many have argued, including those behind the coup, that the whites who carried out most of the violent acts of November 10 were simply out of control in their attempt to take away the other's privileged relation to goods: the good jobs, good housing, good education, and good medical care, all of which were becoming available to the burgeoning black middle class in Wilmington. Lastly, and most importantly for our analysis, is superego-violence. This form of violence most likely erupts to promote the good of the community when the law fails. At a certain point, those in Wilmington who were the city leaders before the Republican/Populists gained such a stronghold decided that matters had to be taken into their own hands, that the city must again be in white hands, for the good of the community. The November 15, 1898, *Wilmington Messenger* article "Northern Papers Slandering Wilmington" reported how just prior to and in furtherance of the riot the South "is determined come what may, to preserve its civilization, to protect its women and children from slanderers and villains and brutal rapists, to maintain orderly and honest government, at any cost" and how white North Carolinians "will steadily pursue what they believe to be the right course." When violence is strongly tethered to some ideological ideal, as it clearly was according to this newspaper report on the Wilmington race riot and coup d'etat, it is of a superegoic nature.

When examined closely enough, Chesnutt's and Thorne's novels show this superegoic motive in their respective fictional accounts of the events leading up to November 10, 1898, in Wilmington. In doing so, they help supplement the historical account by shedding further psychological light on the motive behind a factual event. Historians agree that in post–Reconstruction Southern society there was a "troubled relationship between law and lawlessness" (Bentley and Gunning, viii). Because of the increasing legal and political limitations put on the gains of Reconstruction, lynching and race riots became universally accepted by whites as a way of protecting the community from "Negro rule." As Bentley and Gunning argue, "In a sense then, white supremacists were arguing that anti-black vigilante violence was itself part of the natural law of white racial survival, and therefore could not be considered criminal activity" (quoted in Chesnutt, 335). What one should notice from the beginning is the fact that this form of violence, a violence that Chesnutt's and Thorne's narratives indict as a specifically superegoic violence, is itself more of a supplementary buttress to the failing, traditional, paternalistic law of the South than it is a direct transgression of the law. In fact, the racial violence that erupted in 1898 displays the transgressive and unethical underside of traditional Southern law in its attempt to violently interrupt the process of racial equality, which is based on universal rights, and return to the social relations of the past, which are based on inequality.

In psychoanalytic parlance, the superego emerges where the law fails. Thus, it is not difficult to see how the white supremacist movement, inaugurated in 1896 all through the state of North Carolina, was based on a seemingly paradoxical, unethical moral law. And it would be precisely this law that would restore the traditional rules of the Southern community, which had been turned upside down by Reconstruction reforms. This ideological framework allowed Alfred Waddell to claim in the aftermath of the events of November 10 that "there has not been a single illegal act committed in the change of government." Whites claimed lawfulness, even though fourteen unarmed African Americans were shot dead in the streets and democratically elected city officials were put on train at gunpoint and forced to leave the city (*Collier's Weekly*). The superegoic interpretation of the law also allows *Messenger* editor Thomas Clawson to reinterpret the nature of the mob violence on November 10: "It was not a mob but a Wilmington army of vindication of Wilmington's social security."

Chesnutt portrays this mechanism in his novel by fictionalizing the conspiracy developed by Wilmington's Secret Nine. Since post–Reconstruction Southern society had become more egalitarian than it was in the antebellum days — blacks, after all, were enfranchised — the old, traditional, authoritarian, patriarchal ways that used to be the direct means of rule could now only seep back into social rule in an unethical type of morality. Chesnutt's narrative focuses on the Secret Nine's (reduced to a Secret Three for the novel) dark-room conspiracy meetings to take back the city of Wilmington (fictionally called Wellington in the novel), illustrating how the deposed city leaders based their conspiracy on what was supposedly good for the community. He sets the Secret Three clandestine meetings in the office of the editor-in-chief of Wilmington's Associated Press white daily, thereby illustrating how the coup was orchestrated by the fourth estate, a supplementary ruling body.

This notion of the communal good, which grounds the coup d'etat, is invoked early on in a scene from Chesnutt's novel when Dr. Burns, a Northern and progressive white physician, is called down from Philadelphia. He arrives in Wellington to perform a delicate operation on the only son of Major Carteret, one of the Secret Three conspirators. In order to successfully complete the operation, Burns seeks the assistance of Dr. Miller, a local African American doctor. Of course Major Carteret protests Dr. Miller's involvement on the grounds of racial propriety. Chesnutt goes further, suggesting a critique of this underlying code, as he introduces Dr. Price, a local white doctor, into the scene. In response to Burns's insistence that Dr. Miller be allowed to assist him, Price points out how this northern doctor does not quite appreciate Carteret's refusal to allow a black physician to operate on his only son, a figure of the white heritage: "This is not with [Carteret] an unimportant matter, or a mere question of prejudice, or even of personal taste. It is a sacred principle, lying at the root of our social order, involving the purity and prestige of our race" (Chesnutt, 89).

Later on in the narrative when the Secret Three invoke Barber's (the fictional Alexander Manley) editorial from the city's *Afro-American Banner*, which points out the real reason behind public lynchings as a tool to rally white support in favor of overthrowing the democratically elected municipal government, they claim that Barber's article "violates an unwritten law of the South" (98). This unwritten law, as Chesnutt's novel goes on to argue, is none other than the very unethical superegoic imperative that the Secret Three invoke publicly through Carteret's city newspaper to gather moral support for their planned political coup. Because the coup cannot be justified on legal terms, the three use Barber's editorial negatively to organize a white imperative duty for all to protect the sanctity of white womanhood. This imperative is constantly referred to as the "license" the mob has been granted by duty in its violent and unethical treatment of Wellington's African American population.

This imperative is most effectively challenged at the end of Chesnutt's novel when Major Carteret's wife Olivia is forced to beg and plead with Janet — Dr. Miller's wife and Olivia's half-sister from her father's second marriage to his black housekeeper — to allow her husband to save her son's life, the very life that Major Carteret had earlier forbade Dr. Miller from assisting in saving. Since all of the city's white doctors are unavailable due to the events of the riot instigated in part by the major, Olivia must violate the unwritten law of the South through devotion to a particular maternal superegoic imperative.

The fact that women can see the imaginary nature of this unwritten law of the South much more effectively than men seems to be the sole concern of Thorne's novel *Hanover*. While Chesnutt offers the reader a glimpse into the mechanism of the race riot by fictionalizing the superegoic imperative set up by the actual male conspirators, Thorne ingeniously exposes the superegoic nature of the mob violence by directing his narrative almost exclusively to women's — both black and white women's — ability to see through the flimsy imperative lurking behind the male violence. Although Freud's assertion that a woman's superego is weaker than a man's is often criticized by feminists because it leads to the conclusion that women are therefore somehow less moral, Thorne's fictional narrative seems to expose another, more complex, understanding of this Freudian claim. Because a man's relation to the world heavily relies on the law, he needs to cover over the law's lacking foundation with some sort of notion of the Good — a notion that is always superegoic by nature. But since a woman, according to Freud, develops a certain mistrust of the law — a law that doesn't seem to offer as much for her as for her male counterpart — she more readily acknowledges its lacking foundation. And it is this awareness that is displayed in Thorne's female characters' skepticism about the male population's imperative to protect the sanctity of Southern white womanhood.

While Thorne's novel, essentially a combination of journalism, fictional narrative, historical account and personal correspondence, is much less literary than Chesnutt's (in fact, Thorne's novel has often been cited as an historical source), it adds the most to the historical account precisely when it is most fictional — in its portrayal of women as those who are most ignored in the historical account. While Gleason has recognized that Chesnutt seems fully aware that "women are at the very core of the race question in the South," he recognizes that only Thorne sees the women of both races as "more strong-willed, intelligent, and morally sound than men" (37, 38). Yarborough likewise agrees that Thorne depicts women as superior in "morality, intelligence, and courage" (246). Although the municipal coup portrayed in *Hanover* is also constructed around the violation of the unwritten law enacted by Manley's editorial, Thorne almost never focuses on the male conspirators in his account. There is, in fact, only a six-page chapter devoted to the male political conspiracy, and this chapter is immediately followed by a chapter devoted to one of the white leaders of the planned coup being castigated by his wife for the lacking foundation of his plan. When Teck Pervis attempts to justify the white supremacist plan to disenfranchise blacks through the threat of violence as supremely sanctioned, Thorne has his wife simply ask him whose teaching he's "follerin" and precisely what scripture he's using to back up his planned "devalmint" (Thorne, 31). Although Thorne devotes a chapter to a black women's civic organization — the Union Aid Society — and its criticism of the underhand motive of the impending race riot and political coup, his portrayal of the white women's criticism of the motive offered by the male members of their own race for the political coup even more effectively exposes the superegoic nature of the 1898 race riot.

After Dr. Jose, a prominent white minister, calls on his congregation to help deliver the city from "Negro rule," a rule that has allowed the insults initiated in Manley's editorial against the sanctity of white womanhood, his wife explains to him that vengeance belongs only to the Lord. The minister, however, ignores his wife's point and presses his justification: "'But Mary,' [persists] the minister, 'you don't understand the situation. We, the men of

Wilmington, see utter ruin in store for us unless something is done to check the Negro. Our women can scarcely venture out alone after dark, so ugly and bold has he become under our lenient treatment.'" To this supposed imperative for the injustice that is soon to be perpetrated in the city of Wilmington, Mary responds perceptively: "'This is all imaginary my dear ... Our homes, our firesides, our women are perfectly safe. The only uneasy ones among us are those who want offices'" (59–60).

Towards the end of the novel, Thorne strategically puts some of his most important observations about the unethical nature of the 1898 coup into the mouth of Mrs. McLane, "an old and wealthy white citizen" (111). While partaking of tea with some of her closest friends two weeks after the coup, Mrs. McLane systematically exposes the false foundation of the recent reactionary revolution. Contradicting the claim that the riot rested on divinely sanctioned motives, she claims, "'My people are to-day imbued with the feeling of boastfulness in their own strength rather than thankfulness to God. For can any of us feel that God has countenanced the murder, pillage and intimidation which the whites of Wilmington have resorted to?'" (111). With this direct challenge to Rebecca Latimer Felton's editorial call to lynch the "black brute," Thorne has Mrs. McLane further argue that the mob and its leaders "in their blind zeal to restore white supremacy, and to defend women, have unmistakably demonstrated their weakness. White supremacy cannot be maintained by brute force, neither can the women of one race be protected and defended while the defender of virtue looks upon the destruction of the other race as only an indiscretion.'" (113). She further complains how mere boys were "licensed" by an imperative that allowed them to insult women by strip searching them in the middle of the street during the riot. "'The Negro woman,'" she further argues, "'should be considered a woman in the fullest sense of the term, and those men and boys who in their zeal to protect white women humiliated and disgraced black ones, insulted and humbled their own mothers, sisters and sweethearts; for what disgraces one woman disgraces another, be she white, black, red or brown'" (114). She further illustrates to her friends how the anti-miscegenation attacks against blacks are completely misguided since "'the best white blood of the South flows through the veins of Negroes'" (116). But, in the end, when Thorne has Mrs. McLane complete her harangue by arguing that "'the passing of laws since the war prohibiting the intermarriage of the races is proof that the men do not trust us [white women] as implicitly as they pretend'" and that "'the lynchings and burnings that are daily occurring in the South are intended as warnings to white women as well as checks to Negro men'" (117), he forces his readers to examine precisely why the supposed impossibility of a white woman ever desiring a marriage with an African American man needs to be explicitly prohibited. And when Thorne has Mrs. McLane finish her argument with the proclamation that "'it is time for us [white women] to rise up and let our voices be heard against the making of our protection an excuse for crime'" (117), the reader can glimpse Thorne's perceptive insight that the original political threat that was disguised as a sexual threat by the conspirators of the riot is itself really a displacement of a sexual conflict within the white race itself. This leads to the final conclusion that the antagonism between white men and white women is ideologically overcome only by maintaining that this inherent antagonism only exists because of the intrusion of an external force. Thorne's novel subtly exposes the ideological mechanism where the illusion of a state of fullness is maintained as lacking.

So, while it is important to recognize precisely how these two novels by Chesnutt and Thorne added to and at times corrected the prevailing historical and journalistic accounts of the events surrounding the race riot of November 10, 1898, it is just as vital, if more difficult, to understand the less obvious critique of the racist ideology they provide. In various ways critics have noticed and commented on the differing means in which both Chesnutt and Thorne have elicited sympathy for their race, how they have provided a more accurate picture of African American desires, ambitions and economic differences, how they have protested the inaccuracy of the historical register, and how they have even promoted a form of black resistance. However important it is to recognize these writers' contribution to representing the African American experience, readers should always pay close attention to how these two writers' characterization of their white characters reveals the psychological complexity behind racist motivated actions and beliefs.

WORKS CITED

Cecelski, David S. and Timothy B. Tyson. *Democracy Betrayed: The Wilmington Race Riot of 1898 and Its Legacy*. Chapel Hill: University of North Carolina Press, 1998.

Chesnutt, Charles W. *The Marrow of Tradition*. Edited by Nancy Bentley and Sandra Gunning. Boston: Bedford/St. Martin's, 2002.

Du Bois, W.E.B. *The Souls of Black Folk*. New York: Fawcett, 1961.

Gilmore, Glenda E. "Murder, Memory, and the Flight of the Incubus." In *Democracy Betrayed: The Wilmington Race Riot of 1898 and Its Legacy* by David S. Cecelski and Timothy B. Tyson, 73–93. Chapel Hill: University of North Carolina Press, 1998.

Gleason, William. "Voices at the Nadir: Charles Chesnutt and David Bryant Fulton." *American Literary Realism* 24 (1992): 22–41.

Lacan, Jacques. *The Seminar of Jacques Lacan, Book VII: The Ethics of Psychoanalysis, 1959–1960*. Translated by Dennis Porter. New York: Norton, 1992.

Prather, Leon. "We Have Taken a City: A Centennial Essay." In *Democracy Betrayed: The Wilmington Race Riot of 1898 and Its Legacy* by David S. Cecelski and Timothy B. Tyson, 15–41. Chapel Hill: University of North Carolina Press, 1998.

Thorne, Jack. *Hanover; or The Persecution of the Lowly. A Story of the Wilmington Massacre*. New York: Arno, 1969.

Wilmington Messenger. 8 November 1898: 1.

Yarborough, Richard. "Violence, Manhood, and Black Heroism: The Wilmington Riot in Two Turn-of-the-Century African American Novels." In *Democracy Betrayed: The Wilmington Race Riot of 1898 and Its Legacy* by David S. Cecelski and Timothy B. Tyson, 225–51. Chapel Hill: University of North Carolina Press, 1998.

Zupancic, Alenka. *The Shortest Shadow: Nietzsche's Philosophy of the Two*. Cambridge, Mass.: MIT, 2003.

CHAPTER 2

"The fruit of my own imagination": Charles W. Chesnutt's *The Marrow of Tradition* in the Age of Realism

Willie J. Harrell, Jr.

The very marrow of tradition's shown.
And all that history, much that fiction weaves.
— Charles Lamb, *"To the Editor of the Every-Day Book"*

The title of the book fairly embodies the theme, which is an attempt
to picture, through the medium of dramatic narrative, the atmos-
phere in which these problems must be worked out— an atmos-
phere of which the dominant note is Tradition.
— Charles W. Chesnutt, 20 October 1901

'The Marrow of Tradition' is one of the first fruits of the new agi-
tation. Whether it will be helpful remains to be seen. But it is a
very strong and virile story.
—*The Brooklyn Daily Eagle*, 9 November 1901

When Charles W. Chesnutt wrote that his fiction was "the fruit of my own imagination," he was focusing on how his pragmatist style of writing presented the litigious and complex question of race relations in the American South to his reading public. "Imagination can only act upon data," Chesnutt discovered. "One must have somewhere in his consciousness the ideas which he puts together to form a connected whole ... there is nothing new under the sun." Chesnutt believed that the "brilliant touches" to his fiction were "awaiting only the spur of imagination to bring them again to the surface" ("Superstitions and Folk-Lore," 231). One of his aims, then, for writing *The Marrow of Tradition*, was to shed light on the ills of racial prejudice by bringing those issues "again to the surface." It was imagination itself that made it realistic for Chesnutt in *Marrow* to ardently examine the social and political powers in both the black and white community. "The power of such a book," a reviewer writes of the novel, "lies in its searching truthfulness." As *Marrow* tackles concerns "over which there is the deepest feeling," the novel's importance should lie, this critic suggests, in "the fidelity with which it portrays the conditions" of racial discrimination (*Literature and Literary Topics*, 17).

Since Chesnutt did not "like the South" ("Letter to Booker T. Washington," 158),[1] a novel dealing with Southern racism was of keen interest to him around the turn of the century. Chesnutt understood that timing was of the essence in pursuing such a project, and he could not have chosen a better time to initiate his investigation into American racism. Race riots and lynchings were taking place not only in the South, but all across the country. In 1900, the City of New Orleans suffered a race riot and later 106 reported lynchings of African Americans; in 1904, and again in 1906, race riots engulfed Springfield, Ohio; and the "Red Summer" of 1919 resulted in racial attacks in just about every major American city starting in Chicago, moving even to Cardiff, Wales. Chesnutt realized that had he written *Marrow* at any time other than at the height of Jim Crowism, it would have been simply a tale laudable of note and nothing else. His understanding of what constituted the construction of an accepted "literary style," however, was an important element in his decision to fashion *Marrow* as a text to deal with Southern prejudice. Two years before writing *Marrow*, Chesnutt came to the realization that a successful novel would have to have "humor, pathos, plot, [and] dramatic intensity" as well as "well drawn or strongly contrasted characters" ("Why is a Book Popular?" 5). This essay, then, is an attempt to explore Chesnutt's examination of what would become of the traditional white constituents of a Southern town when they attempted to suppress black socio-political participation, which was the basis for the continuation of Southern traditions, and what becomes of that supposed supremacy when their notions are goaded by the subject of racial injustice. Overall, this essay will examine Chesnutt's contribution to what has been called the Age of Realism through one of his more representative works.

***

This essay begins like many other discussions on Charles Waddell Chesnutt with Cleveland, Ohio. Chesnutt's witnessing race and color prejudice both in Cleveland, where he was born on June 20, 1858, as the grandson of a white man and the son of free blacks who had moved to Cleveland from North Carolina two years earlier, and in Fayetteville, North Carolina, where he spent his childhood and eventually worked as assistant principal of a normal school, had a grave impact on his racial consciousness. Early in his life, he realized how his own race affiliation would be a critical point on the subject of constructing a text on racial issues; he discerned distinctions between a group of people he dubbed "true" blacks, and those who were "people of mixed blood." Affiliated with the latter group, Chesnutt recognized that his own position in society was "similar to that of Mahomet's Coffin." He considered himself "neither fish, flesh, nor fowl — neither 'nigger,' white, nor 'buckrah.'[2] Too 'stuck-up' for the colored folks, and, of course, not recognized by the whites" (*The Journals of Charles W. Chesnutt*, 157–56).[3] It was the Southern states, Chesnutt charged, that were responsible for the manifestation of and division that the color line perpetuated:

> Vary slightly in regard to what constitutes a mulatto or person of color, and as to what proportion of white blood should be sufficient to remove the disability of color. As a general rule, less than one-fourth of Negro blood left the individual white — in theory; race questions being, however, regulated very differently in practice.... The color-line is drawn at one-fourth of Negro blood, and persons with only one-eighth are white ["What is a White Man?" 5].

In *Marrow*, Chesnutt relied on the impact of these Southern laws to awaken a consciousness in blacks to a degree of social reform by presenting life as it was for blacks in the South. His realistic approach, which was typical of texts belonging to Realism that explored complex race relations during his time,[4] examined a revolutionary representation of light-complexioned African Americans during a time when racial awareness was heightened by the predisposed definitions of race placed on the African American community as African Americans consciously and simultaneously struggled with the ambivalence of being African *and* American. Joseph R McElrath, Jr. has argued, however, that Chesnutt was not a realist because he does not fit into William Dean Howells's realm of Realism. Howells declared an author's work Realism when the work represented even the most minuscule particulars of characterization by challenging problems that often arose from social differences. Howells's convictions about Realism and essays on European writers were the foundation for shaping the face of American Realism. McElrath suggests that Chesnutt, then, "instead merits consideration as a remarkable romancer" because of his "typical subject matter," "didactic intentions and considerable imaginative powers." (92). It was because of Chesnutt's persuasive "imaginative powers," however, that he was able to envision *Marrow* as a work that would "sketch in vivid though simple lines the whole race situation" ("Letter to John P. Green," 156). As a realist, then, Chesnutt made "good use of the material at his hand," writes a contemporary critic. Chesnutt's "picture of the South" and racial attitudes of Southern whites, "as viewed from the Negro standpoint," are represented "with real effectiveness" in *Marrow* ("The Race Question in Fiction," 16). In the midst of McElrath's difficulty in seeing Chesnutt as a realist, the common approaches to reading *Marrow* all become, to some degree, subjective. McElrath's unease about Chesnutt's use of Realism, then, stems from his social ideas of what constitutes the "real" for African Americans during the apex of Jim Crowism.

This essay, however, is not an attempt to argue that Chesnutt was or was not a realist. Many scholars have already demonstrated his realistic worldview and technique of writing. When considering how one perceives realistic notions, it is important to bear in mind that, autonomous of the human psyche, Realism exists. Chesnutt used Realism in *Marrow* to respond to the need for social change for the betterment of African American life. His argument in *Marrow*, as I see it, is that the "Traditions" of Southern racism cannot be seen visibly, but only in their effects, like the wind, just as "race" is a construction that really has little to do with what we see (hence the emphasis on the mulatta/o) but with what we think. Chesnutt is more like the psychological realists such as Henry James and Edith Wharton, although, in technique, he has an affinity with writers such as Paul Laurence Dunbar, Frank Norris, and Theodore Dreiser. Chesnutt's infinite exploration into the insight of the ways psychologically complex characters deal with ambiguous racial, social, and intellectual problems can be seen clearly in *Marrow*. Readers see Chesnutt's attempts to promote an awareness of realistic ideologies as largely Southern traditions with remarkable authority and control. The most important element of Chesnutt's use of Realism is his representation of not only black life in the South, but white racism as well.

While collecting, for example, "a great deal of material" in Wilmington, North Carolina, in preparation for *Marrow*, Chesnutt found "the people there were eager to tell him all the details of the riot" (Helen Chesnutt, 159). As they set out to ruin property, homes, and buildings in black neighborhoods, the vigilantes included members of every layer of Wilmington's white communities: lawyers, businessmen, and even clergymen. Several hours of rioting claimed the lives of ten to thirty Wilmingtonites. The "'revolution,' as the white people call it, or the 'massacre' according to the Negroes," Chesnutt writes, led him to conclude that blacks "in the South are not yet free, and social odium at the North is deemed, by many, preferable to the same thing at the South, with oppressive and degrading legal enactments superadded" ("The White and the Black," 13). Chesnutt attempted to agitate his Northern audience by fashioning *Marrow* to impact the degree to which the influential whites of Wellington — his fictionalized Wilmington — would adapt to protect their traditions even at the cost of annihilating Southern blacks. "But so long as the traditions of the past remain," Chesnutt writes, "and until the North has changed much more than it has, the Negro will feel that the North is more friendly to his aspirations than the South" ("The Negro's Franchise," 18). Chesnutt's attention to involving the North in solving the Southern race problem left Northerners with a "feeling of resentment toward the dominant race at the South." Although Chesnutt's representation of Southern racism in *Marrow* "does not stir with a sense of righteous wrath at race hatred and injustice of all kinds," a reviewer writes, the *Marrow* does present "truer and more agreeable impressions of the Southern gentleman than most Northern men possess and quite as much consideration for the white ruffians of the South as they deserve" (*The Public*, 688).

Although only about a third of *Marrow* is based on the actual riots, Chesnutt intended for the novel to improve the "incongruity that characterizes the racial fabric of the South" because he believed these factors were important for understanding the relationships between whites and blacks both North and South (Pettis, 109–110). Since literary Realism is difficult to characterize, the way a person perceives *Marrow* is what will most likely comprise his or her ideologies about Realism. As Bernard W. Bell has suggested, *Marrow* is read in terms of the "antireferential bias of modern criticism and the deconstructionist theory of the indeterminant meaning of texts" (102). What I would like to explore, then, is why Chesnutt chose Realism and how he employed experiences and factual events to create the realist novel.

***

The hunt for Realism in American literature will take us to novels of the mid to latter part of the nineteenth century, an era which Marshall Brown calls "the period and genre that gave it currency" (224). In considering literary Realism and what role African Americans have played in its development, this essay is an attempt to explore Chesnutt's contribution to what has been dubbed the Age of Realism through one of his most important works, one that he conceived would shed "light upon the vexed moral and sociological problems which grow out of the present" ("Chesnutt's Own View," 5). African Americans' contribution to the Age of Realism, then, offers an insight into their continuing struggle in searching for their cultural identities in the hostile environment of the racial prejudice of Jim Crowism. *Marrow* was a response to Jim Crowism and other racial injustices that goaded African American writers to represent their lives as they saw them in America. What was the remedy to the race animosity that plagued the country, especially in the South? Chesnutt understood that the answer to this question lay in the elimination of the hostilities that caused racial prejudice by taking away their foundations. Chesnutt believed that the racial oppression of both the North and South would cease to exist if these issues were confronted. He knew, however, it would not happen over night; *Marrow* was only an iota of Chesnutt's measures to break down the structural fabric of racial prejudice.

Historians suggest that the realist novel, however, developed in the latter part of the nineteenth century with the rise of industrialization, amidst social ideals about what represented the "real." Today the varying ideologies of the "real" are eagerly debated by scholars and historians. How did Americans deal with the revolutionary changes that shifted their preexisting worlds between the periods of the Civil War and World War I? Roger B. Salomon suggests that Realism became a "response and a solution to the problem of the past":

> The picturesque tradition was unable to deal with the present, and so realism made a religion of newness and contemporaneity. It dismissed the problem of artistic form (associated with the past) by refusing to acknowledge any distinction between art and life; the writer was not, in fact, a creative artist at all, but rather a reporter, a social commentator, or a psychologist [537].

Writers such as Mark Twain, William Dean Howells, Henry James, and John W. DeForest, whether self-consciously or not, saw Realism as a means of refuting the British romanticism that had maintained a stronghold on American arts and letters for some time. Howells, one of the most significant advocates of American Realism, writes that Chesnutt's previous collections of short stories had "won the ear of the more intelligent public" for his detailed representation and unmistaken "knowledge of the life he has chosen in its peculiar racial characteristics." Howells further remarks:

> Yet these stories, after all, are Mr. Chesnutt's most important work, whether we consider them merely as realistic fiction, apart from their author, or as studies of that middle world of which he is naturally and voluntarily a citizen. We had known the nethermost world of the grotesque and comical negro and the terrible and tragic negro through the white observer on the outside, and black character in its lyrical moods we had known from such an inside witness as Mr. Paul Dunbar; but it had remained for Mr. Chesnutt to acquaint us with those regions where the paler shades dwell as hopelessly, with relation to ourselves, as the blackest negro. He has not shown the dwellers there as very different from ourselves ["Mr. Charles Chesnutt's Stories," 700].

Howells's comments on Chesnutt's work definitely affected the content of his later fiction. Chesnutt opens *Marrow* by introducing readers to the christening party of the Carteret baby, Theodore Felix, whose destiny is inextricably linked with the larger progression of the plot and structured around the opening problem which throws the conventional cultural and signifying practices into disarray and creates, as Chesnutt suggests, "an atmosphere of which the dominant note is Tradition" ("Chesnutt's Own View," 5). Chesnutt's attempt to expose Southern prejudice traditions is the most important element that connects *Marrow* to the "movement of literary realism" (Bently, 22).

In Chesnutt's time, Theodore Dreiser defined Realism as a representation of "a struggle between the forces of light and darkness" (Bowron, 268).

Salomon suggests that critics' definition of Realism has been irrationally concerned with the unjust treatment of Realism and its "national origin":

> For some [Realism] reflects the triumph after 1860 of science and patriotism — of the new empirical vision mingled with a heightened national consciousness. It has been described as the product of a society shaken by war, transformed by technology, and discovering the sound and look of its own regions, especially the West. A less nationalistic version of our literary history minimizes the influence of native elements and describes American realism as largely the local response to literary currents already widespread in Europe [532].

Although there are numerous definitions, today Realism can be broadly defined as "the faithful representation of reality" or "verisimilitude" (quoted in Campbell). Lilian Furst suggests that Realism is "an artistic movement" that "is the product and expression of the dominant mood of its time: a pervasive rationalist epistemology that turned its back on the fantasies of Romanticism and was shaped instead by the impact of the political and social changes as well as the scientific and industrial advances of its day" (1). With this in mind, Samara Kawash's argument that *Marrow* was goaded by two political agendas — the revealing of "violence and lawlessness of White supremacy" and the interfering with "Black debates regarding the best course of future action" — plays a central role in Chesnutt's use of Realism, because the fictional account of the race riot is what gives *Marrow* its political power (89). The political connection to *Marrow* becomes apparent: as Chesnutt attempted to illustrate disfranchisement as it was for African Americans in the South, he employed irony throughout the text to represent the incongruities in the South's racial traditions. Of *Marrow*'s political association, Chesnutt writes, "The political element of the story involves a fair statement, I believe, of the course and the underlying motives of the recent and temporarily successful movement for the disfranchisement of the colored race in the south, and particularly in North Carolina, where there was less excuse for it than in any other state where it has been carried through" ("Chesnutt's Own View," 5).

The disfranchisement of African Americans, Chesnutt decided, leaves them with "no direct representation in any Southern legislature, and no voice in determining the choice of white men who might be friendly to their rights" ("The Disfranchisement of the Negro," 88). Since African Americans had no political representation and no voice planning their own future, Chesnutt aimed to reflect in *Marrow* the reality of African American disfranchisement to his reading public. As in any realist text, Chesnutt asked his readers to draw their own conclusions from this mirrored outlook of disfranchisement and African Americans' role in the future of the American governmental system. In doing so, Chesnutt undertakes the political turmoil of white supremacy in Wellington. He uses Jerry's analysis of a meeting between Major

Carteret, Captain McBane, and General Belmont to illustrate the political mayhem he imagined in the South. Overhearing parts of McBane's, Carteret's, and Belmont's plan to eliminate black socio-political participation, Jerry, Carteret's servant, misinterprets "no Nigger domination" as "no Nigger damnation." Jerry concludes that whatever "damnation" is, if McBane is involved, "niggers" would be better off with "damnation." Jerry says of McBane:

> "Dat's a gent'eman, a rale ole-time gent'eman," he said to himself when he had closed the door. "But dere's somethin' gwine on in dere,— dere sho' is! 'No nigger damnation!' Dat soun's all right,— I'm sho' dere ain' no nigger I knows w'at wants damnation, do' dere's lots of 'em w'at derserves it; but ef dat one-eyed Cap'n McBane got anything ter do wid it, w'atever it is, it don' mean no good fer de nigger,— damnation'd be better fer 'em dan dat Cap'n McBane! He looks at a nigger lack he could jes' eat 'im alive'" [*Marrow*, 67].

Chesnutt tells readers that the purpose of this meeting at the *Morning Chronicle* was to inform Carteret that:

> The unfitness of the negro to participate in government — an unfitness due to his limited education, his lack of experience, his criminal tendencies, and more especially to his hopeless mental and physical inferiority to the white race — the major had demonstrated, it seemed to him clearly enough, that the ballot in the hands of the negro was a menace to the commonwealth. He had argued, with entire conviction, that when white and black races could never attain social and political harmony by commingling their blood; he had proved by several historical parallels that no two inassimilable races could ever live together except in the relation of superior and inferior [*Marrow*, 62].

Realism for Chesnutt was in response to the call of what Nancy Bentley and Sandra Gunning called "cultural segregation" (26). By the time Chesnutt envisioned *Marrow*, he was becoming increasingly concerned about the moral fabric of America, and *Marrow* illustrates his determination and willingness to appropriate his fiction to reveal the existing conditions, without the confines of race, which is not always true of his Southern contemporary writers.

Chesnutt's use of dialect and characterization are essential elements that account for his use of Realism. His notions were present in the writings of contemporaries like Paul Laurence Dunbar (*Sport of the Gods*) and Joel Chandler Harris (Uncle Remus stories). Phillip Barrish suggests that "literary dialect can serve as a terrain for readers" to demonstrate "certain specialized forms of taste and cultivation, or their lack" (*American Literary Realism*, 17). Chesnutt believed in the power of dialect. "The lines seem to be drawn pretty tight for the colored race just at present," he wrote, "and it ought to be a source of great satisfaction to them that there is certainly one high forum from which they can speak for themselves" ("Letter to Walter Hines Page," 117).[5] Dialect cleverly serves Chesnutt's purpose of conveying the atmosphere and describing his characters much more poignantly than standard English. By doing so, Chesnutt seemed to be against the sentimentalism of African American culture. It was over-romanticizing he sought to avoid, which he felt destroyed the reality of African American Southern dialect. Chesnutt's use of dialect enhances the setting, mood, and atmosphere of *Marrow* as a realist text. He creates an atmosphere for his audience through the use of dialect designed to draw them into assurance of *Marrow*'s realism. By 1900, in preparation for writing *Marrow*, Chesnutt commented about the difficulties of writing a text to tackle racial issues suitable for white readers. Feeling, as he did, that novels whose content dealt with race should be mostly aimed at white readers ("Letter to John P. Green," 156), Chesnutt believed that *Marrow* was not a lesson in despair. *Marrow* was his contribution toward the advancement of eliminating not only racial injustices but other social evils ("Chesnutt's Own View," 5).

***

Chesnutt believed in the morality of the oppressed African American, and he felt it his calling to illustrate how racism confined the masses of blacks for the benefit of whites. As *Marrow* presented racial prejudice in "its ugliest shape," it also connected the ascension "of the educated negro into social possibilities" ("With Ye Books," 28). Chesnutt's travel to Wilmington on a reading and lecturing tour and gathering resources for *Marrow*, marked a dramatic shift of his ideas as he entered a great productive period; criticism would become foremost to the success of his fiction. One critic suggested that Chesnutt "pictured such a community with faithful realism, and the passions, prejudices, sentiments, and ideas of his characters are fairly representative of the people of the South" ("The Literary World," 260). Chesnutt's most significant critic, William Dean Howells, seemed to be dubious with his criticism of *Marrow*. "It cannot be said," Howells writes, that Chesnutt's "aesthetics or his ethics are false." Although calling *Marrow* a "bitter, bitter" text, Howells acknowledged that "if the tables could once be turned" and blacks "triumphed in the bloody revolution at Wilmington, North Carolina ... what would we not excuse to the white man who made the atrocity the argument of his fiction?" (quoted in Bentley 26). Contemporary reviews of *Marrow* attribute its success to Chesnutt's Realism. One critic saw *Marrow* as a "strong, virile and exciting novel of contemporary Southern life" that was "tremendous in emotional interest." Chesnutt's story "sweeps the reader along to an end at once artistic and satisfying" while it illustrated a "clear conception of the difficult problems which confront the South" (*New York Press*, 7). Yet another suggests that the novel was "skillfully written," however, "quite unfair" ("Mr. Chesnutt's 'Marrow of Tradition,'" 939). Another critic saw Chesnutt's portrayal of "his enemy" as "too rash" and "too personal." This review ends: "There is no color line in its eternal fairness" (*Independent*, 582).

For Chesnutt, however, an examination of the "color line" became more of a moral movement than a fictional one. Conceiving that *Marrow* was meant to shed "light upon the vexed moral and sociological problems which grow out of the present, in our southern states" ("Chesnutt's Own View," 5), Chesnutt offered an understanding of the complexities of the African American experience by shaping the text to suit a white audience. His contribution to Realism has clearly been a factor in the development of what is called American Realism. Critics in Chesnutt's day saw the need for a text that tackled racial prejudice. As one contemporary critic writes, "to militate against such lack of discrimination," *Marrow* represents "a plea upon the racial question, which is worthy of consideration" (*Books and Authors*, 3). Therefore, *Marrow*, representing a fictional, yet historical, account of the 1898 Wilmington race riot, also offers a piercing psychoanalysis of "cultural segregation" (Bentley, 26). Chesnutt saw that the "solution of the race problem is an old cry, replete with historic significance":

> It has been wrought out in blood in other lands; it may quite as easily be enforced by peaceful means: "Liberty, Equality, Fraternity"; liberty to all, on equal terms; equality to every man as soon as he shall have won it — nay, more, for every man at all times equality with those who are no wiser or better than he; fraternity, for only with this can equality or true friendship exist ["The Negro's Franchise," 18].

His reason for choosing to structure *Marrow* in the manner in which he did suggests that his text's primary focus thus becomes whether white supremacy is harmful to blacks, as Chesnutt forces his reading public to consider the inevitable consequences if the issues are not confronted. As a prelude to his novels, Chesnutt came to the realization that writing a book would elevate Americans and bring them to a level of consciousness about racial prejudice. "The object of my writing," Chesnutt writes, "would not be so much the elevation of the colored people as the elevation of the whites." "For I consider the unjust spirit of caste which is so insidious as to pervade a whole nation, and so powerful as to subject a whole race and all connected with it to scorn and social ostracism — I consider this a barrier to the moral progress of the American people: and I would be one of the first to head a determined, organized crusade against it" (*Journals*, 139–140).

Chesnutt's fundamental premise toward an endeavor of this magnitude, the cornerstone for his novels, would act as a "moral revolution which must be brought about in a different manner" than that of "an appeal to force" (*Journals*, 140). A novel of this caliber, Chesnutt continues, should have a "twofold character": to prepare blacks for "social recognition and equality," while leading them on, "imperceptibly, unconsciously step by step to the desired state of feeling." In a book review of Booker T. Washington's *The Future of the American Negro*, Chesnutt posited that "the race problem can be settled." He further conjectured that racism had "grown to too great proportions to be permanently disposed of along any other lines than those of equal and exact justice" ("A Plea for the American Negro," 63). Chesnutt's endeavor, then, to help shape blacks' consciousness while fostering their understanding of the manifestation of race relations in the American South, was something he was prepared to "gladly devote [his] life to" (*Journals*, 140).

All throughout *Marrow*, Chesnutt juxtaposes two opposing forces, the old Southern traditions vs. the new Southern traditions, in order to heighten his reading public's awareness of racial issues; thus, the more appropriate title would have been *The Marrow of Traditions*. Chesnutt's interpretation of Charles Lamb's verse, "I like your book, ingenious Hone! / In whose capacious, all-embracing leaves / The very marrow of tradition's shown" (*The Watchman*, 15), suggests his awareness of racial prejudice grown not only from his own experiences as a light-complexioned African American, but also from the injustices that the Negro endured "in the public estimation, from loose and hasty generalizations with reference to his intelligence, his morals, his physical characteristics, and his social efficiency" ("A Defamer of His Race," 351) becomes the title of his text. As he continued to illustrate his authority over his great effort throughout the text, Chesnutt made use of a former slave driver, a Southern dignitary turned editor and his wife, an honored Confederate general and his morally wronged grandson, a liberal young newsman, a white-supremacist politician, and an aging woman of good family and little humanity. These characters are balanced with African American characters: a young laborer whose rebelliousness will not allow him to acquiesce to white supremacy, an adroit medical doctor and his nearly-white wife, an intimidated young servant boy who is subject to white protectors (Keller, 190), and the "typical old 'mammy,'" and a "faithful servant who is willing to die for his master and an ideal old aristocrat who practically sacrifices his life to save that of his servant" ("Chesnutt's Own View," 5). *Marrow* portrayed a "white uprising ... for the overthrow of the ascendancy of the colored race in a southern city" that contemporary critics assumed "to be based on what really occurred in a locality in North Carolina" ("The Race Question in Fiction").

In a November 9, 1901, review of *Marrow*, *The Brooklyn Daily Eagle* suggested that *Marrow* highlights the "forces and the problems" that "the American race question" symbolizes more readily "than the story itself that gives it importance." In this power struggle, Mammy Jane, the Carteret family nurse, represents the "relic of antebellum time" (*Marrow*, 70). The new nurse, of course, "belonged to a younger generation of colored people" who possessed "neither the picturesqueness of the slave, nor that unconscious dignity of those of whom freedom has been the immemorial birthright." The new nurse, Chesnutt reveals to his reading public, thought that "old-time negroes" were degrading the race "with their slavering over white folks" (*Marrow*, 69–70). When Mammy Jane and the new nurse are confronted early in the text, Jane is left with a "feeling bordering upon awe." Carteret, "the quintessence of aristocracy," nullifies Jane's astonishment by telling her:

> "The old times have vanished, the old ties have been ruptured. The old relations of dependence and loyal obedience on the part of the colored people, the responsibility of protection and kindness upon that of the whites, have passed away forever. The young negroes are too self-assertive. Education is spoiling them, Jane; they have been badly taught. They are not content with their station in life. Some time they will overstep the mark. The white people are patient, but there is a limit to their endurance" [*Marrow*, 70–71].

Using Carteret's statement, "the old times have vanished" to echo his own sentiments, Chesnutt, at the end of the text, attempts to further eliminate the old Negro's ideologies with the death of Mammy Jane and Josh Green. Although Green may be read by some critics as the revolutionary character that is needed to forge a rebellious consciousness among blacks, Chesnutt's killing of Green is evidence that he did not plan for him to be read as such.

This debate on Chesnutt's choice of characterization for Green has been fueled by scholars' interpretation of Chesnutt's stand on assimilationism (Wilson 112). Idyllically, ideas that forge a new consciousness are fostered and sometimes accepted by society. A revolutionary ideology is needed, Chesnutt believes, but not in Green's radical manner. Green's death is paralleled by that of Captain McBane, who represents the old Southern plantocracy. Hence, throughout the text Chesnutt presents a balancing of the old vs. the new and it is imperative that the old "traditions" be eliminated. From his own perspective on *Marrow*, Chesnutt later writes:

> Tradition made the white people masters, rulers, who absorbed all the power, the wealth, the honors of the community, and jealously guarded this monopoly, with which they claimed to be divinely endowed, by denying to those who were not of their caste the opportunity to acquire any of these desirable things.
> Tradition, on the other hand made the negro a slave, an underling, existing by favor and not by right, his place the lowest in the social scale, to which, by the same divine warrant, he was hopelessly confined.
> The old order has passed away, but these opinions, deeply implanted in the consciousness of two races, still persist, and "The Marrow of Tradition" seeks to show the efforts of the people of a latter generation to adjust themselves in this traditional atmosphere to the altered conditions of a new era ["Chesnutt's Own View," 5].

Since the "old order has passed away," it is important that the threat the old —
Negro/southern plantocracy — characters pose to society is shattered so that
the new can emerge. Given that the "latter generation" has "to adjust themselves in this traditional atmosphere to the altered conditions of a new era,"
Green's arrogant idealism, and Mammy Jane's subservience, would somehow
hinder this growth and development.

Since the realist novel is concerned with re-establishing diplomacy by
restoring confidence in the reader that his cultural practices are in peril, readers can assume that Dr. Miller's *real* work will now begin: forging a new
socio-political and socio-economic consciousness — a new representative
image for African Americans. Believing that *Marrow* was his greatest work,
Chesnutt hoped that readers of his previous fiction would find *Marrow* pleasing and tasteful ("Chesnutt's Own View," 5). Over 20 years before Alain
Locke's call for the elimination of the old Negro with the rise of the new was
heralded in his essay "Enter the New Negro,"[6] Chesnutt was already attuned
to the needs of the African American community. *Marrow* would demonstrate
in remarkable style the development of repression and domination of blacks
in the South. The elevation of both his race and the white race becomes the
crucible for which *Marrow* is examined, because Chesnutt believed blacks'
condition in the South was anomalous. Adding a warning that will echo
throughout later criticism of African Americans' contribution to the Age of
Realism, Chesnutt continues: "When every Negro has learned to read and
write, unless the Constitutional guarantees of his liberty are maintained, some
other means will be sought to preserve intact the power and prestige of the
white race" ("The Negro's Franchise," 18). What Chesnutt here posits is exactly
the problem that continues to consume scholars' interpretation of his fiction:
the awareness that his pragmatist style in writing *Marrow* saw its charge as
telling the truth about the ordinary life of African Americans who went against
Southern traditions.

***

When did realist writers start to employ Realism in their texts? Can we
readily point to a single text that gave Realism birth? As with any literary
movement, Realism's origins are convoluted, for no one truly knows where it
begins, or ends. What we are certain of, however, is that it was born from the
"conception [that] reality had become increasingly problematic" (Brown, 227)
in mid nineteenth-century America. Chesnutt's contribution to the Age of
Realism, then, stems from his ability as a writer to elevate African American
fiction to innovative plateaus. To understand why Chesnutt chose Realism in
Marrow, one asks that readers categorize the text for its beneficial aspects, not
only for what it contributes to the world of Realism, but for how it affects
readers, for that is the single most important element that truly characterizes

any realist text. This more than anything attaches Chesnutt's notions in *Marrow* to the Age of Realism. What Realism offers readers is a window through which they can gaze and see what the author suggests is reality. With his imagination, Chesnutt was able to draw from the events of the race riot and present readers, as they peer through his window, the opportunity to view Southern racism. Even though, as Charles Hackenberry suggested, the last line of *Marrow* is prophetic, "There's time enough, but none to spare," (201) Chesnutt does not offer a solution to racial problems because he recognizes that the future of his race is a dilemma yet uncertain. Depending on one's reading of the text, then, Miller has "time enough" to forge the new consciousness, but "none to spare." Even though he lost his own son amidst the mayhem, Miller's decision to fix whatever *ails* the Carteret baby is his first step toward repairing the *ills* of Southern racism. It is an important step, one that, Chesnutt suggests, the light-complexioned African American is responsible for in forging this new consciousness because Chesnutt understood that the mulatto would be more easily accepted into white mainstream America than a dark-complexioned African American.

Chesnutt believed that African Americans should progressively speak out against their injustices. The power of "free speech" was a vital part of Chesnutt's convictions for he believed it would animate blacks' desire to protect their right to control their destiny. Not only does *Marrow* illustrate Chesnutt's use of Realism, but the novel convinces us that its author was full of racial criticism, more than *The House Behind the Cedars* (1900) or *The Colonel's Dream* (1905) set forth. Chesnutt used *Marrow* to expose what he considered the basis for racial prejudice instead of indulging in literary prudence as an author. "If the colored people of the South could voice in one cry all the agony of their twenty-five years of so-called freedom," Chesnutt said, "the whole world would listen, and give back such an indignant protest as would startle this boasted land of the free into seeing itself, for a moment at least, as others see it — as a country where prejudice has usurped the domain of law, where justice is no longer impartial, and where the citizen deprived of his rights has no redress" ("A Multitude of Counselors," 5). *Marrow* is Chesnutt's response to conditions and his argument that in a reconstructionist Southern town, the conflict between African Americans and Southern whites suggests that the outcome of the traditional behavior of the South will explode in a dynamic and vengeful confrontation.

NOTES

1. Reprinted in *To Be an Author: Letters of Charles W. Chesnutt, 1889–1905*. Ed. by Joseph R. McElrath, Jr. and Robert C. Leitz, III. Princeton: Princeton University Press, 1997, 158.
2. Derived from an African word meaning either "monster," "master" or both, depending

on the context in which it is used, Chesnutt's use of the term "buckrah" is in reference to the slave term which was employed by blacks in the mid–1850s in relation to poor white people, or white trash. Chesnutt later employed the term in many of his conjure woman tales.

3. *The Journals of Charles W. Chesnutt*, edited by Richard Brodhead (Durham: Duke University Press, 1993) will henceforth be referred to as *Journals* when cited parenthetically within the text.

4. Novels such as Paul Laurence Dunbar's *Sport of the Gods*, Booker T. Washington's *Up from Slavery* and W.E.B. Du Bois's *Souls of Black Folks,* although not intended to be Realism as a genre of fiction, are very much so as they, too, represent the reality of African American life.

5. Reprinted in *To Be an Author: Letters of Charles W. Chesnutt, 1889–1905,* 117–118. Chesnutt, in his 27 December letter to Page, was referring to his recent published short story, "Hot-Foot Hannibal," in *Atlantic Monthly*.

6. Published in 1925, Alain Locke's pioneering essay, "Enter the New Negro," calls to African American writers, "the younger generation" which is "vibrant with a new psychology," to awaken in masses a "new spirit" that will transform "what has been a perennial problem" of African Americans "into the progressive phases of contemporary Negro life" (*Survey Graphic,* 4:6, March 1925, p. 631). Sutton Griggs's *Imperium in Imperio* (1899) and *Pointing the Way* (1908) also illustrate the ideology Locke posits in his essay.

WORKS CITED

Andrews, William L. "William Dean Howells and Charles W. Chesnutt: Criticism and Race Fiction in the Age of Booker T. Washington." *American Literature* 48.3 (November 1976): 327–339.

Barrish, Phillip. *American Literary Realism, Critical Theory, and Intellectual Prestige, 1880–1995.* Cambridge: Cambridge University Press, 2001.

Bell, Bernard W. *The Contemporary African American Novel: Its Folk Roots and Modern Literary Branches.* Amherst: University of Massachusetts Press, 2004.

"Book Review of *The Marrow of Tradition.*" *The Independent* 54 (March 1902): 582.

Bowron, Bernard R. "Realism in America." *Comparative Literature* 3.3, A Symposium on Realism (Summer 1951): 268–285.

Brown, Marshall. "The Logic of Realism: A Hegelian Approach." *PMLA* 96.2 (March 1981): 224–241.

Campbell, Donna M. "Realism in American Literature, 1860–1890." *Literary Movements* (September 2003).

Chesnutt, Charles W. "Charles W. Chesnutt's Own View of His Story 'The Marrow of Tradition.'" *Cleveland World,* (20 October 1901): 5.

_____. "A Defamer of His Race." *Critic* 38.4 (April 1901): 350–51.

_____. "The Disfranchisement of the Negro." In *The Negro Problem.* Edited by Bernard R. Boxill. New York: Humanity Books, 2003. 77–124.

_____. *The Marrow of Tradition.* Edited by Nancy Bentley and Sandra Gunning. Boston: Bedford/St. Martin's, 2002.

_____. "A Multitude of Counselors." *The Independent* 43 (2 April 1891): 4–5.

_____. "The Negro's Franchise." *Boston Evening Transcript* (11 May 1901): 18.

_____. "On the Future of his People." *Saturday Evening Post,* (20 January 1900): 646.

_____. "Superstitions and Folk-Lore of the South." *Modern Culture* 13 (May 1901): 231–5.

_____. "What Is a White Man?" *The Independent* 41 (30 May 1889): 5–6.

_____. "The White and the Black" *Boston Evening Transcript,* (20 March 1901): 13.

_____. "Why is a Book Popular?" *The Index* 2.1 (1 September 1899): 5.

Chesnutt, Charles W., Joseph R. McElrath, Jr., and Robert C. Leitz, III. *To Be an Author: Letters of Charles W. Chesnutt, 1889–1905.* Princeton: Princeton University Press, 1997.

Chesnutt, Helen. *Charles Chesnutt: The Pioneer of the Color Line.* Chapel Hill: University of North Carolina Press, 1952.

Hackenberry, Charles. "Meaning and Models: The Uses of Characterization in Chesnutt's *The Marrow of Tradition* and Mandy Oxendine." *American Literary Realism* 17.2 (Autumn 1984): 193–202.

Howells, William Dean. "Mr. Charles Chesnutt's Short Stories." *Atlantic Monthly* 85 (1900): 699–710.

"The Literary World," *Modern Culture* 14 (1901): 260–261.

Loewen, James W. "Telling History on the Landscape." *Poverty & Race*, March/April 1999.

Kawash, Samira. *Dislocating the Color Line: Identity, Hybridity, and Singularity in African-American Literature.* Stanford: Stanford University Press, 1997.

Keller, Frances Richardson. *An American Crusade: The Life of Charles Waddell Chesnutt.* Provo, Utah: Brigham Young University Press, 1978.

McElrath, Joseph R., Jr. "Why Charles W. Chesnutt Is Not a Realist." *American Literary Realism* 32.2 (2000): 91–108.

Pettis, Joyce. "*The Marrow of Tradition*: Charles Chesnutt's Novel of the South." *North Carolina Literary Review* 11.1 (Spring 1994): 108–118.

"The Race Question in Fiction, a review of 'The Marrow of Tradition.'" *The Sunday Herald* (27 October 1901): 16.

"Review of 'The Marrow of Tradition.'" In "Among the Books." *The Watchman* 82 (12 December 1901): 15.

"Review of 'The Marrow of Tradition,'" In "Books and Authors." *Boston Courier* (16 November 1901): 3.

"Review of 'The Marrow of Tradition.'" *The Brooklyn Daily Eagle* (9 November 1901).

"Review of 'The Marrow of Tradition.'" *New York Press.* (2 November 1901): 7.

"Review of 'The Marrow of Tradition.'" *The Public.* 4 (1 February 1902): 687–88.

"Review of 'The Marrow of Tradition,'" *The Times Literature and Literary Topics*, (15 December 1901): 17.

"Review of 'The Marrow of Tradition.'" In "With Ye Books," *The Evening Star* (9 November 1901): 28.

Salomon, Roger B. "Realism as Disinheritance: Twain, Howells and James." *American Quarterly* 16.14 (Winter 1964): 531–544.

Wilson, Matthew. *Whiteness in the Novels of Charles W. Chesnutt.* Jackson: The University Press of Mississippi, 2004.

CHAPTER 3

"I shall leave the realm of fiction"[1]: Conjure, Genre, and Passing in the Fiction of Charles W. Chesnutt

Christopher Bundrick

As part of his larger discussion of "the relationship of two conflicting yet coalescing cultural traditions ... that have produced a sustained tradition of the most significant literature of race in America," Eric Sundquist introduces his ambitious *To Wake the Nations* (1993) by arguing that the cultural work of several minority literary traditions (especially those traditions most closely associated with African American writing) are unintelligible to readers who can only approach them through the veil of a dominant ideology (6). Beginning with the premise that a study of the racism entrenched in nineteenth-century American literature "seems frequently to lock readers into rigid, unimaginative structures of analysis," Sundquist outlines instead a more flexible strategy that works to "understand the authorial context, the historical moment, and reigning cultural pressures, even the deliberate strategies employed for producing signs of both racial consciousness and racial antagonism" (9). Claiming that Chesnutt's literary career "was one of extruding richness," that he "wrote successfully in a number of forms," and most interestingly, that his short stories, "offer an unparalleled bridge between the art of black folk vernacular and published literature," Sundquist emphasizes the important role that Chesnutt's work plays in the emerging African American literary tradition of the late nineteenth and early twentieth century (12–13). At the heart of his argument that Chesnutt's fiction is central to issues of race and literature in the U.S. at the turn of the century is Sundquist's emphasis on historical context and rhetorical fluidity, which, he claims, shows us that "Chesnutt worked within the confines of literary high culture but did so by locating premises of modern black literature in the historical memory and vernacular practice of slave culture and its implied African resources" (13). Careful not to oversimplify this dynamic, however, Sundquist reminds us that "neither perspective [white or black] is by itself adequate to account for the ongoing crisis over race in American cultural or political life, just as neither black nor white authorship guarantees any sort of univocal vision or moral advantage" (7). No matter how complex or mitigated this division might be, the reality of American culture at the end of the nineteenth century is that the color line remained a very real boundary and anyone who attempted to cross it risked serious consequences. Considering the way he focuses on Chesnutt's position within the American canon, however, Sundquist seems to be offering him as a figure through which we might reconcile the cultural traditions of African American storytelling and the (then) white tradition of ostensibly high culture literary publication. That Chesnutt's work (especially his conjure tales) offered a subtle critique of the structures of white superiority and racial segregation is something of a commonplace. Focused primarily on demonstrating that Chesnutt's texts do, in fact, resist structures of racism, much of the existing scholarship on this topic ignores the remarkable way the formal and aesthetic dimensions of his work speak to the actual mechanics of that resistance. Here, one can examine more closely the way Chesnutt's fiction confronts these issues not only through the overt commentary that narration provides, but also by engaging questions of race and culture through a nuanced exploration of the way literary and social traditions intersect. The purpose of this essay is to examine the manner in which Chesnutt's work necessarily subverts genre conventions in the process of undermining the cultural conventions that they represent. Using his unusual position as a commercially successful African American author in the 1800s to rewrite some of the more popular genre forms of his time, Chesnutt, in an attempt to subtly reorient his white readers' sympathies, was able to offer them a brief glimpse of life from the other side of the color line.

We can see the most conspicuous and propagandistic example of this strategy in "Marse Jeems's Nightmare," the third story in Chesnutt's 1899 *The Conjure Woman*. As do all of the stories in *The Conjure Woman*, "Marse Jeems's Nightmare" follows the same basic dialect tale formula that we find in Murfree and Page. This story opens with John, the white frame narrator who has recently purchased the North Carolina plantation on which Julius had been a slave, musing over the old man's character. Even though John recognizes that Julius "had a thorough knowledge of the neighborhood, was familiar with the roads and watercourses, knew the qualities of various soils, and what they would produce, and where the best hunting and fishing were to be had," he returns to the old racist stereotypes and ignores Julius's lifetime of experience with the property, deciding instead that Julius's talents must be the result of an innate and specifically racialized relationship to the land, something that John describes as "a peculiar personal attitude" (25). "He had been accustomed," John concludes, "to look upon himself as the property of another" and after Emancipation, John reasons, Julius doesn't accept owner-ship of himself so much as he transfers title to the old plantation grounds (25). Effectively reducing Julius from human subject to "appurtenance" of the property, John's attempt to rationalize his sense of Julius as both part and prod-uct of the landscape is really just an attempt to further inscribe him within a limited frame of discourse and thus, essentially, re-enslave him (25). While this peek into John's psyche certainly reveals the frame narrator's essential racism, John's reluctance to recognize Julius's subjectivity is more important for its contribution to the complex structure of narration and authority that Chesnutt's stories construct around Julius's relationship to him. John's thoughts about Julius are not without context, as his part of the narrative seems designed to compare Julius to Tom, his seventeen-year-old grandson, who (at Julius's urging) John hires "to help about the stables, weed the gar-den, cut wood and bring water, and in general to make himself useful about the outdoor work of the household" (25).[2] Unlike Julius, whose willingness to conform — superficially at least — to the old stereotypes puts John at ease, Tom the proverbial "new Negro" cannot or will not play that part and so John finds him to be "very trifling" and fires him (26)[3]. Julius asks John to give him another chance, but John, who tells us sanctimoniously that he has "always been too easily imposed upon" is "determined to be firm as a rock in this instance" and refuses (26). Of course, Julius's special talent, like that of all tricksters, is using the inflexibility of authority as the very means of shat-tering that which will not bend.

Later the same day, Julius drives John and Annie to a nearby mineral spring in order to collect some of its water. Along the way, they encounter a neighbor going in the other direction. Having difficulty with his horse, the young man is "beating him furiously with a buggy whip" (27). After he's past, John and Annie both express their disgust for such cruelty and Julius agrees, adding, "'A man w'at 'buses his hoss is gwine ter be ha'd on de folks w'at wuks fer 'im.... Ef young Mistah McLean doan min', he'll hab a bad dream one or dese days, des lak 'is granddaddy had way back yander, long befo' de wah'" (27). Forced to wait before they can fill their jugs, John asks Julius to tell them the rest of the story, since, as he puts it, "'we might as well put in time listening to Julius as in any other way'" (27). Seeing his opportunity, Julius tells them the story of Marse Jeems, who was "'a ha'd man, en monst'us stric' wid his han'" (27). Marse Jeems, Julius tells his new employers, not only expected his slaves to work longer hours than any of the other slave owners in the region, but he expected them to do it on short rations. At the same time, Jeems refused to allow any singing or dancing as he "'bought his han's ter wuk, en not ter play, en w'en night come dey mus' sleep en res', so dey'd be ready ter git up soon in de mawnin' en go ter dey wuk'" (28). Worst of all, Jeems disallowed any courtship among his slaves, and whenever two slaves showed any sign of romance Jeems would ship one to his other plantation in order to break up the lovers (28). Anyone who dared to break the rules had to face Nick Johnson, the overseer whose cruelty led the slaves to call him (behind his back, of course) Ole Nick.

When Jeems begins courting Libbie McSwayne his attention is distracted from the slaves and some of his more strict regulations go briefly unenforced. But before things can get too serious, Libbie, who worries that Jeems "'mought git so useter 'busin' his niggers dat he's 'mence ter 'buse his wife atter he got useter habbin' her roun'" breaks off her relationship with Jeems (28).[4] "'De niggers wuz all monst'us sorry w'en de match wuz bust' up,'" Julius tells us, but their sorrow didn't come from sympathy for the rejected suitor as much as the understanding that they would bear the brunt of the spurned lover's frustration (28). Sure enough, Jeems uses the time he had once spent on courtship "'findin' fault wid de niggers,'" and, as one might imagine, when Jeems discovers that two of his field hands have entered into a surreptitious romance under the cover of his own failed courtship the punishment is direct and merciless (28). Jeems sends the woman to his distant plantation in Robeson County and gives Solomon, her lover, forty lashes. Sore from his lashing, but sorer still from the loss of his love, Solomon goes to Aunt Peggy, the local conjure woman, to see if she can do anything to reunite them. Although she hesitates at first, explaining that conjuring white people is sometimes a dangerous business, Peggy finally agrees to help Solomon and gives him a concoction of roots and herbs that he is to slip into Jeems's soup — and a strict warning to return in a month to report on the effects. Solomon manages to slip the mixture into Jeems's soup the very next day, but before anything can happen Jeems announces that he's going to the Robeson County plantation for a month or so and leaves it to the overseer Johnson "'ter run dis year plantation fer all it's wuth'" (30).

A few days after Jeems's departure, Duncan McSwayne comes by the plantation, offering a slave as payment for a bet he'd lost to Jeems. "'He's kinder brash,'" McSwayne says to the overseer, "'but I knows yo' powers, Mistah Johnson, en I recon ef anybody kin make 'im toe de ma'k, you is de man'" (31). Moved both by Jeems's command to wring as much profit as possible from the plantation and a sycophantic pleasure at McSwayne's confidence in his cruelty, Ole Nick invests considerable time and energy into beating the new slave into submission. Johnson's efforts are to no avail; the new slave is either unwilling or unable to obey. As Julius puts it, he simply "'could n' 'pear ter git it th'oo his min' dat he wuz a slabe en had ter wuk en min' de w'ite folks'" (32). Deciding that he would risk killing the man if he continued to beat him, Johnson gives up and returns the new slave to McSwayne who plans to send him downriver to the markets of New Orleans. Later the same day, Aunt Peggy arrives, checking up on the effect of her medicine. When Aunt Peggy's interest peaks at Solomon's mention of a new slave, readers must acknowledge what they most probably already suspected — that Peggy's conjure actually transformed Marse Jeems into a slave. That night Solomon takes the new slave a drugged sweet potato that will undo the conjure and sure enough Jeems returns the following morning, explaining his ragged appearance by telling everyone that he's been waylaid and robbed. After he's had a chance to change into proper clothing Jeems calls Johnson to account for his supervision of the plantation. In particular, Jeems grills the overseer about his treatment of the new slave. Having learned his lesson, Jeems discharges Johnson at the end of the interview and immediately relaxes the rules on the plantation by shortening the workday and allowing dancing and singing. He even returns Solomon's sweetheart to him

Making his motives a little too obvious, Julius uncharacteristically tips his hand and in doing so, seems to reveal Chesnutt's narrative purpose as well. The moral of Julius's story is that "'w'ite folks w'at is so ha'd en stric', en doan make no 'lowance fer po' ign'ant niggers w'at ain' had no chanst ter l'am, is li'ble ter hab bad dreams, ter say de leas' en dat dem w'at is kin' en good ter po' people is sho' ter prosper en git long in de worl'" (38), sounds suspiciously similar to the language Julius used when he pled his grandson's case asking John to "'make some 'lowance fuh a' ign'ant young nigger, suh'" (26). Even John, who is not very perceptive, recognizes Julius's story for what it is and facetiously tells Julius "'I am glad ... that you told us the moral of the story; it might have escaped us otherwise'" (38). Richard Baldwin argues that Julius's "sententious moralizing reveals Uncle Julius's awareness of the white man's guilt and his willingness to exploit that sense of guilt unscrupulously," however, there is much more to Julius's approach than simple, venial opportunism (396). In that it convinces Annie to rehire Julius's grandson, the story of Marse Jeems's transformation seems wholly successful, but in thinking that Julius is primarily interested in taking advantage of his new employers for short-term material gain, Baldwin makes the same mistake that John does. The clumsiness and transparency of Julius's gambit in this sketch suggests a simplicity of approach that isn't at all characteristic of Chesnutt's fiction. Certainly, Julius must take some pleasure in gulling the white man, but his goal (and Chesnutt's as well) is much more ambitious than simply getting the better of John in these petty swindles. Chesnutt explains his ambition to go beyond traditional stories about African American tricksters in an entry from his journal dated May 29, 1880, in which he writes, "The object of my writings would be not so much the elevation of the colored people as the elevation of the whites" (Chesnutt, Helen, 21). He understands that this is a delicate business and goes on, "The subtle almost indefinable feeling of revulsion toward the Negro ... cannot be stormed and taken by assault; the garrison will not capitulate, so their position must be mined, and we will find ourselves in their midst before they think it" (21). Chesnutt's martial language signals just how serious an issue this is for him, but his plan of attack, "to accustom the public mind to the idea; to lead people out, imperceptibly, unconsciously, step by step" represents a restrained and patient, long-term attempt to develop a counter hegemony capable of undermining the ideology of white superiority until an ideology of racial equality can take its place (21). As we'll see over the course of *The Conjure Woman*, Julius wants to do much more than simply fleece his employer; in fact, his tricksterism is really part of his long-term plan to bring John over to something closer to a black way of seeing the world.

Chesnutt's (mis)appropriation of the frame narrative is crucial to understanding this dynamic. Borrowing from Kenneth Lynn's arguments as well as his own earlier work on the social aspects of the frame narrative in Southwest humor, Lorne Fienberg writes that the frame in *Conjure Woman* "creates the illusion of distance for the comfortable reader, a kind of *cordon sanitaire* which makes it safe to contemplate the words and deeds of social and racial inferiors.... Put another way, the frame is a strategy of containment which returns the freed slave to a state of narrative bondage" (164). The frame that Chesnutt employs, however, only imitates the sort of barrier that Fienberg describes. Constrained by his own incontrovertible faith in racial difference, John, the white, upper-class frame narrator is incapable of understanding his relationship with Julius except in terms of a natural superior and satisfied inferior — a stereotype very effectively reaffirmed by the plantation romance rhetoric that has informed his sense of the South from the very beginning. In Chesnutt's alternate frame narrative, however, the frame reverses polarity and rather than marking the regionalized inferior's social distance from the superior frame narrator, it demonstrates how these ostensibly superior figures are bound and limited by their faith in the frame's ability to act as a barrier, while less thoroughly convinced subalterns, who are not invested in the rhetoric of hierarchy, are free to move back and forth across both social and narrative frames. In Chesnutt's version of the frame narrative the frame doesn't enclose marginalized figures so much as it generates a literary space in which they can use their capacity for social and rhetorical flexibility to reshape the relationship — a relationship that dominant figures are compelled to understand as fixed and immutable — between center and periphery.

While Chesnutt's application of this strategy as a way of signifying genre is more sophisticated in *The Marrow of Tradition*, he first used it in *The Conjure Woman*, a collection of plantation dialect sketches he began writing in the mid 1880s and first published in 1899. Although, in the mode of Harris's *Uncle Remus* (1881), *The Conjure Woman* doesn't attempt to reframe the Old South as a sort of plantation utopia so much as it tries to hijack Harris's pastoral motif in an effort to reveal the other side of what Matthew Martin calls "the two-faced South" (17). Lacking any established models for writing the kind of stories he wanted to write, Chesnutt adopted the genre popularized by conservatives like Harris and Page and bent it until it was capable of telling the story of the other — as well as the *othered*— South. The sketches that are the result of this experiment represent a complex kind of signifying that not only uses indirection to revise the cultural significance of the nostalgic plantation school, but also works to codify a literary model for African American literary subjectivity in the South. It's become something of a commonplace to discuss the narrative strategy that Chesnutt uses in *Conjure Woman* as being, itself, a kind of conjure. Gloria Odem, for instance, invokes Chesnutt's narrative conjure as a kind of parallel to the conjure that enslaved African Americans used as a survival strategy, writing "Chesnutt knew that conjure filled a deep need in the slave's life for a weapon to invoke against the arbitrary and often violent circumstances that made up his existence" (39). No matter how much Chesnutt was aware of the problems of slavery in the Old South, his South was the Reconstruction South — the South of the Wilmington Massacre — which, while certainly violent and arbitrary, required a subtly different kind of conjure. John Wideman seems to understand this when he broadens his examination of Chesnutt's fiction to consider the role of the black voice throughout the span of American literature. Emphasizing the way Chesnutt's fiction "juxtaposed the dialect voice with standard literary discourse (a code for the real), dramatizing the inadequacy of the assumptions (encoded in literary discourse as part of the real) which locked black voice and black character into conventional formulaic molds," Wideman points out the way Chesnutt's strategy empowers Julius in a specifically literary way (81). Unlocked from the conventional and marginalized role of black speaker, the old storyteller, Wideman argues, "peeks around the frame [and] uses it for his own purposes, ultimately demolishing its restrictions" (81). Comparing *Conjure Woman* with Ovid's *Metamorphosis*, Karen Magee Myers, like Wideman, comes to see this conspicuous circumvention of the frame as an essential element of Chesnutt's strategy. "It is immediately obvious," she argues, "that the white narrator is insensitive to the material he records. He interprets the stories on the basis of superficial detail and consistently fails to respond to deeper meanings" (15). Since it's an essential part of Julius's (and thus, by extension, Chesnutt's) narrative strategy, we can't blame John entirely for failing to understand the full significance of Julius's stories. Chesnutt knew that his goal of transforming American white consciousness into something that could understand or at least empathize with an African American point of view was, at best, a delicate piece of work. As such, the narrative progression throughout *Conjure Woman* models a gentle process of acculturation through which Chesnutt's readers come to understand Julius, in part, by recognizing John's inability to do so. Julius represents Chesnutt's attempt to develop a narrator capable of operating within the bounds of established white literary and social authority at the same time that he presents a serious challenge to the foundational values and assumptions that prop up that authority.

Richard Brodhead explores this narrative paradox in the introduction to his edition of *The Conjure Woman and Other Conjure Tales* when he writes, "These tales are programmed to produce a display of standard, correct, literate speech that then calls up a different speaker, the bearer of a local dialect barbarously deviant from official literate English, yet fully expressive on its own terms, who is invited to pronounce his vernacular for the other person's hearing" (2). Brodhead's analysis of the frame in Chesnutt's conjure tales quickly adopts a more conservative reading that can't conceive of the frame operating as anything except the *cordone sanitare* that Lynn defined in 1959. Seeming almost to apologize for what he sees as a weakness in Chesnutt's approach, Brodhead continues:

> This formula [the frame] might be called the operative condition of authorship in Chesnutt's conjure stories, so fully does it govern the production of the tales. But to understand the nature of Chesnutt's work as an author it is essential to grasp that the formula he subscribes to here is by no means his own invention. It represents a convention already massively conventional when he adopted it, a formula fully established in the literary system of his time [2–3].

Trying to understand the frame as defining a space in which the definitions of the culture are unsettled, however, Scott Romine argues that the frame narrator wields a kind of "interpretive authority" (63) through which he "attains a style that socializes previously alien and disruptive members of the community" (62). Explicitly trying to move beyond Kenneth Lynn's *cordone sanitare*, Romine's reading re-imagines the frame as a permeable boundary through which the aristocratic narrator and regionalized subject join in a genuine give and take that irrevocably alters both parties. Accepting the frame less as a boundary and more as a zone of convergence that offers the narrator access to the regionalized subject at the same time that it exposes him to that subject is an essential step to understanding the experiment that Chesnutt undertook in *The Conjure Woman*. Chesnutt's plantation sketches, like those from earlier collections, still focus on mediating difference, but unlike the fundamentally conservative versions of this genre that we see in Longstreet, Harris or Page, Chesnutt's sketches ultimately invest authority not in the upper-class, white frame narrator, but in Uncle Julius. Shaping stories of the antebellum South to serve his purposes, Julius uses this authority to reconcile racial difference by using the frame not as a device that heightens difference, but rather emphasizing the frame's ultimate inability to construct clear racial and social boundaries across the inherently ambiguous continuum through which we experience race and class in the U.S. Using a literary form that traditionally specialized in dividing the ambiguous into easily managed hierarchical categories, Chesnutt's strategy in *Conjure Woman* is to signify on the values of this literary tradition the same way that Julius's stories of the Old South slyly signify against the racist social tradition of the region.

The first sketch, "The Goophered Grapevine" introduces the complex frame narrative strategy that Chesnutt will continue to use throughout his conjure stories. Setting the tone for the rest of the collection, "Goophered Grapevine" opens with a lengthy passage in which John, the white, Northern frame narrator, introduces himself and explains that his wife Annie's poor health has forced them to move somewhere with a milder climate. Clearly understanding the postwar South as an improbable combination of Old World agrarian aristocracy and New World frontier, John's sense of the region reveals his limited and self-serving grasp of the political, social and economic complexities that defined the postwar relationship between North and South. Inadvertently positioning himself as a colonizer — an outsider come to extract value from the less civilized South — John's perspective clearly comes out of an essential faith in regional structures of race, gender and economic dominance which, not coincidently, confirm his sense of superiority to those around him. The reader will notice that John has certain, conspicuous blind spots regarding that superiority. Explaining why he favored the old McAdoo vineyard, for instance, John tells us that "shiftless cultivation had well-nigh exhausted the soil" of the McAdoo vineyard, which he believes has gone unattended since the war (2). In nearly the same breath, however, John tells us that the local scuppernong vines, supposedly "lapsed into utter neglect," have grown into a "wild and unpruned luxuriance" (2). Not seeming to recognize the obvious fact that these vines must be the result of active cultivation, John chooses instead to believe that the healthy vines represent only a potential in the soil of this vineyard that "with a little attention, could not have been better" (3). In many ways, this inability to draw reasonable conclusions based on clear evidence is John's defining characteristic. John cannot see that the vines are under cultivation because, for him, the absence of a white landowner necessarily signifies the absence of cultivation. John's crucial inability to understand the world around him suggests that the same ideologies that maintain his authority tend to circumscribe his subjectivity the same way it constrains that of marginalized African Americans.

When John takes Annie to see their future home he discovers Julius eating grapes from the vineyard. There is an awkward pause when the black man realizes that he's no longer alone and, true to form, John mistakes what is almost surely the old man's reflexive impulse to flee as him rising in a show of respect. Fundamentally refusing to acknowledge the obvious, John asks him if he knows anything about the last attempt to cultivate grapes in the McAdoo vineyard and Julius replies, "'Lord bless, suh, I knows all about it. Det ain' na'er a man in dis settlement w'at won't tell you ole Julius McAdoo 'uz bawn en raise' on dis yer same plantation'" (4). Julius's answer is, at least in part, an attempt to stake a claim on the old vineyard whose grapes he has both tended and enjoyed since the McAdoos left. Negotiating a careful course that acknowledges both the desire to retain his *de facto* possession of the vineyard and the necessary prudence of avoiding open confrontation with a white man, Julius's reply is constructed around his recognition of a power dynamic that John either fails to notice or assumes exists unchallenged. Although native-born to the McAdoo plantation and inculcated in the real experience of the South, Julius must at least superficially defer to John, who only knows the region through the self-serving and second-hand narratives of white male superiority he wants to recreate. At the same time that Julius's response reassures John by enacting the pandering character of what Thomas Nelson Page would call "the old-time negro," it also works to challenge the hierarchies implicit in John's attitude by accentuating that it's Julius who inhabits a position of the authority in regards to the McAdoo vineyard and John who is the alien *other*. It's specifically this local authority that Julius invokes when he offers the story of Henry's tragic encounter with the cursed grapevine as proof of why John shouldn't buy the vineyards. Before he can get to the story, Julius seems to make a crucial misstep that threatens to waste all his efforts at subtlety. Tipping his hand, Julius finishes introducing himself by asking John, "'Is you de Norvern genman w'at's gwine ter buy de ole vimyard?'" (4). Of course concern over this kind of transaction demonstrates an understanding that tends to undermine the simple ex-slave persona that John has already begun to construct for Julius, but this is perhaps where we see the old man's true genius. Julius, who seems to be aware that his audience extends beyond John's frame plays directly to the reader. This approach confronts the narrative hierarchy implicit in traditional readings of the frame narrative, the most obvious of which is the assumption of racial superiority on the part of the frame narrator. In a sense, then, missing the point is John's most important duty throughout the conjure tales. His doing so shores up not only Julius's

authority, but also the reader's sense of superiority to John, which short cir-
cuits Lynn's *cordone sanitare* by inviting the reader to identify with Julius and
his signifying sensibility rather than John's obviously inadequate frame for
reading the world. When John asks Julius to go on, Julius tells him matter-
of-factly, "'I dunno whe'r you b'lieves in cunj'in er not,—some er de w'ite
folks don't, er says dey don't,—but de truf en de matter is dat dis wer ole
vimya'd is Goophered'" (5). Citing an understanding that he clearly identifies
along racial lines—even to the point of using a term he must know would be
unfamiliar to his white audience—Julius establishes himself as a harmless,
superstitious darky even as he evokes an authority that simply isn't available
to John. Setting up the context for not only the tale but also its telling, Julius
becomes his own frame narrator after a fashion and defines, in the first
moments of their acquaintance, a dynamic that will characterize his relationship to John and Annie throughout *The Conjure Woman*. Emphasizing the
difference between the relationships that African Americans and whites have
to conjure while also implying that the story will only serve to pass the time
(a device he will use repeatedly), Julius invites John to disregard the tale as
little more than additional local color. At the same time Julius's frame clearly
situates racial difference at the forefront of his story about the travails of a
slave who eats from the goophered grapevine.

Julius begins the tale by explaining that Ole Marse Dugal' McAdoo, the
previous owner, had been distressed by the failure of traditional safeguards,
"spring guns en steel traps," to curb the extent to which his grapes were pil-
fered (6) and so undertook the extreme measure of hiring Aunt Peggy, the
local conjure woman, to curse them so that, as she explains it to the slaves
on the plantation, "a'er a nigger w'at eat dem grapes 'ud be sho ter die insid-
e'n twel' mont's" (7). That Aunt Peggy specifically aims the goopher at the
slaves bears special attention. The implication is clearly that although McAdoo
doesn't really believe in Peggy's power to conjure, he trusts that his slaves'
superstitious faith in the goopher will keep them away from the grapes.
McAdoo's ruse proves to be very effective and wine production takes a sharp
rise. This arrangement gets complicated when Henry, a new slave, eats some
of the grapes before he could be told about the goopher. Henry is so distressed
that the overseer carries on with the ruse by taking him to Peggy's house to
see if she can't remove the curse. Although she recognizes Henry's innocence,
Peggy must observe the internal logic of the curse so while he can't be cured
outright the effects of the curse can be deferred if Henry rubs the grapevine
sap on his head every spring. An unexpected result of this treatment is that
Henry's vitality becomes linked to the vineyard's so that, as Julius tells it, in
the spring Henry "'got young ag'in, en so soopl en libely dat none er de young
niggers on de plantation could n' jump, ner dance, ner hoe ez much cotton'"

and in the fall "'his j'ints ter git stiff, en his ha'r drap off, en de rheumatiz begin ter wrestle wid im'" (9). Something of a trickster himself, McAdoo recognizes in Henry's condition a unique opportunity for profit and hatches a complex scheme in which he sells the young vital Henry every spring for fifteen hundred dollars and then buys back the ailing Henry for five hundred. Coming out a thousand dollars ahead every year, Julius tells John and Annie, in just five years McAdoo makes enough money to buy a second plantation. Before McAdoo can sell Henry for a sixth time a Northern stranger arrives with a plan that he claims will double the vineyard's production. McAdoo's greed compels him to follow the con man's questionable advice to dig up the roots of the vineyard and pack the earth around them with lime and ash. Predictably, the vines all die and without the spring sap to restore his youth and energy, Henry dies as well. Furious over losing both his sources of wealth, McAdoo welcomes the outbreak of war and rushes off swearing to kill a Yankee for every dollar he lost. "'En I 'spec' he would 'a' done it, too,'" Julius affirms with a little more amusement than he can hide, "'ef de Yankees had n' s'picioned sump'n, en killed him fus'" (12).

After he buys the vineyard, it finally get through to John that Julius had been cultivating the grapes. Not understanding that he is the very last one to grasp the painfully obvious, he tells us smugly that this "doubtless accounted for his advice to me not to buy the vineyard" (13). It's in John's obvious pleasure in figuring this out that Julius's seemingly clumsy question about John's intentions to buy the vineyard makes sense. Recognizing John's need to feel in charge, Julius has constructed for himself the persona of an artless and harmlessly venial trickster against whom John can demonstrate his superiority both by seeing through and indulging his petty scams. In "The Functions of Folklore in Charles Chesnutt's *The Conjure Woman*," Robert Hemenway observes that "the key to understanding the relationship between the two narrators [John and Julius] is not in the trickster schemes, since Julius's tricks are often transparent," but what Hemenway is missing is the second, crucial trick that Julius is hiding behind the first. As already argued, Julius's long-term project is to transform white understanding of blackness and in order to do this he performs a version of blackness that, in turns, reassures and challenges his white audience. While he doubtless enjoys the incidental material advantage that his tricks help him gain, Julius is mostly a rascal because he understands that John expects a certain amount of sass from him. Offering his new master what he expects is a kind of second-order signifying since Julius does it to help John maintain an illusion of superiority at the same time that his stories of the Old South oblige John and Annie to gradually adapt their vision of the social structures of racial hierarchy to something more like Julius's point of view.

Although it wasn't included in *The Conjure Woman*, "Dave's Neckliss," another of Chesnutt's conjure tales featuring Julius, is very interesting in the way it demonstrates the effectiveness of this approach. "Dave's Neckliss" is set long enough after the events of "Goophered Grapevine" for John and Annie to have made themselves perfectly at home on the old McAdoo plantation. In fact, the frenetic northern industry that John was so eager to bring south has been replaced by a sense of ease and leisure that seems to confirm the portrait of southern living in which the plantation romances of the late 1800s were so invested.[5] Following the pattern that Chesnutt established with John and Annie's first encounter with Julius, "Dave's Neckliss" begins with John, as frame narrator, ostensibly establishing the context for Julius's story. After Annie invites Julius to have some of the luncheon leftovers, John, observing from a distance, notices that Julius seems to have a particular affinity for ham, "slice after slice of which," he tells us, "disappeared in the spacious cavity of his mouth" (90). However, after Julius finishes his sixth helping John sees him pause, "as if struck by a sudden thought," and unexpectedly "a tear rolled down his rugged cheek and fell upon the slice of ham before him" (91). His curiosity piqued, John invites Julius to explain this show of emotion by impishly asking if the mustard was too spicy. John's approach here sounds like the beginning of a signifying sensibility. Uncomfortable with directly asking about the tear (perhaps on some level, John recognizes the moral ambiguity of spying on Julius), John instead enters into a kind playful exchange that indirectly invites rather than directly commands an explanation. "'No, suh,'" Julius replies solemnly, "'it wa'n't de mustard. I wuz studyin' 'bout Dave'" (91). Explaining that "the conditions were all favorable" for storytelling, John asks Julius to go on.

Before allowing Julius to begin, however, John steals back narrative control in order to reemphasize his sense of Julius's difference. "His way of looking at the past seemed very strange to us," John explains. "His view of certain sides of life was essentially different from ours" (91). John's persistent use of the infinitely inclusive "us" is so obviously an appeal for the reader to identify with the white frame narrator rather than the regionalized black speaker that we might wonder if John hasn't begun to sense Julius's other motive. Careful to maintain this him and "us," construction, John further develops his portrait of Julius:

> While he mentioned with a warm appreciation the acts of kindness which those in authority had shown him and his people, he would speak of a cruel deed, not with the indignation of one accustomed to quick feeling and spontaneous expression, but with a furtive disapproval which suggested to us a doubt in his own mind as to whether he had a right to think or feel, and presented to us the curious psychological spectacle of a mind enslaved long after the shackles had been struck off from the limbs of its possessor [91].

As his pathos-laden, but almost surely crocodile tear suggests, however, Julius is not only much more aware of the reality of his condition than John suspects, but he also understands the way John's assumptions about the limitations of an ex-slave leave him vulnerable to manipulation.

Finally allowed to begin his story, Julius is careful to make it clear that, above all else, Dave was a sober, religious man whose morals were uncompromising. Julius's description of Dave as "one er dese yer solemn kine er men, en nebber run on wid much foolishness" seems to invite the reader to compare him to the ostensibly superior white overseer, Walker, whose anger at discovering that Dave has learned to read the Bible comes, as Julius tells it, from his anxiety over his own illiteracy (92). "'Mars Walker w'an't nuffin but a po' bockrah,'" Julius explains dismissively, "'en folks said he could n' read ner write hisse'f, en co'se he did n' lack ter see a nigger w'at knowed mo' d'n he did'" (92). When Walker brings Dave before McAdoo the reader sees that Dave is not only upstanding, but shrewd as well. When McAdoo asks Dave what he's learned from reading the Bible, Dave replies, "'Marster, I l'arns dat it's a sin fer ter steal, er ter lie, en fer ter want w'at doan b'long ter yer; en I l'arns fer ter love de Lawd en ter 'bey my marster'" (92). Forgetting right away that Dave had violated one of the keystone laws of slave culture by learning to read, McAdoo responds to Walker as much to Dave, that reading the Bible hasn't seemed to have done any harm. Of course, given the precedent that Julius has already offered, there's good reason to believe that Dave is employing a similar signifying strategy in which he acts the part of the child-like and obedient servant — hiding the ways he's breaking the rules behind a facade that falsely confirms all his master's stereotypes and assumptions. When another slave frames Dave for the theft of a ham from the smokehouse, all McAdoo's kindly paternalism vanishes. Not satisfied with the traditional forty lashes, after he finishes whipping him, McAdoo hangs the stolen ham around Dave's neck on a heavy chain. Beaten and humiliated, Dave carries the heavy ham around his neck night and day. "'It wuz monst'us hard on Dave,'" Julius tells John and Annie, "'w'at wid dat ham eberlastin' en etarnally draggin' roun' his neck, he 'mence' fer ter do en say quare things'" (97). In his madness, Dave begins telling stories about a secret grove of ham-bearing trees he's discovered in the swamps and one day, while picking cotton with Julius, Dave leans in conspiratorially and asks, "'Did yer knowed I wuz turnin' ter a ham, Julius'" (99)? Emerging, as it does, from the distress of carrying a heavy ham around his neck, it's no surprise that ham should play such a central role in Dave's madness. At the same time, however, Dave's insanity is essentially the logic of slavery. Julius and the rest of the slaves think that Dave has lost his mind for thinking that he's becoming a ham, but when we remember that Julius himself had explained that meat from a smokehouse worked as a sort of universal currency, that "it wuz mon-st'us easy fer ter swop off bacon fer sump'm ter chaw er ter wa'm yer up in de wintertime," Dave's belief that he has begun to transform into a tradable com-modity seems perhaps less like insanity and more like epiphany (94). Dave's seemingly nonsensical vision of himself as a ham actually signals a final rejec-tion of his master's culture, one which doesn't have the capacity to express the kind of profound loss that defines Dave's experience. Alienated not only from authority, but also from the white constructs of reason, Dave's madness directs him to a perhaps more essential language of signifying that allows him to express relationships of power and identity that the master's language — for obvious reasons — cannot consider. Understanding the full extent of his dehumanization, Dave's grief is so inexpressible that he can only hope to articulate it by literally embodying the reality of this inhuman condition. Dave's story ends when Julius discovers his body in the smokehouse where he had "'tied a rope roun' his neck, des lack de hams wuz tied, en had hung hisse'f up in the smoke'ouse fer ter kyo'" (101). Circuitously returning to the question that had prompted the story in the first place, Julius concludes his tale by saying, "'Ever sence den ... w'eneber I eats ham, it min's me er Dave'" (101–2). We find out how much Annie has taken Dave's story to heart when she admits to John the next morning that "'I couldn't have eaten any more of the ham, so I gave it to Julius'" (102). On a very superficial level, Julius succeeds by getting the rest of the ham for himself, but more importantly he succeeds by offering a challenge to the pastoral sense of the Old South that John and Annie had begun to internalize, offering a vivid reminder to his white audience that the "Arcadian joyousness and irresponsibility" they associate with the golden age of the southern plantation was built on an institution that reduced human beings to meat (91). Having transformed the ham into a painfully conspicuous symbol of the human suffering indelibly connected to the history of slavery, we can begin to measure Julius's mounting success in Annie's refusal to eat any more, which serves as a symbolic refusal to coop-erate with the ideologies of dominance.

The sketch in which we can best see the fruits of Julius's labor, however, is "Sis Becky's Pickaninny." In the fifth of seven stories that make up *The Con-jure Woman*, a close reader will immediately recognize that the frame narra-tive with which John opens this sketch focuses not on Julius but Annie, who he tells us has become "the victim of a settled melancholy, attended with vague forebodings of impending misfortune" (51). John attempts to cheer his wife using various approaches, including reading novels to her and arranging for the workers to entertain her with old plantation songs, but nothing seems to draw her out of the depression into which she has sunk. One afternoon while the two of them are sitting on the porch (which John is determined to call the piazza), Julius approaches and asks Annie how she is feeling. "'She is not very cheerful,'" John answers for her, and asks Julius to sit. Noticing that Julius is holding "some small object in his hand," John asks what he has and Julius tells him, "'Dis is my rabbit foot, suh'" (52). John scoffs when Julius tells him that he carries the rabbit's foot for luck, and comments, as he tells us, "half to him and half to my wife," that "'your people will never rise in the world until they throw off these childish superstitions and learn to live by the light of reason and common sense'" (52). Clearly John is associating women with African Americans based on his assumption that both are overly emotional and, thus, prone to bouts of irrational behavior. Julius disagrees, maintaining that everybody knows about the luck of a rabbit's foot and suggesting that "'ef it has ter be prove' ter folks w'at wa'n't boen en raise' in dis naberhood, dey is a' easy way to prove it'" (52–3). Julius's proof, of course, is the story of Becky and her baby. A field hand on a nearby plantation, Becky loses her husband (who belongs to a different man) when he's sold to pay his dead master's debts. Becky takes comfort in their son Mose, however, and tries to get by the best she can. But before long, her master Colonel Pendleton decides that he needs a racehorse badly enough to trade Becky away from her child for it. The separation is hard on both mother and child. In fact, Mose's health gets so bad that his nurse takes him to Aunt Peggy, who immediate diagnoses the problem. The nurse leaves Mose with Peggy and she changes him into a hummingbird so he can fly off to see his mother. This covert visit seems to satisfy both mother and child, but before long Mose's health begins to worsen again. This time Aunt Peggy transforms him into a mockingbird and even though this second visit seems to revive them both, the nurse recognizes that what Mose needs is to be permanently reunited with his mother. She asks Aunt Peggy to fix it so that Becky can return for good, so the conjure woman convinces a hornet to sting the racehorse's knees so they swell painfully. Convinced that he's been sold a horse with "'a ringbone er a spavin er sump'n,'" Colonel Pendleton calls off the trade (59). When the horse trader balks, Aunt Peggy fixes "a little bag wid some roots en one thing er ernudder in it" and arranges to have it delivered to Becky's doorstep. Convinced she's been conjured, Becky takes to her bed with quickly failing health (59). Thinking that it's better to have a sick horse than a dead slave the trader agrees to cancel the deal and returns Becky. Of course, both Becky and Mose's health improve almost immediately upon the reunion and Julius goes on to explain that Mose grew up to be a blacksmith and "'bimeby he bought his mammy en sot her free, en den he bought hisse'f, en tuk keer er Sis' Becky ez long as dey bofe libbed'" (61). Annoyed, John remarks petulantly, "'That's a very ingenious fairy tale, Julius,'" to which Annie responds, "'Why John ... the story bears the stamp of truth, if ever a story did'" (61). Unwilling to drop the matter, John nonchalantly observes to Julius "'your story doesn't establish what you started to prove,— that a rabbit's foot brings good luck,'" but Annie cuts him short explaining, "'I rather suspect ... that Sis' Becky had no rabbit's foot'" (61). "'You is hit de bull's-eye de fus' fire, ma'm,'" Julius tells her. "'Ef Sis' Becky had a rabbit fot, she nebber would 'a' went th'oo all dis trouble'" (61).

That Annie supplies the moral to this story is absolutely essential to understanding how important it is. Robert Hemenway suggests the "Sis Becky's" concentrates on the way "belief informs the most complex use of folklore," but, again, it's even more complicated than that. In *Charles W. Chesnutt: A Study of the Short Fiction*, Henry Wonham comes closer when he argues that

> while Julius does not prove the validity of folk traditions to John's satisfaction, he does effectively associate John's skepticism with the trader's questionable therapeutic disposition ... John doesn't laugh at Annie, but his condescension toward Julius's folk beliefs is directed at least half in her direction, implying that John's disbelief in the legitimacy of the rabbit's foot as a cure may be taken as an extension of his belief in the reality of the illness itself [35].

Connecting Julius's superstitions with Annie's melancholy, "Sis Becky's Pickaninny" invites the reader to recognize the similarities between Annie and Julius, who — like her — must submit to the will of a dominating white man. Offering the moral of Julius's story before he himself can deliver it, Annie reveals that her point of view has shifted to the extent that she can actually connect with Becky and thus, by extension, Julius. This isn't really all that surprising since — as a woman in the late nineteenth century — Annie's social position has certain, undeniable parallels to what Becky's would have been before Emancipation. Recognizing that her relationship to John has some disconcerting parallels to Becky's relationship to Colonel Pendleton, Annie's transformation (the consequence of Julius's narrative conjure) is evidence of the ultimate success of Chesnutt's plan for the "elevation of the whites." Oblivious as ever, John closes the narrative by remarking that Annie's health took a turn from the better, "from this day forward" (61). Leading us to understand that Annie's recovery is really the effect of the freedom that her newly acquired ability to signify has offered her, John's final comment only proves that, as has been Julius's plan all along, the agent of white male dominance is left holding the bag.

Chesnutt continues to explore race and questions of the color line in *The House Behind the Cedars* (1900). His approach in this novel is radically different. Certainly, there are familiar themes, chief of which is the way the novel articulates Chesnutt's dissatisfaction with racial constructions that rely on the sense of clear boundaries between black and white. Delaying racial identification of either Rena or John, for instance, the novel participates in their attempt to pass and, as William Andrews puts it, "Chesnutt hoaxes his readers in a way reminiscent of the initial concealment" (155). Stories about passing in general, and The *House Behind the Cedars* in particular, as William Andrews puts it, "ridiculed the fiction of 'Anglo-Saxon racial purity' and the social and legal means by which this delusion was perpetuated" (140). A comparatively conventional story about a tragic mulatto, the traditional narrative structures of *House Behind the Cedars* seems to limit Chesnutt's capacity to signify in it. Chesnutt relied on the rhetorical and ideological friction that is the result of the innate contradictions in the socially conservative Plantation Sketch to shape his approach in the conjure stories. The already overtly activist nature of the tragic mulatto plot left Chesnutt in the unfamiliar territory of working within a genre model that didn't resist his ideologies. Working within a literary tradition willing to cooperate with him seems, ironically, to have restricted Chesnutt much more than when he put himself in the position of writing against the grain. Left without any structures to undermine, Chesnutt's attempt at a straightforward narrative becomes just another example (albeit a particularly good one) of a pre-established model of genre and ideology. Sally Ann Ferguson ultimately judges *The House Behind the Cedars* to be "a vehicle for racial propaganda" (80). While this is, to one degree or another, true of everything that Chesnutt ever wrote, the unoriginal approach that the confluence of genre and ideology forces Chesnutt to take leads to equally unoriginal conclusions that William Andrews emphasizes when he claims the novel "retreats with its still largely unrealized heroine into the sentimental byways of the novel of seduction" (166). Relying on convention rather than bucking it simply wasn't Chesnutt's strength, but whatever minor failures *The House Behind the Cedars* might represent, Chesnutt's next novel is a clear demonstration that he learned from them.

To see the best example of the way Chesnutt creatively misapplies genre conventions, we must look ahead to *The Marrow of Tradition* (1901), the novel that many critics consider Chesnutt's finest work. A fictional exploration of the political and cultural forces that culminated in the 1898 Wilmington Massacre, *Marrow* frames the story in the familiar conventions of the romance; however, as he does in *Conjure Woman*, Chesnutt only creates a false impression of genre in order to thwart the fundamentally conservative sense of hierarchy that the form represents. Interestingly, although the readers' foreknowledge of the killing looms large in the background, Chesnutt's plot, in the best tradition of the historical saga, organizes itself around a series of family rather than political crises. Although they are carefully interrelated, Chesnutt draws the novel's chief conflicts around the tensions surrounding Olivia Carteret's refusal to acknowledge Janet Miller as her sister and co-heir to their father's estate, and the intergenerational conflict between the austerely respectable old Mr. Delamere and his dissipated grandson, Tom Delamere. Olivia Carteret's husband, Major Carteret, is editor of *The Morning Chronicle* and chief of the "big three," the secret committee through which he, aristocratic General Belmont and coarse Captain McBane have devised an extensive campaign of misinformation with the aim of undermining Reconstruction policies and keeping African Americans from polls and elected office. Although their efforts ultimately culminate in a bloody riot, it is important to note that, while Chesnutt's novel certainly uncovers the full scope and horror of the massacre, the text plainly follows the conventions of the romance in that it makes a determined attempt to reimagine this violent clashing of social, political and racial ideologies as a breakdown of traditional familial harmony. Refiguring such a bloody rejection of the Constitutional rights granted to African Americans as a kind of family disagreement allows Chesnutt (as it did Page) to transform the clash of essentially abstract ideas into the very specific and comprehensible terms of familial relationships. Operating as a regionalized kind of reconciliation romance, Chesnutt's version refuses to support the inflexible structures of patriarchal, hierarchical authority at the center of the conventional romance. Although this approach is generally in line with the reading of *Marrow* that that we find in William Andrews's *The Literary Career of Charles Chesnutt*, Andrews seems to restrict his attention to the specifically overt manner in which the novel's plot and narration comment on U.S. race relations at the beginning of the twentieth century. Making his conclusions about *Marrow*, Andrews writes:

> Chesnutt made his novel of the New South investigate the dynamics of Wellington's sociopolitical system against the backdrop of its history and tradition in order to seek out some principles of reasonable hope for the welfare of southern blacks.... Chesnutt sought to find in Wellington's historical, political, and moral record evidence of both positive and negative traditions at work [184–5].

He is exactly right regarding the way *Marrow* confronts the cultural and political aspects of the color line. Chesnutt's novel is also (and perhaps more importantly) investigating models of African American expression capable of crossing that line. Confining his reading to the novel's explicitly sociopolitical context and overlooking the ways *Marrow* subtly considers the roles genre convention and literary tradition play as part of this sociopolitical dynamic, Andrews — literally — is only scratching the surface.

In her introduction to *Culture of Sentiment*, Shirley Samuels argues against the traditional view that the sphere of the romance is limited to domestic writing, claiming instead that "sentimentality acts in conjunction with the problem of the body and with it embodies how social, political, racial and gendered meanings are determined through their different embodiments" (5).

In *Sensational Designs*, Jane Tompkins takes this argument to its next logical step, declaring that the romances of the late nineteenth century "have designs upon their audience, in the sense of wanting to make people think and act in a particular way" (xi). The key to Tompkins's reading is her suggestion that the stereotyped characters who inhabit the romance aren't supposed to be real but rather "operate as a cultural shorthand," and are valuable not for their verisimilitude, but their capacity to quickly convey "complex clusters of value" (xvi). As *Marrow* clearly demonstrates, Chesnutt thoroughly understood both the way that racialized bodies expressed a specific set of social meanings within nineteenth-century culture and the manner in which the aesthetic of the romance related to those larger cultural values. Recontextualizing an obviously political problem as a family problem, *The Marrow of Tradition* seems to function in essentially the same manner as the rest of the reconciliation romances coming out of the South at the turn of the century. However, instead of looking at the socio-geographic rift between North and South that occupied novels like *Red Rock* (1898) or *Lovell's Folly* (1833), Chesnutt's version of the romance examines the racial divide.[6] At the same time, Chesnutt's version of the romance as a text of African American equality sheds a new light on the way he takes advantage of the social function of the genre in his attempt to slowly acclimate the reading public to the idea of black subjectivity.

If indeed the transformation from political problem to family problem that characterizes the traditional romance serves as a way to resolve otherwise impossible conflicts, Chesnutt's appropriation of the romantic mode for his historical novel would seem perfectly reasonable. Representing the otherwise impossibly complicated race problems in the U.S. through Olivia Carteret's estrangement from her half-sister Janet Miller, *Marrow* should, as is customary with the genre, offer their (albeit grudging) reconciliation at the end of the novel as a model for a more widespread racial reconciliation. For Chesnutt the issue of family is absolutely central to the question of race, something his version of the race romance reveals in the way that it uses the figure of the family to explore a race problem that has as one of its fundamental causes the white refusal to acknowledge familial relationships that cross racial lines. While traditional reconciliation romances can imagine intermarriage and family connection as figurative solutions to the division between North and South, Chesnutt's adaptation of the form seems designed to examine the possibility of using such a solution to imagine a way of reuniting the portion of the nation divided across racial lines. That anxiety about race so often manifested itself in concerns over miscegenation (which was outlawed as soon as Reconstruction ended) and that accusations of rape were the most common excuse for lynching seem to suggest that framing a narrative of race reconciliation as a romance is to miss the point altogether. In this novel, such an approach is an essential part of Chesnutt's attempt to question the conventions that helped maintain so strict a divide. Disguised as a conventional romance, *The Marrow of Tradition* serves as a kind of Trojan horse that allows Chesnutt to argue his position on the race question to a white readership that he saw as the key to any movement toward racial equality. Chesnutt ultimately rejected passing, but he clearly remained fascinated by the implications of the act. As is the case with any boundary, that the color line could be crossed in any fashion suggested that it was neither as "natural" nor as fixed as the race hierarchies of the U.S. suggested it was. Attempting a kind of complex literary passing, *The Marrow of Tradition*— fascinated by the fluidity between the performance of race, identity, and social status — experiments with different combinations of racial and familial "places" in an effort to construct a place for African American subjectivity within the national family.

Eric Sundquist's reading of Chesnutt's canon in *To Wake the Nations* centers around the tradition of the cakewalk, which Sundquist claims is "an example of the principles of subversion and indirection essential to the evolution of African American cultural expression in the nineteenth century" (279). What Sundquist's cakewalk chapter really offers is an exceptionally thorough examination of one of the ways dominant societal structures control the means of expression and, in the process, defines the marginalized, racialized, or regionalized *other* that best serves the interests of continued dominance. We see an obvious example of this dynamic at work, as Sundquist points out, in the case of Tom Delamere's impersonation of Sandy at the cakewalk staged for the benefit of potential investors from the North, but we also see it in his murder of Mrs. Ochiltree. Dressed in "a long blue coat with brass buttons, and a pair of plaid trousers," Delamere's version of the old family servant relies heavily on the stereotype of the comic darky (118). In fact, after winning the cake, the narrator tells us, Delamere fascinates the audience with a speech that "sent the Northern visitors into spasms of delight at the quaintness of the darky dialect and the darky wit" and "danced a buck dance with a skill and agility that brought a shower of complimentary silver" (118). Clearly, there's some serious wish fulfillment in Delamere's depiction of the comic black man, so eager to please that even his personal dignity is fodder for the amusement of his white audience. That Delamere chose the cakewalk as the venue for his reverse passing is telling as well. If we understand, as Sundquist puts it, that the cakewalk is "a takeoff on the high manners of the folks in the 'big house,'" (279) it becomes pretty clear that when Delamere pretends to be Sandy in a cakewalk expressly organized to demonstrate "the joyous, happy-go-lucky disposition of the Southern darky and his entire contentment with existing conditions," he is specifically usurping the means of black expression and black rebellion (*Marrow*, 117). The novel suggests that Delamere pulls this prank out of simple boredom, but at the same time, it's also very clear that his performance comes out of an awareness of the serious fiscal interests at stake in the cakewalk. Appropriating what began as a subtle mockery of white wealth and leisure and transforming it into nothing more than clownish buffoonery, Delamere's version of black subjectivity not only reassures the Northern audience that Southern whites have things well in hand, it also reinforces the mythology of the African American as irresponsible and childish and happiest under white guardianship.

In his second performance as Sandy, Delamere disguises himself as the faithful servant in order to rob and murder Mrs. Ochiltree. In this instance Delamere is enacting the other stereotype — that of the African American man as violent brute — but something in the narrative suggests that the act perhaps went further than he actually intended it to. Earlier in the novel when Major Carteret cautions the old woman about keeping so much money in her house, Mrs. Ochiltree blusters, "I have a revolver, and know how to use it. Whoever attempts to rob me will do so at his peril" (26). However, there's no sign of any struggle at the scene of the crime, simply the woman's body with a "gaping wound in the head," and the contents of a broken chest scattered across the room (177). As Tom Delamere knew they would, the white people of Wellington immediately assume the killer to be a black man. As the narrator puts it:

> Suspicion was at once directed toward the negroes, as it always is when an unexplained crime is committed in a Southern community. The suspicion was not entirely an illogical one. Having been, for generations, trained up to thriftlessness, theft, and immorality, against which only thirty years of very limited opportunity can be offset, during which brief period they have been denied in large measure the healthful social stimulus and sympathy which holds most men in the path of rectitude, colored people might reasonably be expected to commit at least a share of crime proportionate to their numbers [178–9].

In the process of seemingly justifying the town's racism, Chesnutt's narrator subtly manages to redirect blame so that it lands not on the ostensibly morally weak African Americans, but instead on the former white masters whose dominance so limited African American options in the first place.[7] Once Ellis and Jerry confirm this suspicion by identifying Sandy as the prime suspect, the community immediately assumes that Sandy is guilty of not only murder and robbery, but also rape. As the narrator casually explains, "The criminal was a negro, the victim a white woman; — it was only reasonable to expect the worst" (182). Assuming such, the text demonstrates the community's inability to understand the murder as anything but a "black" crime and its corresponding inability to imagine blackness as anything but a violent, brutish, and corrupted version of humanity. The necessary sexual component of the town's understanding of the crime is, in part, simply the response of a racist community looking for an excuse for mob violence. At the same time the assumption of rape brings the Ochiltree murder into a very interesting parallel with the crisis surrounding Olivia Carteret's refusal to acknowledge her relationship to Janet Miller. In both instances, the main issue seems to coalesce around relationships that cross the color line. In the case of Samuel Merkel, the problem is not that he dallied with his black servant, but that he actually validated their relationship by marrying her. History shows that black women had never been beyond the sexual attention of white men in the antebellum South, but when Merkel marries his black mistress and thus legitimizes Janet as both daughter and heir, he breaks one of the fundamental rules of white hegemony, that authority — sexual, social, or political — must remain exclusively in the hands of white men. Polly Ochiltree tries to rectify this lapse when she steals the documents that confirm the marriage as well as the will in which Merkel leaves Julia half his estate, but as the continuation of this conflict between Merkel's two daughters makes clear, especially in a society built on the fragile absolutes of paternity and blood, these kinds of secrets simply can't be kept.

While the blackface was primarily a means of hiding his identity, Delamere's talent for performing the white idea of blackness in that context should make us wonder if his seemingly unnecessary violence against the old woman isn't also somehow part of the performance of this other white stereotype of blackness. Perhaps Delamere, who understood the white assumptions about blackness at least as well as anyone else in Wellington, didn't think the robbery would be a convincingly black crime unless the white woman was murdered as well. If, as it seems, this is Delamere's motive for the murder, then we must recognize the way this killing demonstrates that the system of racial dominance that defines Wellington equally denies the autonomy of a supposedly aristocratic and privileged young white man as it does that of African Americans or women. Either way it's clear that Polly Ochiltree's murder is as much a result of the culture of white superiority as the Wellington massacre was. That Delamere, regardless of the racial identity he was acting out, could murder the old woman with such apparently casual indifference makes it clear that in his estimate she is as disposable as Sandy, whom he frames for the murder. Conflating the oppression of white women with that of black men, the romance that *Marrow* pretends to be establishes a new kind of family made up of those dispossessed through the structures of white male dominance. Very much resembling one of Benedict Anderson's imagined communities (which he characterizes as "indefinitely stretchable nets of kinship and clientship") this alternate model attempts to reconcile not the races, but the black men and white women that the sham threat of racially-motivated rape have worked to keep separate and so incapable of resisting white male authority (Anderson, 16).[8] It can't simply be coincidence that Tom Delamere picks Ochiltree as his victim. The obvious reason to rob Ochiltree is that she tells him that she doesn't keep any of her money in the bank, but it's in the same conversation that she proudly boasts, "I've proved a match for two husbands, and am not afraid of any man that walks the earth, black or white, day or night" (26). While this scene partly plays to the humor of a salty old woman bragging about her courage, the swagger in her claims of self-sufficiency makes it clear that Ochiltree represents a very real, very visible challenge to the social, political and economic dominance of the masculine order. In the first chapter, when Jane tells Doctor Price about the quarrel over Samuel Merkel's refusal to discharge Janet Brown after his wife's death, she makes it very clear that Merkel refuses his sister-in-law's help because he is afraid of her. The doctor, for his part, isn't surprised. "'I don't wonder,'" he replies, "if she was anything like she is now'" (5). Jane explains that Samuel Merkel's fear was not only real — it was warranted. She tells Doctor Price:

> "'Wuss, suh, fer she wuz younger, an' stronger. She always would have her say, no matter 'bout what, an' her own way, no matter who 'posed her. She had already be'n in de house fer a week, an' Mars Sam knowed ef she once come ter stay, she'd be mist'ess of eve'ybody in it an' him too. But w'at could he do but say yas?'" (5)

Since apparently everyone in Wellington is acquainted with a version of this story, it's unlikely that young Delamere doesn't know the history of Ochiltree's ferocity in the face of her ostensible superior. Having repeatedly defied the aristocratic system of privilege that preserves male social authority, Ochiltree essentially threatens to undermine the very structures of white male hegemony that have propped up the obviously morally and intellectually questionable Delamere. His gambling debts and drinking getting worse, Tom Delamere's problems are on the verge of completely overwhelming him. When McBane uses an enormous poker debt to pressure the younger man into vouching for the ex-overseer's membership in the exclusive Clarendon Club, Delamere tries to win the money he needs in a crooked card game at that same club. He is caught, of course, and the club offers to keep his infraction quiet on several conditions — the chief of which being that he pay off his remaining card debts in seventy-two hours. Faced with bankruptcy, the total loss of what little reputation he had left, and the wrath of McBane as well as his grandfather, Delamere goes out into the night a desperate man, whose thoughts "touched a depth of scoundrelism far beyond anything of which he had as yet deemed himself capable" (165). Plumbing new depths of immorality, Tom Delamere arrives at a dangerous plan that, had it succeeded, would have not only restored

his finances, but also allowed him to silence Ochiltree's rejection of the patriarchy.[9] Delamere doesn't fall from grace because he suddenly begins to behave
badly, but rather because the people he's been mistreating for some time finally
stop offering him special consideration for his position as a young, aristocratic, white man. According to the narrator, Delamere's aristocratic gra-
ciousness was never anything more than "the shadow without the substance"
(96). Chesnutt doesn't use Delamere's pursuit of Miss Pemberton to rehabil-
itate the dissipated gentleman. Chesnutt's version of romance isn't interested
in propping up the structures of race and gender domination entrenched in
the analogy of familial relationships and instead offers an entirely new structure that inverts the old system by rejecting the antagonism between African
American men and white women that so effectively served to keep both these
groups under the yoke of aristocratic, white male dominance.

Chesnutt rewrites the cultural significance of the romance by applying
its conventions to a plot that, although it retains the superficial markers of
the genre, organizes itself around conflicts that specifically uncover the bigoted cultural ideologies that the romance (in its straightforward iteration)
works to uphold and preserve. In the case of *Marrow*, Chesnutt specifically
works to expose the inadequacy of the familial model of resolution in the case
of racial conflict made popular with both the plantation and reconciliation
romances. Chesnutt recognizes that, as an already marginalized African American, he is writing from a position that, by definition, is excluded from all
the meaningful systems of cultural authority. His voice, like those we read in
the slave narratives of the mid to late nineteenth century, must be validated
by an external and recognized figure of authority that, in essence, approves
the message. The same way Tom Delamere uses his performance of Sandy to
invoke a culturally over-determined version of blackness, Chesnutt's bitter
criticism of race relations at the turn of the twentieth century *passes* as
romance, an already culturally approved literary form. Delamere's caper at
the cakewalk is supposed to allay the moral concerns that potential Northern
investors have over the treatment of African Americans in Wellington and
Chesnutt's performance of the romance similarly puts his readers at ease by
seeming to enact a specific aesthetic form and, by extension, the social and
cultural forms of discourse that go with it. Delamere's version of blackness
reveals his commitment to the ideologies of universal white male superiority,
but Chesnutt's manipulation of the conventions of romance forces his readers to acknowledge that white male dominance alone cannot manage the problem of race relations in the U.S. By accepting the miscegenation required to
complete the romance plot by bringing Samuel Merkel's two daughters
together as equals, he metaphorically reconstructs the social fabric that Major
Carteret's massacre has torn apart.

NOTES

1. This comes from a journal entry that Chesnutt made on March 16, 1880, in which he outlines his plan to write a book to rival Tourgée's *Fool's Errand*, declaring, "I intend to record my impressions of men and things, and such incidents or conversations which take place within my knowledge, with a view to future use in literary work. I shall not record stale negro minstrel jokes, or worn out newspaper squibs on the 'man and brother.' I shall leave the realm of fiction, where most of this stuff is manufactured and come down to hard facts" (Wonham, 86). Rejecting as sentimentalized or malicious the depictions of African Americans that he saw in, for instance, Stowe's Topsy or Page's Dr. Moses, Chesnutt's approach seems to be offering his readers a realist version of blackness in that it isn't imitative but actually is a native utterance. From this strategy we can clearly see that Chesnutt's view of the "literary" has been shaped by critics like Garland and Howells, however, at the same time, Chesnutt's rejection of used-up types suggests a rejection of Romance for Realism, but there are equally pragmatic and political motives behind his attempt to move beyond these limited depictions of blackness in the U.S.

2. Reminiscent of the passage in which Sam, the ex-slave storyteller in Page's "Marse Chan," celebrates the old days by telling the white frame narrator, "'Dem wuz good ole times marster — de bes' Sam, ever see! Dey wuz, in fac'! Niggers didn' hed nothin' 't all to do — jes' hed to 'ten' to de feedin' an' cleanin' de hosses, an doin' what do marster tell 'em to do." Chesnutt's passage works to reveal the (not entirely) hidden irony in this kind of praise for the Antebellum South (10).

3. Reading this Tom as a revised version of Stowe's Uncle Tom, we begin to see that Chesnutt is rejecting the stoic ideal for a more active pursuit of African American subjectivity.

4. While only superficially connected to the main plot, this detail suggests that white women and slaves — as mutual victims of white male dominance — might have concerns in common. As we'll see even more clearly in *The Marrow of Tradition*, this attempt to identify the similarities of both black and female experience in the U.S. reveals one of the most interesting ways Chesnutt will attempt to revise the dynamics of race in the nineteenth-century United States.

5. Although not an exhaustive list, some popular examples of plantation romances are John Pendleton Kennedy's *Swallow Barn* (1832), William Gilmore Simms's *The Partisan* (1835), Caroline Hentz's *Lovell's Folly* (1833), Thomas Nelson Page's *Red Rock* (1898) and, more recently, Margaret Mitchell's *Gone with the Wind* (1933).

6. For a more comprehensive look at the reconciliation romance see Karen Keely's "Marriage Plots and National Reunion: The Trope of Romantic Reconciliation in Postbellum Literature," *Mississippi Quarterly*, Fall 1998, Vol. 51, No. 4 (621–28).

7. This strategy echoes a critical scene in *Uncle Tom's Cabin* in which St. Clair similarly defends the moral character of African Americans by questioning the structures of white authority, suggesting that, in the circumstances they must endure under slavery, "cunning and deception become necessary, inevitable habits. It isn't fair to expect anything else of him.... For my part, I don't see how they can be honest" (235).

8. As mentioned already, given the established racist hierarchy that upheld anti-miscegenation laws, the romance was simply the wrong vehicle for imagining any sort of racial reconciliation. Within the context of an "imagined community" made up of similarly subjugated white women and black men, Chesnutt's romance suggests a novel solution to the problem of white male hegemony.

9. At this point, the parallels between Polly Ochiltree and Josh Green are difficult to ignore. Each of them is a strong, stubborn character who refuses to play by the rules of white male dominance, and each of them is killed, essentially for standing in the way of complete white male hegemony. Perhaps aiming to temper the humor in Ochiltree's threat to shoot anyone who tries to rob her, Josh Green makes a similar pronouncement in the face of Carteret's riot, telling Dr. Miller, "We ain' gwine ter stan' up an' be shot down like dogs. We're gwine ter defen' ou' lives, an' we ain' gwine ter run away f'm no place where we've got a right ter be; an woe be ter de w'ite man w'at lays han's on us" (281).

WORKS CITED

Anderson, Benedicy. *Imagined Communities: Reflections on the Origin and Spread of Nationalism*. Norfolk, U.K: Verso, 1983.

Andrews, William L. *The Literary Career of Charles W. Chesnutt*. Baton Rouge: Louisiana State University Press, 1980.

Baldwin, Richard E. "The Art of *The Conjure Woman*." *American Literature* 43 (1971): 385–398.

Chesnutt, Charles W. *Conjure Tales and Stories of the Color Line*. Edited by William L. Andrews. New York: Penguin, 1992.

_____. *The Conjure Woman and Other Conjure Tales*. Edited by Richard H. Brodhead. Durham, N.C.: Duke University Press, 1993.

_____. *The Marrow of Tradition*. Edited by Eric J. Sundquist. New York: Penguin, 1993.

Chesnutt, Helen M. *Charles Waddell Chesnutt: Pioneer of the Color Line*. Chapel Hill: University of North Carolina Press, 1952.

Ferguson, SallyAnn. "Rena Warden: Chesnutt's Failed 'Future American.'" *Southern Literary Journal*, 15 (1982): 74–82.

Feinberg, Lorne. "Laughter as a Strategy of Containment in Southwestern Humor." *Studies in American Humor* 3 (1984): 107–22.

Martin, Matthew R. "The Two-Faced New South: The Plantation Tales of Thomas Nelson Page and Charles W. Chesnutt." *Southern Literary Journal*, 30 (2) (1998): 17–36.

Myers, Karen Magee. "Mythic Patterns in Charles Waddell Chesnutt's The Conjure Woman and Ovid's Metamorphoses." *Black American Literature Forum* 13 (Spring 1979): 13–17.

Oden, Gloria C. "Chesnutt's Conjure as African Survival." *MELUS* 5 (1) (1978): 38–48.

Page, Thomas Nelson. *In Ole Virginia: Or Marse Chan and other Stories*. Nashville: J.S. Sanders, 1991.

Romine, Scott. *Narrative Forms of Southern Community*. Baton Rouge: Louisiana State University Press, 1999.

Samuels, Shirley, ed. *The Culture of Sentiment: Race, Gender, and Sentimentality in Nineteenth-Century America*. New York: Oxford University Press, 1992.

Stowe, Harriet Beecher. *Uncle Tom's Cabin, or Life Among the Lowly*. Boston: Houghton Mifflin Company, 1852.

Sundquist, Eric J. *To Wake the Nations: Race in the Making of American Literature*. Cambridge, Mass.: Harvard University Press, 1993.

Tompkins, Jane. *Sensational Designs: the Cultural Work of American Fiction, 1790–1860*. New York: Oxford University Press, 1985

Wideman, John. "." *Black American Literature Forum* 11 (1977): 79–82.

Wonham, Henry B. *Charles W. Chesnutt: A Study of the Short Fiction*. New York: Twayne Publishers; Prentice Hall, 1998.

CHAPTER 4

"Those folks downstairs believe in ghosts": The Eradication of Folklore in the Novels of Charles W. Chesnutt

Wiley Cash

The cover of the first edition of Charles W. Chesnutt's *The Conjure Woman* (1899) features a picture of the book's main character, Uncle Julius MacAdoo, beset on both sides by a white, floppy-eared rabbit. Considering Julius' wit, coupled with his ability to mask his chicanery in plantation lore, it is no surprise that the African trickster figure of the rabbit was chosen to accompany Julius on the cover of Chesnutt's first book-length publication. In his essay "Post-Bellum — Pre-Harlem" (1931) Chesnutt does not explicitly align Uncle Julius with the trickster figure and even glosses over the significance of the juxtaposition of Julius and the rabbit. He simply recounts that the book "was bound in brown cloth and on the front was a picture of a white-haired old Negro, flanked on either side by a long-eared rabbit" ("Post-Bellum," 101). Concerning Uncle Julius's manipulation of the paternalistic and often overly sentimental white couple in the book, Chesnutt states that Julius merely "had an axe to grind" ("Post-Bellum," 100). In reading his early journal entries, it is apparent that Chesnutt himself had a very real axe to grind with white America and would do so behind the heft of his pen throughout the course of his career.

According to his famous "high, holy purpose" in which his goal "would be not so much the elevation of the colored people as the elevation of the whites," Chesnutt, like Uncle Julius, wished to enchant America's white readership by entertaining them with the palatable and much loved plantation lore of the kindhearted slave while simultaneously chipping away at the very prejudice and stereotypes that fostered and propagated the same image (*Journals*, 139). In part, he was successful. He was the first black novelist of literary merit, which is to say, the first black novelist to be deemed worthy of consideration by the white literary world. *The Conjure Woman* was both a critical and monetary success for Chesnutt and Houghton Mifflin. However, the formula of using folklore to attain literary success was not one by which Chesnutt would long abide.

Following *The Conjure Woman*, Chesnutt's novels take a marked turn from the use of folklore as a means to reach and influence white audiences and focuses instead on the injustice of race prejudice. By the publication of *Marrow of Tradition* in 1901, Chesnutt's popularity had begun to wane. His third novel *The Colonel's Dream*, a denouncement of Washington's plan of industrial education, was released in 1905 and went unheralded and largely unnoticed. His recently published novels *Paul Marchand, F.M.C.* (1999) and *The Quarry* (1999), completed in 1921 and 1928 respectively, also focus on the color line, proving that Chesnutt's turn from folklore as a theme in his fiction was final and distinct.

Although Chesnutt's aspirations remained in focus, his means of attaining them abandoned the use of folklore and even turned against it in his works following *The Conjure Woman*. Considering this, Chesnutt can be placed somewhere in the folklore canon, not necessarily as a folklorist or folk artist, but as someone who knew the importance and power of folklore in the South's disenfranchised black communities, as well as white America's fascination with it. Second is Chesnutt's exposure to and synthesis of folklore and the ways in which he relates these assumptions and experiences in his fiction in order to better understand the reasons for its frequent brutalization and eventual eradication in his later novels. In collecting folklore, writing in the tradition of folklore and embodying one of African folklore's most significant figures, Chesnutt enters into a three-tiered stratum of liminality that indeed finds him "betwixt and between" three separate and definable states; that of collector, artist, and trickster figure. It is in this conscious state of liminality that Chesnutt approaches the problem of race prejudice in *The Conjure Woman* and his subsequent works as well.

The characterization of Chesnutt as "not necessarily a folklorist or folk artist" seems apropos considering the modest measure Chesnutt gives of his own knowledge of folklore in his essay "Superstitions and Folklore of the South" (1901). Again downplaying folklore's significant role in *The Conjure Woman*, Chesnutt explains that his representations of "'conjuration' and 'goopher,' [were lifted from] my childish recollection of which I have elsewhere embodied into a number of stories" ("Superstitions," 58). The claims of the novice later prove to be somewhat misleading as he details his acts of interviewing people and collecting material. After interviewing "half a dozen old women, and a genuine 'conjure doctor,'" Chesnutt understood that the stories he had "created" were but "dormant ideas, lodged in my childish mind" and that "creative talent, of whatever grade, is, in the last analysis, only the power of rearrangement" ("Superstitions," 60, 59). Donald M. Winkleman argues that "the material the folk artist uses is completely assimilated in his mind and culture" (130). Considering Winkleman's assessment of the material from which the folk artist draws, one could argue for Chesnutt's placement as a folk artist in that, although he claims to have been unaware of the effect folklore had on his literary development, he nonetheless refers to the stores of folklore material filed away in his memory. In this sense, he is more folk artist than folklorist in that, although he uses the staples of conjuration and goopher in his tales, he also adds his own fictive elements and devices in order to serve his literary and, as shall be discussed later, moral purposes.

However, the tales in *The Conjure Woman* are not wholly products of Chesnutt's buried psyche. In his essay "The Functions of Folklore in Charles Chesnutt's *The Conjure Woman*" (1976), Robert Hemenway highlights "Chesnutt's admission to the retelling of a folktale in 'The Goophered Grapevine'" and that this "would seem to indicate that he serves primarily as a literary redactor for the tale" (288). This admission also serves to show that Chesnutt was concerned with, not only the retelling of the tale, but with the collecting of it as well. The faculties and compulsions of the neophyte folklorist are also apparent much earlier than the publication of both *The Conjure Woman* and the writing of "Superstitions and Folklore of the South." In a journal entry dated 11 March 1880, Chesnutt, when discussing his inclination to collect folk music, considers that "a collection of the ballads or hymns which the colored people sing with such fervor, might be acceptable, if only as a curiosity to people, literary people, at the North" (*Journals*, 121). Chesnutt fully comprehended the interest that Northern "literary people" had in black Southern folklore and dialect works. In a journal entry dated five days later on 16 March 1880, he expounds upon his interest in collecting music, not necessarily as a means to benefit financially from the effort, but to bring interest to the plight of African Americans in the "hazy moral and social atmosphere" of the South (*Journals*, 125). He also shows an understanding of the interest that Northern whites had in Southern black folklore. "Men are always ready to extend their sympathy to those at a distance, than to the suffering ones in their midst" (*Journals*, 125).

Although Chesnutt is discussing the need for Northern interest to be directed to the suffering of Southern blacks several years before the publication of his first conjure tale in *The Atlantic Monthly*, his career goal of writing with a "high, holy purpose" becomes apparent. Chesnutt understood that in order to elevate whites to a new level of consciousness that would render them free of race prejudice he must first play upon their sentiments. Like Uncle Julius, Chesnutt "is trading in bits of local lore and superstition, artistic trinkets which have a value only because his listeners are outsiders" (Fienberg, 166). Expounding upon the important role that whites would have to play in a restructuring of racial sentiment, Chesnutt, in "An Inside View of the Negro Question" (1889), explains that "in the united and aggressive public opinion of the North, the Negro sees his chief hope for the speedy and peaceful recognition of his public rights at the South" (64). According to Melvin Dixon, Chesnutt, in writing *The Conjure Woman*, "[Chesnutt] is aware that he is writing for a predominately white audience who have a strong nostalgia for the antebellum southern tradition" and "just as trickster Julius masked his moral lesson in the fictive world of his folklore to serve his own gains, so too did Chesnutt use the fictive medium of the novel to accomplish his professional goals" (187, 196). Although one can disagree with Dixon in that Chesnutt's goals were not solely professional, but also moral, one can agree that Chesnutt, like Julius, masked his intentions under the veil of folklore in order to manipulate the white readership. He realized that once he held the "sympathy and cooperation of the vast majority of the white people all over the country" it would be much easier to attempt his goal of enlightening white America on the evils of race prejudice ("Inside," 64).

Regardless of Chesnutt's commitment to stamping out race prejudice, his aforementioned journal entry from 16 March 1880, in which he designates "the southern Negro" as "commonplace and vulgar," cannot be excused away or simply unexplained. Considering that it is the "commonplace and vulgar" for which he has taken up his charge, his attitude towards his own race seems insipid, condescending and, in light of other journal entries, racist. In order to understand the duality of Chesnutt's cause for, as well as his aversion to, Southern blacks, it is imperative to consider his early exposure to and synthesis of folklore.

After the Civil War, Chesnutt's mother and father returned to North Carolina and settled in the elder Chesnutt's hometown of Fayetteville, a town fictionalized in many of Chesnutt's works. In Fayetteville, Chesnutt divided his time between the Howard School, an educational institute created by the Freedmen's Bureau, and his father's store, where he "kept the books, waited on customers, swept out the place-and listened to and reflected upon everything he heard" (Helen M. Chesnutt, 5). In her biography of her father, Helen M. Chesnutt discusses Chesnutt's encounters with folklore and culture while working in his father' store. "The store was the natural meeting place for all the people of the neighborhood. Here the more intelligent met and discussed freely the latest political developments. Here the more ignorant told each other stories of superstition and conjuration, and the boy Charles took in everything with wide open ears" (5). Ms. Chesnutt's designation of those who "told each other stories" as "ignorant" is similar to her father's note of the Southern black as "commonplace and vulgar." Because of his education and light complexion, Chesnutt did indeed hold himself above the darker-skinned and less educated African Americans with whom he came into contact.

At the age of fourteen, Chesnutt, under the encouragement of the principal of the Howard School, relocated to Charlotte, North Carolina, where he taught at the Peabody School. He spent the summer of 1875 teaching on the outskirts of Spartanburg, South Carolina, in the foothills of the Appalachian Mountains. It was in the countryside of South Carolina that Chesnutt's journal chronicles his first negative reactions to folklore. While boarding with an African American family, an exasperated Chesnutt records his shock at what he perceives as their lack of education and enlightenment. "Well! uneducated people, are the most bigoted, superstitious, hardest headed people in the world! Those folk downstairs believe in ghosts, luck, horse shoes, cloud signs and all other kinds of nonsense" (*Journals*, 81).

In an act of self-congratulatory triumph at escaping such a fate, largely through his own pursuit of self-education, Chesnutt proclaims that "education is a great thing" (*Journals*, 81). Although Chesnutt's entry shows an immature and presumptuous opinion of the people with whom he is boarding, it also exhibits a disdain for what he perceives as ignorance.

In his introduction to Chesnutt's collected journals, Richard H. Brodhead argues that "uneducated rural blacks seem (as they always do) profoundly *other* to this writer, the outlook he has taken in through his schooling organizes his sense of difference" (Brodhead, 14). Chesnutt's sense of otherness and organization of difference also stems from his awareness of the blackness of others, in that he organizes blacks into a hierarchy depending upon their complexions.

This hierarchical organization of blacks is first evident as Chesnutt, while looking for employment at a school just north of Charlotte in June 1875, chronicles his awareness that, although the people with whom he comes into contact are "black," the shades of their complexions differ greatly. He writes of "a little yellow girl" who the previous teacher had "treated better than the other scholars" and argues that the others must have been jealous because "they are the blackest colored people up there that I ever saw" (*Journals*, 60). Later, in the same entry, he refers to a "buxom young woman" and ironically and maliciously notes that she is "not quite as black as the 'ace of spades'" (Brodhead, 61). The differences between himself and others were apparent to Chesnutt early in his life. Helen M. Chesnutt documents the favoritism shown him by a wealthy, white bookstore owner in Fayetteville. "There were few books in his home and no libraries in town, but there was a very good book-store run by Mr. George Haigh, a member of one of Fayetteville's first families. Mr. Haigh took an interest in Charles because he was such an intelligent and well-bred little lad, and gave him the freedom of the store" (6). However, Haigh's racial liberality cannot be assessed simply based upon his treatment of Chesnutt. In a journal entry dated 16 March 1880, Chesnutt details a conversation with Haigh in which the bookstore owner is lamenting the end of slavery and arguing that blacks "don't work like they used to" (*Journals*, 126). Chesnutt counters by explaining "that is one of the results of slavery," to which Haigh further complains that "it's hard work to get a servant who won't steal.... You *can't* superintend them" (*Journals*, 127). Considering the abject racism that Haigh shows in Chesnutt's journals, it is apparent that Chesnutt has the "freedom of the store" because he is light-skinned and highly educated.

Chesnutt's assessment of his own racial identity is first noted in his journals on 31 July 1875 in the countryside of South Carolina. "Twice today, or oftener I have been mistaken for 'white.' At the pond this morning one fellow said 'he'd be damned' if there was any nigger blood in me.... I believe I'll leave here and pass anyhow, for I am as white as any of them" (*Journals*, 78).

It is clear that in Chesnutt's realization that he could "pass" for white, he is acknowledging that blackness and black folk belief, something by which the precocious and ambitious young man did not wish to be defined, are impediments to the social mobility that he will need to fulfill his own professional goals.

With this in mind, it is interesting that Chesnutt chose the folklore laden theme of conjure stories to drive his initial attempts at publication, especially considering his apparent aversion to folk belief and the people who sustained its practices. However, after returning to Fayetteville in 1877, Chesnutt's journals exhibit a softening interest in folklore.

In 1879, Chesnutt took a trip to Washington, D.C., in order to measure the possibility of retaining "employment in some literary avocation" (*Journals*, 106). After discussing the matter with Dr. Haigh, who thought Chesnutt could "succeed in the North, for there are more opportunities and less prejudice," he decided to "go to the Metropolis" and "test the social problem ... [to] see if it's possible for talent, wealth, genius to acquire social standing and distinction" (*Journals*, 105, 106). On the train North, Chesnutt again comes into contact with blacks in a scene reminiscent of his earlier entries concerning African Americans in Spartanburg. "It was pleasant enough till we took on about fifty darkies who were going to Norfolk to work on a truck farm. They filled the seats and standing room, and sat in each other's laps for want of seats. As the day was warm and the people rather dirty, the odor may better be imagined than described" (*Journals*, 112). However, unlike Chesnutt's stigmatization of the blacks in Spartanburg, the group on the train to Norfolk "was a merry crowd" (*Journals*, 112). Chesnutt recounts "one young fellow who would gravely line out a hymn and then sing it himself, with all the intonation of a camp meeting" (*Journals*, 112). Again, Chesnutt expresses the same interest in black folk music exemplified in earlier journal entries.

It must have seemed ironic to Chesnutt that in attempting to escape the South where "the home folks cannot appreciate my talents" to the great and hopeful North where "there is more life and activity, more openings for business, more opportunities" he is accompanied by "fifty darkies" who are attempting to do the same (*Journals*, 141, 117). Whether or not his trip North and the company along the way had any impact on Chesnutt's sentiments toward blackness and folklore is not clear; however, a tempered attitude towards what was once the belief and practice of the "commonplace and vulgar" is apparent in his subsequent journal entries. His journal entry of 8 September 1881 marks his first attempts at writing in the dialect that he would use in *The Conjure Woman*. In another entry written one year later on 8 September 1882, Chesnutt seems to be recording ideas and sketches for stories and recollections. After a series of notes, Chesnutt again attempts to write in dialect.

In these sketches, it is evident that Chesnutt is highlighting the "commonplace and vulgar;" however, it is also evident that he is beginning to come to terms with his understanding of folk practices, practices which, according to Chesnutt, were "one source of their popularity" (Brodhead, 125). The popularity of and desire for black folklore became crystallized to Chesnutt upon the publication of Albion Tourgee's *A Fool's Errand*. In an entry dated 16 March 1880, Chesnutt discusses that Tourgee's book "is about the South" and that "nearly all his stories are more or less about colored people" (*Journals*, 124, 125). Considering Tourgee's subject, as well as his $20,000 profit from the novel, Chesnutt questions how "Tourgee, with his necessarily limited intercourse with colored people, and with his limited stay in the South, can write such interesting descriptions ... of Southern life and character" (*Journals*, 125). In his journal Chesnutt questions why a black man could not write the same type of novel and enjoy the same type of success. "Why could not a colored man if he possessed the same ability, write a far better book about the South than Judge Tourgee or Mrs. Stowe has written?" (*Journals*, 125). Considering that Chesnutt saw both Tourgee and Stowe as social crusaders who could also benefit financially from their message, it is no surprise that he chose black folklore as the central theme for *The Conjure Woman*, his first fiction of purpose.

However, in his works following *The Conjure Woman*, Chesnutt did not use folklore as either a crutch to aid him or a divining rod to point him in the direction of literary success. In *The Wife of His Youth and Other Stories of the Color line, The House Behind the Cedars,* and *The Marrow of Tradition,* blackness and folklore are not something to which Chesnutt repairs, but a hindrance from which he and his characters attempt to escape.

In the title story from *The Wife of His Youth and Other Stories of the Color Line* (1899), Mr. Ryder is a light-skinned black man who fled slavery and headed north to Groveland (Cleveland, Ohio) in search of possibility and equality. Upon settling in Groveland, Mr. Ryder becomes a member of the influential Blue Veins, a social group whose members are "more white than black" (*Wife,* 1). Although Mr. Ryder postures himself as a successful man and even the "dean of the Blue Veins," he is unable to escape the power of his past in the form of 'Liza Jane, the dark-skinned wife to whom he was betrothed while both were slaves (*Wife,* 1).

When 'Liza Jane confronts Ryder as to the possible whereabouts of "my man Sam," she declares that Sam must be alive because she has had a succession of dreams in which she finds him. When Ryder hints that Sam may be dead, 'Liza Jane counters by explaining, "Oh no, he ain' dead. De signs an' de tokens tells me. I dremp three nights runnin' on'y dis las' week dat I foun' him" (*Wife,* 14). 'Liza Jane's folk belief, coupled with her appearance in that she "looked like a bit of the old plantation life, summoned up from the past," is held in stark contrast with Mr. Ryder's light-skinned complexion and gentlemanly refinement (*Wife,* 10). Also held in stark contrast with 'Liza Jane is the twenty-five-year old Ms. Dixon, Ryder's love interest and potential wife who is younger, lighter-skinned and more educated than even himself. The story ends with Ryder acknowledging 'Liza Jane as "the wife of his youth" and surrendering to the inescapable power of his own past and his wife's strong ties to folk belief.

Like the characters in "The Wife of His Youth," Rena Walden of *The House Behind the Cedars* is inextricably tied to her own blackness because of her susceptibility to the power of folk belief. Rena is a light-skinned black woman who leaves home and attempts to pass as white under the guidance of her brother John, who has rejected "black life without regret" and has become "the novel's standard for black success" (Ferguson, 75, 76). Upon joining John, Rena becomes engaged to a dashing, white aristocrat named George Tryon and plans to marry him. However, after having a succession of three dreams in which her mother appears ill and dying, Rena is compelled to return home to care for her, proving that although she is posing as white, her blackness and folk belief play as strong a role in her conception of reality as they do for 'Liza Jane.

Although Rena assumes whiteness and lives as white, she remains, according to SallyAnn H. Ferguson, "psychologically black" as "she gives into super-stition because of her inability to reason" (Ferguson, 77). Her return home "outs" her as black when Tryon discovers her in the streets of Patesville. Even-tually, Rena dies in the swamp from exposure after being lasciviously pursued by Tryon because her race now makes her an object of perverse sexual desire.

The Marrow of Tradition contains two characters who, like Rena, suffer the fate of death as they either rely on folklore practices or merely exhibit the uneducated ignorance that Chesnutt abhorred. The novel opens with the birth of a first child, a son, to Major Carteret and his wife. Although the deliv-ery is difficult, the child is born healthy and Mrs. Carteret survives, much to the relief and surprise of the family. However, Mammy Jane, the couple's ser-vant who belonged to Mrs. Carteret's mother before Emancipation, is con-cerned about a mole she spies under the ear of the child.

In his essay "The Mole on the Neck: Two Instances of a Folk Belief in Fiction" (1983), James S. Hedges discusses the folk belief that holds that "if you have a mole on your neck, you will be hanged" and argues that, like the child's foreboding possible fate, the town of Wellington experiences a cul-tural strangulation in the face of heightening racial tensions (43). Another focus is on the popular folk belief Chesnutt uses in *Marrow*. As before, in the writing of "Goophered Grapevine," Chesnutt is using an already existing folk-tale, proving foreknowledge of the tradition in which he is writing.

Because of Mammy Jane's concern for the welfare of the child, she pays a visit to a "wise old black woman, who lived on the farther edge of the town and was well known to be versed in witchcraft and conjuration" (*Marrow*, 10). After visiting the conjure woman, Mammy Jane heeds her advice as to how to protect the newborn child. "She filled a small vial with water in which the infant had been washed ... [and] the conjure woman added to the con-tents of the bottle a bit of calamus root, and one of the cervical vertebrae from the skeleton of a black cat, with several other mysterious ingredients, the nature of which she did not disclose" (*Marrow*, 11). Later, under a full moon, Mammy Jane buries the vial in the Carterets' backyard as "a good-luck charm to ward off evil spirits" (*Marrow*, 11). In "Superstitions and Folk-lore of the South," Chesnutt contends that "most of the delusions connected with this belief in conjuration grow out of mere lack of enlightenment" (60). Mammy Jane is indeed "unenlightened," not only in her obsessive belief in conjuration, but also in her dog-like fealty to the Carterets. This dedication is most grossly displayed as Mammy Jane is dying in the street after being attacked during the race riot. Dr. Miller, the novel's protagonist, comes "upon the body of a woman lying upon the sidewalk" and realizes that "the pros-trate form was that of old Aunt Jane Letlow" (*Marrow*, 296). Realizing that Mammy Jane is dying, Miller bends down in an attempt to comfort her, only to hear her utter her last words, "Comin', missis, comin'!" (*Marrow*, 296). The irony of Mammy Jane's last locution is not lost on the narrator in that "not all her reverence for her old mistress, nor all her deference to the whites, not all their friendship for her, had been able to save her from this raging devil of race hatred" (*Marrow*, 297).

The black reaction to the race riot centers around two characters in the novel; dark-skinned Josh Green, the quintessential black folk hero reminiscent of Nat Turner, and a mulatto named Dr. Miller, whom Robert M. Farnsworth, in his introduction to *Marrow*, argues is Chesnutt's "most viable possibility of racial accommodation" and, like John Walden from *House*, is "the novel's standard for black success" (Farnsworth, xi).

Dr. Miller, who, according to Farnsworth, "recognizes the overwhelming white power and who thus insists there is no choice but accommodation to it" tries to convince Green not to react violently to the riots (Farnsworth, ix).

> "Listen men," he [Miller] said. "We would only be throwing our lives away ... my life would pay the forfeit. Alive, I may be of some use to you, and you are welcome to my life that way, — I am giving it to you. Dead, I should be a mere lump of carrion" [*Marrow*, 282].

In her essay "Some Implications of Womanist Theory" (1986), Sherley Anne Williams argues that Dr. Miller forges a path for the non-aggressive hero as he "avoids physical aggression" and reaches "intellectual equality with — not dominance over — the collective white man" (Williams, 220). She contends that Miller achieves this equality in that he "is a husband, father, son, and founder of a hospital and school for blacks" (Williams, 221). However, Williams fails to cite Josh Green as an example of the black male character who uses "physical force ... which is almost always defensive, especially against white people" (Williams, 220). Green, whose father was murdered by the Ku Klux Klan, feels there is no option short of physical confrontation, whether defensive or otherwise. "'De w'ite folks are killin' de niggers, an' we ain' gwine to stan' up an' be shot down like dogs. We're gwine to defen' our lives, an' we ain' gwine ter run away f'm no place we got a right ter be; an' woe be ter de w'ite man w'at lays han's on us!'" (*Marrow*, 281). Miller's attempt to enlighten and dissuade Green from action is similar to Chesnutt's attempt to do the same with "those people downstairs" in Spartanburg, S.C. The parallel between Miller and Green is similar to the aforementioned parallels of Mr. Ryder and 'Liza Jane and John and Rena Walden. The former in each grouping is able to reject black life without regret, while the latter is unable to free him or herself from the ties that bind them to folklore and blackness. Green's fate is the same as Rena's and Mammy Jane's in that Green is killed after not heeding the advice of Miller and fighting to the death during the riots.

Considering the brutal deaths of Rena Walden, Mammy Jane and Josh Green, as well as the survival of John Walden and Dr. Miller, why does Chesnutt seemingly turn against blackness in his later novels? Perhaps the answer can be found in his aforementioned journal entries, especially those detailing the differences between himself and the blacks with whom he was surrounded. The fact that, as Brodhead argues, uneducated blacks are considered "profoundly *other*" to Chesnutt could explain why he simply eliminates them as they are considered serious impediments to the social mobility (and, in Green's case, stability) upon which the race's future hinges.

In his remarks upon accepting the NAACP Spingarn Medal in 1928, Chesnutt states, "My physical makeup was such that I knew the psychology of people of mixed blood in so far as it differed from that of other people, and most of my writing ran along the color line" ("Remarks," 99). Chesnutt closes by making clear that his focus on his characters of mixed race "was perfectly natural and I have no apologies to make for it," and, in "Post-Bellum — Pre-Harlem," he concedes that "substantially all of my writings, with the exception of *The Conjure Woman*, have dealt with the problems of people of mixed blood" (99, 104) He adds that "in some instances and in some respects [the problems are] much more complex and difficult of treatment, in fiction as in life" ("Post-Bellum," 104). Chesnutt clearly excludes *The Conjure Woman* from "substantially all of my writings," proving that his venture into folklore and the culture of blackness was a singular experiment with an exact purpose.

Chesnutt initially wished to assuage his readers' hunger for folklore and blackness in order to beguile them into accepting a palatable dose of didactic color line literature. However, he did so as an outsider in both instances, inhabiting a precarious state, writing for a white audience to which he clearly did not belong and drawing from a black tradition of which he adamantly did not wish to be part, ensuring that the "other," even in his fiction, remained to him distinctly so.

WORKS CITED

Andrews, William L. *The Literary Career of Charles W. Chesnutt*. Baton Rouge: Louisiana State University Press, 1980.

Chesnutt, Charles W. "An Inside View of the Negro Question." In *Charles W. Chesnutt: Essays and Speeches*. 1889. Edited by Joseph R. McElrath, Jr., Robert C. Leitz, III, and Jesse S. Crisler. Stanford, Calif.: Stanford University Press, 2000. 57–68.

_____. *The Journals of Charles W. Chesnutt*. By Charles W. Chesnutt. Edited by Richard M. Brodhead. Durham, N.C.: Duke University Press, 1993.

_____. *The House Behind the Cedars*. Athens, Ga.: University of Georgia Press, 2000.

_____. *The Marrow of Tradition*. Ann Arbor, Mich.: University of Michigan Press, 1996.

_____. "Post-Bellum — Pre-Harlem." In *Charles W. Chesnutt: Selected Writings*. Edited by SallyAnn H. Ferguson. Boston: Houghton Mifflin, 2001. 100–105.

_____. "Remarks of Charles Waddell Chesnutt, of Cleveland, in Accepting the Spingarn

Medal at Los Angeles, July 3, 1928." In *Charles W. Chesnutt: Selected Writings*. Edited by SallyAnn H. Ferguson. Boston: Houghton Mifflin, 2001. 94–100.

_____. "Superstitions and Folklore of the South." In *Charles W. Chesnutt: Selected Writings*. Edited by SallyAnn H. Ferguson. Boston: Houghton Mifflin, 2001. 58–65.

_____. *The Wife of His Youth and Other Stories of the Color Line*. Ann Arbor, Mich.: University of Michigan Press, 1999.

Chesnutt, Helen M. *Charles Waddell Chesnutt: Pioneer of the Color Line*. Chapel Hill, N.C.: University of North Carolina Press, 1952.

Dixon, Melvin. "The Teller as Folk Trickster in Chesnutt's *The Conjure Woman*." *CLA Journal* 18.2 (December 1974): 186–197.

Ferguson, SallyAnn H. "Rena Walden: Chesnutt's Failed 'Future American.'" *Southern Literary Journal* 15 (1982): 74–82.

Fienberg, Lorne. "Charles W. Chesnutt and Uncle Julius: Black Storytellers at the Crossroads." *Studies in American Fiction* 15.2 (Autumn 1987): 161–173.

Hedges, James S. "The Mole on the Neck: Two Instances of a Folk Belief in Fiction." *North Carolina Folklore Journal* 31.1 (Spring-Summer 1983): 43–45.

Hemenway, Robert. "The Functions of Folklore in Charles Chesnutt's *The Conjure Woman*." *Journal of the Folklore Institute* 13.3 (1976): 283–305.

Williams, Sherley Anne. "Some Implications of Womanist Theory." In *African American Literary Theory*. Edited by Winston Napier. New York: New York University Press, 2000. 218–223.

Winkelman, Donald M. "Three American Authors as Semi-Folk Artists." *Journal of American Folklore* 78.307 (January-March 1965): 130–135.

CHAPTER 5

The Fiction of Race: Folklore to Classical Literature

Maria Orban

"We live amid the interminable reproduction of ideals, phantasies, images and dreams which are now behind us, yet which we must continue to reproduce in a sort of inescapable indifference"

Moving from short fiction to the novel for Chesnutt also meant moving away from folklore and what Brodhead in his introduction to *The Conjure Tales* calls "cultural tourism," usually a white character filtering black voices and their tales told in dialect. Chesnutt never thought much of superstitions and folk tales. His sentiments are echoed in the tales: "your people will never rise in the world until they throw off these childish superstitions and learn to live by the light of reason and common sense" (*The Conjure Tales*, 52). They are also amply recorded in his journals. In his essay "Superstitions & Folklore of the South" he argues that "most of the delusions connected with this belief in conjuration grow out of mere lack of enlightenment" (McElrath, 156). He used them, nevertheless, because there was an audience for them and thus they facilitated his literary debut.

Chesnutt's first novel *The House Behind the Cedars*, published in 1900, marks a shift in terms of literary sources employed from the conjure tales: Brer Rabbit to Cinderella. In terms of narrative strategy and point of view, whereas the conjure tales presented black folklore filtered through white characters, this time he will reverse the pattern using classical literary sources interpreted by people of color. The move from folklore to classical literature was justified especially since Chesnutt considered that "the novel, even more than sculpture or painting, is the flower of culture" (McElrath, 516). And by culture he meant erudition. The particular novel he had in mind reflects the pragmatic approach to literature he elaborated on in a speech to the Bethel Literary and Historical Association in 1899:

> Literature may be viewed in two aspects — as an expression of life, past and present, and as a force directly affecting the conduct of life, present and future....
> History is instructive, and may warn or admonish; but to this quality literature adds the faculty of persuasion, by which men's hearts are reached, the springs of action touched, and the currents of life directed [McElrath, 114].

He chooses to fashion the culmination of his romance of race liberation on the model of Walter Scott's *Ivanhoe*, another narrative about the triumph of the underdog in the face of adversity, in hopes that he will accomplish just that.

The questions raised by his choice are: what is the relevance of his choice for his narrative and, particularly, in what ways is his choice of identification and imitation relevant for his construction of race.

In *The Politics of Postmodernism*, Linda Hutcheon argues that "we only have representations of the past from which to construct our narratives or explanations. In a very real sense postmodernism reveals a desire to understand present culture as the product of previous representations" (58). Chesnutt may well have seen his day and age in the struggle between the Normans and the Saxons about to bring in a new age in *Ivanhoe*. The novel is a representation of the cultural conflict between the old ways of the defeated Saxons and the new victorious Norman feudal system, run by the upstarts that invaded the land who are victimizing and just about to wipe out the old inhabitants. It also dramatizes the conflict between two races and two cultures about to merge into a new nation. Scott's fiction focuses on the relationship between the individual and history, on the arbitrariness with which some individuals are crushed to favor others, and conveys a romantic triumphalist message about the power of the individual to change history by standing up to the powerful forces that shape it, and winning against all odds.

Marilyn Butler notes that Scott "could convey a portrait of a contemporary society, and at the same time represent as central the plight of individuals whose lives were caught up in an impersonal mechanism"(109). This was exactly Chesnutt's lifelong struggle: to show the unfair plight of colored people caught up in the mechanism of history. He also had another motive, since Scott was "the literary idol of the South" (*House*, 161) and Chesnutt tried to educate white audiences and make them sympathetic to the plight of black people discriminated against on racial grounds. Modeling part of his plot on *Ivanhoe*, a well-known and loved classic, could make it easier for a white audience to transfer its understanding and emotional response to the demise of the Saxon race to Chesnutt's characters. Thus, he could use the "Sir Walter disease" (*Life on the Mississippi*, 242) to his advantage.[2]

When deGategno argues in *The Mask of Chivalry* that Scott's characters in *Ivanhoe* "do not display complex psychological impulses; instead they embrace their fates as determined in the variety and contradictions of the historical moment," he could have well been discussing Rena Walden (9).

The similarities between the two historical junctures, the new English nation emerging from the collision of the defeated Saxons and the Norman conquerors and the new American order struggling to emerge from the post–Civil War era collated with Chesnutt's philosophy of history alone would make his choice pertinent.

The generic choice can be justified, too. Fashioning his novel on the conventions of the romance novel, this genre of Western culture developed by Scott, suits the fiction of heroism and romantic love, the elements of the plot, the rise and decline of the heroine, and, most of all, the emotional involvement on the part of his audience for the plight of his characters Chesnutt clearly was seeking to achieve.

But what are the political implications of his multilayered narrative for his authorial position? Chesnutt was himself the embodiment of the conflict between the law and individual freedom. He was in the ambivalent position of being caught between worlds. His body was subverting the established categories and the epistemological validity at the core of the dominant system. He was both a representative and an outsider at the same time for both the white and black cultures, belonging to a culture that excluded him on racial grounds and part of a culture he could not identify with. "As the product of his education, Chesnutt's response to the culture of his illiterate black countrymen is usually one of estrangement, embarrassment, and an anxious attempt to guard his distance from it" (Brodhead, 23).[3] Fashioning his novel on the illustrious literary model paradoxically gives him the possibility to illuminate the intricacies of these contradictions and work out the complexities into a coherent pattern. Decoding the norms and techniques that construct Rena's trajectory will help us follow Chesnutt's motivation.

The House Behind the Cedars revolves around Rena Walden, initially the title character of the novel, and her struggle of race liberation in an attempt to gain access to the life of opportunity available to the white upper class and denied her on racial grounds. She is guided in her goal to challenge history by her brother John, who already succeeded in beating the system and who is, therefore, living proof that the goal is within her reach.

Her character embodies the unstable opposition between the two main female characters in *Ivanhoe*, Rowena and Rebecca, and dramatizes the destabilizing overcompensation resulting from the carefully orchestrated efforts to suppress one in order to completely identify with the other. In the *Invention of Ethnicity*, Peter Sollors underlines that just like Rena, "desired and forbidden, Rebecca is also the prototype of the American Other "(22). It is this exotic Other Rena who wants to transgress in order to become part and parcel of the dominant order. Her two identities replicate in a tragic pendulum swing the deconstruction of the unstable binary oppositions symbolized by Rowena and Rebecca: winner and loser, dominant and subservient, privileged and disenfranchised. Giulia Fabi argues that Chesnutt "constructs his all-but-white heroine as a composite of such opposite female characters as Scott's Rowena and Rebecca, unsettling the readerly expectations elicited by references to these popular characters" (45). Chesnutt's narrative strategy certainly highlights the arbitrariness of the two constructs, especially since one of them, Rowena, further develops both sets of binaries depending on the perspective used to decode them. Thus, the direction of the painstakingly staged transgression favors the more complex character of the two, the one that will further elaborate on the social construction of difference, being at the same time both winner and loser, dominant and subservient, privileged and disenfranchised.

Rena's coronation as Queen of Love and Beauty at the annual tournament of the Clarence Social Club represents the fantasy of social recognition that grants her a privileged position in society, the epitome of whiteness. It is the fiction of ultimate success at the intersection of race, class, and gender in a hierarchical system based on privilege and disenfranchisement. Greene considers "Rena's new name ... a signification of her change in racial identity, a reconstruction of self from chivalric texts" (70), which only serves to reinforce the fictional construction of identity and race. Her triumph is the *embodiment* of a couple of superlatives that advance a value system. In *American Anatomies: Theorizing Race and Gender*, Robyn Wiegman makes the point that "social hierarchies have been rationalized, in both senses of the word, by locating in the body an epistemological framework for justifying inequality" (2). Rena's new female body is valued because it is white, beautiful, and belongs to the right class, has the right heritage.

The moment also represents the coronation of all the efforts her brother put into reinventing her for a successful deception. "Her year of instruction, while distinctly improving her mind and manners, had scarcely prepared her for so sudden an elevation into a grade of society to which she had hitherto been a stranger" (House, 57). So, then, her reinvented self is a fiction that is celebrated. Beauty she had, but not of the right kind, not white, and manners of the right kind she also lacked. It is erasing the cultural representation of difference consisting of prescribed customs, manners, and rituals, a system of social norms that insulates those who belong from the outsiders, that constructs the fiction since the right kind of beauty and manners define membership.

This fiction is fashioned on lady Rowena, the Saxon underdog in a world ruled by Normans. The privileged position and respect she is entitled to by birth and beauty are only granted to her in Cedric's home, though beauty has traditionally been a facilitator of social mobility for women.

> Formed in the best proportions of her sex, Rowena was tall in stature, yet not so much so as to attract observation on account of superior height. Her complexion was *exquisitely fair*, [my italics] but the noble cast of her head and features prevented the insipidity which sometimes attaches to fair beauties. Her clear blue eye, which sate enshrined beneath a graceful eyebrow of brown sufficiently marked to give expression to the forehead, seemed capable to kindle as well as melt, to command as well as to beseech. If mildness were the more natural expression of such a combination of features, it was plain, that in the present instance, the exercise of habitual superiority, and the reception of general homage, had given to the Saxon lady a loftier character, which mingled with and qualified that bestowed by nature [Ivanhoe, 65].

The insistence in her description is on her superiority and manners. Thus, her value consists of natural beauty and prescribed behavior. If we read Rowena's body as a text, the blue-eyed, pure, white beauty matching the feminine ideal of courtly love, is the fiction of a fiction. She stands for the underdog that fights for the recognition and dignity of her defeated Saxon race. She stands for cultural difference and class difference.

In the outside world, at the Ashby-de-la-Zouche tournament, where a new Norman system of values applies, the fair, blue-eyed Rowena is an outcast like her Saxon race, exiled with the lower classes, separated from the Norman nobility, underscoring the not yet balanced conflicting duality of the social system. To mark this stratification and make his disdain for the Saxons public, Prince John offensively suggests they make room for Isaac and Rebecca, the Jews, amongst them.

When crowned Queen of Love and Beauty, Rowena triumphs over the Norman ladies of the day, over the other side of the paradigm receiving the highest honor as part of the rituals of the Norman conquerors, her body as the Queen both displacing and subverting the established axiology. Thus, in a way, she is part of the erasing of the cultural representation of difference since she gaps the cultural difference spilling into the other side.

Just like Rena who was modeled after her, she lacks economic power. Her voice is muted most of the time; she is a pawn, and her real value is that she has royal blood and is marriageable. In Cedric's hollow dreams of resuscitated Saxon glory she is to ensure the succession of the royal line by marrying Athelstane.

Rowena herself is a fiction of the courtly love, stereotypical representation of the feminine ideal. Literary representations of women within the courtly love tradition combine physical and moral beauty, and most of all purity and nobility. The women are put on a pedestal to be admired for their outstanding qualities. Courtly love is a public recognition and an homage paid to those mutually agreed upon values, a celebration of the norms that shape chivalry. The lady's counterpart is the knight in shining armor, as Ivanhoe is for Rowena and Tryon for Rena. They complete the picture of the lady in distress in need of being rescued, an offspring of the feminine ideal. In the case of Rena, Tryon complements a major vulnerability.

Physically, the lady is the most beautiful in the whole world. Courtly love is a vast and shifting tradition spanning centuries of literary development. The image of women evolves with the cultural perspective. I will take a random example to illustrate the stereotype of feminine beauty from the twelfth century: Marie de France's *Lanval*. The lady of Lanval's love is all made of stereotypical superlatives. "There was none more beautiful in the whole world ... her neck whiter than snow on a branch; her eyes bright and her face white.... A golden thread does not shine as brightly as the rays reflected in the light from her hair" (1323). The main components thus are once again white, blond, and pure, with whiteness also the symbol of purity.

There is insistence in the image of women on nobility, elegance, and the way they conduct themselves. The rules of proper conduct for women are as important as those regulating chivalry. The narrative structure conditions the construction of the female subject but generally they are refined and of noble character. The female voice is muted, the lady herself is often absent, and her idealized and highly eroticized qualities consist mainly of prescribed female behavior, the ideal conduct for women. In the courtly love tradition, as well as in the case of Rowena and Rena, beauty is constructed as a sexist, stereotypical currency.

Inside this Chinese box, race identity based on the fiction of whiteness in *The House Behind the Cedars* is, in fact, the fiction of a fiction of a fiction, thus pointing to an endless network of representations.

Therefore, Chesnutt's choice can also be revealing for the way he defines race. "Why then, Chesnutt's novel seems to ask, should people who look as white as 'whites' and whose cultural affinities and socioeconomic goals mirror those of 'whites' be automatically condemned as racial impostors for simply being what to all appearances they actually are — white men and women" (Andrews, XII).

Chesnutt knew first hand there was no biological basis for race. He was taken for white all the time. He seems to make, in his novel, Appiah's argument:

Because the ascription of racial identities — the process of applying the label to people, including ourselves — is based on more than intentional identification that there can be a gap between what a person ascriptively is and the racial identity they perform: it is this gap that makes passing possible ["Reconstructing Racial Identities," 68].

Chesnutt's cultural identification, though, may be read in a number of ways. Traditional criticism reads his choice as part of the general racist sentiment that pervaded post–Civil War Southern society, an ongoing racist sentiment that included people of color who discriminated against people with darker skin.

In a system built on racial prejudice, Molly and the rest of the lighter-skinned Negroes are equally afflicted, and they look down on former slaves and dark blacks.[4] Frank Fowler, the generous neighbor in love with Rena, is the best example. No matter how kindhearted he is, or how much he helped Molly and Rena, he could only be looked down on because of his race and class. Dean McWilliams argues that "dark skinned Negroes for Rena ... are exotic, bestial inferiors," although he concludes that Rena has a slight change of heart toward Frank at the end of the novel (139).

Chesnutt's own description of black people at times plays into racist stereotypes.[5] When he writes about "the excited Negroes, their white teeth and eyeballs glistening in the surrounding darkness to which their faces formed no relief," one cannot miss the stereotypical racist image of colored people present in movies, musicals, and commercials up until not so long ago (House, 42).

In a similar way, shaped by a worldview rooted in hierarchy, in *Ivanhoe* the wronged and dispossessed Saxons[6] that dream of justice for their race both destabilize and re-enforce the oppressive system by discriminating with impunity against Rebecca and her father Isaac. Even after it is known that they saved Ivanhoe's life and they helped him with his tournament gear, thus being instrumental in the Saxon triumph, they are despised as inferior on racial grounds. The Saxons are as disgusted with the presence of the Jews as the Normans are with the presence of the Saxons.

In both cases it can be argued that the oppressed do not want to change the system, just their place in it. There is a cycle of injustice and oppression perpetuated by all the participants in the game. This is to be expected if we consider Foucault's argument that we are all conditioned by the dominant discourse, that there is no outside the system, and even the form our opposition to the system takes is determined by it.

According to Homi Bhabha, Chesnutt's choice would be a manifestation of internalized oppression, a state in which the colonized completely buy into the value system of the colonizer, which they try to emulate. It is the "colonial desire which alienates the modality and normality of those dominant discourses in which they emerge as 'inappropriate' colonial subjects" (Bhabha, 88). Ivanhoe is accepted by King Richard for his bravery and loyalty, but he crosses the race line to identify with "the colonizer," just as John Warrick completely buys into white supremacist values after he passes for white. The crossover will not resolve the incongruities or blatant contradictions their ambivalent positions are built upon. Rowena's ritual reenactment of the Queen of Love and Beauty is mimicry of recognition at court. In actuality she is despised by the Normans. Similarly, black Rena crowned Queen of Beauty by the white Clarence Social Club of South Carolina will be rejected in disgust by Tryon when her race becomes known to him. It is also noteworthy that the moment of Rowena's triumph at the tournament takes place on Norman terms, after the disinherited knight subscribed to the Norman code of chivalry[7] and she becomes part of the tournament ritual, sucked into the Norman system of prescribed social norms.

Similarly, Rena's moment of glory is defined entirely in terms of white Southern culture after she is sent to school and has learned the proper behavior to fit into high society. Since in both cases the participants, Rowena and Rena, did not have much of a choice in the matter, they are examples of symbolic violence.[8] "Symbolic force is a form of power that is exerted on bodies, directly and as if by magic, without any physical constraint" (Bourdieu, 38). Their choice was carefully orchestrated for them; they acquired it by their upbringing in a particular culture.

> The effect of symbolic domination (whether ethnic, gender, cultural or linguistic, etc.) is exerted not in the pure logic of knowing consciousnesses but through the schemes of perception, appreciation and action that are constitutive of habitus and which below the level of the decisions of consciousness and the controls of the will, set up a cognitive relationship that is profoundly obscure to itself [Bourdieu, 37].

By habitus, Bourdieu roughly means embodied social structures. This would explain how we perceive our choice of action. It can explain why after Emancipation in the South everything associated with blackness is viewed as demeaning: superstitions, beliefs, practices, customs, and tales. It may explain why Chesnutt did not wish to be associated with black folklore, but did not find anything demeaning about Western folklore, about inserting references to Cinderella and the glass slipper in his novel (House, 62 and 71 respectively). It may explain why even to this day a critic like SallyAnn H. Ferguson argues that Rena is "psychologically black" in giving in to superstition "because of her inability to reason"; why believing in superstitions is viewed in dialectical opposition to the ability to reason (Ferguson, 77).

It is the customs, values, and dominant beliefs that act on the bodies shaping their choices, because as Appiah argues: "we do make choices (of self), but we don't determine the options among which we choose" (CC, 96).

Chesnutt's choice to shape his heroine on lady Rowena goes to the core of the definition of race he challenges. In one of his essays, "Race Prejudice," he clearly states his view. For him "race is a modern *invention*" [my italics] (McElrath, 232). The point he dramatizes in his novel is that race is a fiction, just as his Rena's fiction of whiteness is based on a fiction of a fiction. No wonder different states had different, confusing ways of defining race. Chesnutt explains in his novel that in order to be white "you would, at least in South Carolina, have simply to assume the place and exercise the privileges of a white man" (House, 172). As Appiah's insightful analysis points out, "Our account of the significance of race ... mistakes identity for culture" (CC, 92). Thus, race is a social and cultural construct and as such is made up of prescribed rules. Chesnutt was part of Western culture just as much as his writings are today. His sophisticated challenge of race is based on erasing the cultural representation of difference in the form of manners, rituals, and customs, all acquired behavior, all authorized versions of otherness, with simulation at the core of the mechanism that insures the reproduction and implementation of values that do not necessarily define us as individuals but which we cannot escape.

NOTES

1. In "After the Orgy," Jean Baudrillard argues that all the explosion of modernity left us with is simulation; but in fact simulation might always have been at the core of representation, and I don't mean, of course, mimesis here. Sorting out Chesnutt's construction of race underscores the role simulation plays in implementing value systems.

2. In his article "Walter Scott, Postcolonial Theory and New South Literature," Peter Schmidt, among others, has a very different take on Chesnutt's use of *Ivanhoe* in his novel, arguing that his allusions to it are ironic (545).

3. His attitude will change later on, as he will come to appreciate the individuality and uniqueness of African American cultural traditions.

4. For a discussion of Chesnutt's hierarchical organization of blacks see in this volume Wiley Cash, "The Eradication of Folklore," 191.

5. For an analysis of Chesnutt's problematic treatment of blackness see McWilliams's discussion of Trudier Harris's charge of racism in *The House Behind the Cedars*: "Creatures of Our Creation," 143–144.

6. The irony of a white, Anglo-Saxon audience forced by Chesnutt to resonate to Rena's oppression on racial grounds by relating to the oppression of the Saxon race in *Ivanhoe* cannot be missed. In fact, the use of irony in this novel is part the construction of race and deserves consideration as a narrative strategy that highlights the inherent contradictions of an incongruous heritage.

7. Actually, Ivanhoe subscribed to the Norman code of chivalry when he chose to follow King Richard in the crusade. That is why Cedric disinherited him.

8. For more on this see: Bourdieu, "A Magnified Image," in *Masculine Domination*, 37–42.

WORKS CITED

Appiah, Anthony K. and Amy Gutmann. *Color Conscious: The Political Morality of Race.* Princeton, N.J.: Princeton University Press, 1996.

_____, "Reconstructing Racial Identities." *Research in African Literatures* 27.3 (1996): 68.

Baudrillard, Jean. *The Transparency of Evil.* Translated by James Benedict. London, N.Y.: Verso, 1993.

Bhabha, Homi K. *The Location of Culture.* London: Routledge, 2004.

Bourdieu, Pierre. *Masculine Domination.* Stanford, Calif.: Stanford University Press, 2001.

Butler, Marilyn. *Romantics, Rebels, and Reactionaries: English Literature and Its Background, 1760–1830.* New York: Oxford University Press, 1982.

Chesnutt, Charles W. *The Conjure Woman and Other Conjure Tales.* Durham, N.C: Duke University Press, 1993.

_____. *The House Behind the Cedars.* Athens: University of Georgia Press, 1988.

_____. *The Journals of Charles W. Chesnutt.* Edited by Richard M. Brodhead. Durham: Duke University Press, 1993.

_____. "Literature in its Relation to Life." In *Charles W. Chesnutt: Essays and Speeches.* Edited by Joseph R. McElrath, Jr., Robert C. Leitz, III and Jesse S. Crisler. Stanford, Calif.: Stanford University Press, 2000.

_____. "The Negro in Present Day Fiction." In *Charles W. Chesnutt: Essays and Speeches.* Edited by Joseph R. McElrath, Jr., Robert C. Leitz, III and Jesse S. Crisler. Stanford, Calif.: Stanford University Press, 2000.

_____. "Race Prejudice." In *Charles W. Chesnutt: Essays and Speeches.* Edited by. Joseph R. McElrath, Jr., Robert C. Leitz, III and Jesse S. Crisler. Stanford, Calif.: Stanford University Press, 2000.

_____. "Superstitions and the Folklore of the South." In *Charles W. Chesnutt: Essays and Speeches.* Edited by Joseph R. McElrath, Jr., Robert C. Leitz, III and Jesse S. Crisler. Stanford, Calif.: Stanford University Press, 2000.

deGategno, Paul J. Ivanhoe. *The Mask of Chivalry.* New York: Twayne Publishers, 1994.

Greene, Lee J. *Blacks in Eden: The African American Novel's First Century Belles and Beaux.* Charlottesville: University of Virginia Press, 1996.

Fabi, Giulia M. "Reconstructing the Race: the novel after slavery." In *The Cambridge Companion to the African American Novel.* Edited by Maryemma Graham. Cambridge: Cambridge University Press, 2004, 34–50.

Ferguson, SallyAnn H. "Rena Walden: Chesnutt's Failed 'Future American.'" *Southern Literary Journal* 15 (1982): 74–82.

Hutcheon, Linda. *The Politics of Postmodernism.* London: Routledge, 1989.

Marie de France. *Lanval.* In The Norton Anthology of Western Literature. Vol.1. New York: W.W. Norton, 2006. 1318–1324.

McWilliams, Dean. *Charles W. Chesnutt and the Fictions of Race.* Athens: University of Georgia Press, 2002.

Scott, Sir Walter. *Ivanhoe: a romance.* New York: L.A. Burt, 1830.

Schmidt, Peter. "Walter Scott, Postcolonial Theory and New South Literature." *The Mississippi Quarterly* 56, 2003.

Sollors, Peter. *The Invention of Ethnicity.* New York and Oxford: Oxford University Press, 1989.

Twain, Mark. *Life on the Mississippi.* New York: Hill and Wang, 1957.

Wiegman, Robyn. *American Anatomies: Theorizing Race and Gender.* Durham, N.C.: Duke University Press, 1995.

CHAPTER 6

Charles W. Chesnutt's *The House Behind the Cedars*: An Outlaw(ed) Reading

Coleman C. Myron

"It's not enough to rage against the lie ... you've got to replace it with the truth."

— Bono

Post-slavery African American writer Charles Waddell Chesnutt, who like many other African American authors, often had to lessen the blow of his message or employ masks to hide unpleasant truths incurred by African Americans that otherwise might not get voiced in leading American literary magazines and publishing houses, refrains from this technique that he used so marvelously in *The Conjure Woman* (1899) to craft his novel *The House Behind the Cedars* (1900). In *The House Behind the Cedars*, Chesnutt deals directly with the social, cultural, and racial upheavals that the freed African American faced in the post–Reconstruction South.

> If I do write, I shall write for a purpose, a high, holy purpose, and this will inspire me to greater effort. The object of my writings would not be so much the elevation of the colored people as the elevation of the whites — for I consider the unjust spirit of caste ... a barrier to the moral progress of the American people; and I would be one of the first to head a determined organized crusade against it. Not a fierce indiscriminate onslaught; not an appeal to force, for this is something that force can but slightly affect; but a moral revolution which must be brought about in a different manner.... The subtle almost indefinable feeling of repulsion toward the negro, which is common to most Americans — and easily enough accounted for —, cannot be stormed and taken by assault; the garrison will not capitulate: so their position must be mined, and we will find ourselves in their midst before they think of it.... It is the province of literature ... to

accustom the public mind to the idea; and ... while amusing them to ... lead
them on imperceptibly, unconsciously step by step to the desired state of feeling
[Chesnutt, May 29, 1880, *Journals* 139–40].

By crafting a complex, multi-layered novel that makes use of several characters whose identities as mulattoes allow them to cross racial boundaries, Chesnutt exposes the racism of white America while shaping a character in young
Miss Rena Walden, whose heroism places her in line with other great American literary figures, both historical and fictional, such as Thomas Jefferson,
Henry David Thoreau, and Huck Finn. They rebel against society, either real
or imagined, to show people that other truths do exist.

Although African Americans had been granted their freedom, their release
from the chains of slavery provided for them only a physical removal from
their situations. As newly freed people, African Americans remained more
enslaved than if they had been slaves, since their new-found condition involved
a constant struggle to define their role alongside their former oppressors, who
did not accept them as equals but adopted them into the framework of their
lives on an as-need basis. What increased the difficulty of assimilation for these
former slaves was the frequent unwillingness of their fellow Southern brethren
to view their past lives as slaves as egregious. Rather than interpret the facts
in clear terms, those in power romanticized the situation of slavery by publishing works along the lines of Joel Chandler Harris's Uncle Remus tales,
which idealized the view of race relations. The publication of these works and
others similar to it served to disguise the deplorable reality of the past and to
help explain the reasons for the present situation. By choosing this path,
Southerners and Northerners tainted history by painting a picture of themselves as liberators of a pagan people from their roots in a savage and uncivilized world. This story of deceit ameliorated the conscience of white society
and allowed it to move forward, not swayed by the needs of those whom it
had liberated.

Through the tale of mulatto siblings John and Rena Walden, who could
pass for being white, Chesnutt (who could also pass for white but chose not
to) provides in microcosm the theme of the growing race consciousness
between African Americans and whites, which had escalated and even turned
into a conflict between African Americans and African Americans. Former
slaves and even previously freed African Americans now faced life under much
different circumstances than the "system that made it possible to convert
human beings into disposable property with supposedly no more feeling or
consciousness than a tree" (Andrews, 43). As property, African American
slaves owed to their masters and mistresses complete allegiance. If they failed
to provide complete allegiance, they could end up being sold or even killed.
Often for female slaves — more so than males — this allegiance included

fulfilling the base sexual needs of their masters. Sexual intercourse with a young girl or woman was often enticed with gifts and other favors, but more often than not, the woman, as the property of her master, was forcibly raped. In either scenario, women gave birth to illegitimate offspring with their fathers' features but not their name, which would have provided them some measure of legitimacy. Once freed from slavery, however, the situation for African Americans of mixed race changed little, as they often found it necessary to prostitute themselves to survive in society. When Molly's father "died prematurely, a disappointed and disheartened man, leaving his family in dire poverty," Molly's own fortunes as a free woman of color changed, and followed a similar path to the ones her ancestors had traveled:

> The slim, barefoot girl, with sparkling eyes and voluminous hair, who played about the yard and sometimes handed water in a gourd to travelers, did not long escape critical observation. A gentleman drove by one day, stopped at the well, smiled upon the girl, and said kind words. He came again, more than once, and soon, while scarcely more than a child in years, Molly was living in her own house, hers by deed of gift, for her protector was rich and liberal [*Cedars*, 371].

As Chesnutt moves his readers forward in historical time with the presentation of Molly, he also moves them backward in time, showing that even though slavery had ended, the mindset of those who had inflicted this social institution on human beings and those who had suffered it endured. In this view, history repeats itself, and Molly follows the precedence of her parents and ancestors, "old issue free negroes," who had "mingled their blood with great freedom and small formality" among the "many Indians, runaway negroes, and indentured white servants from the seaboard plantations" (*Cedars*, 370). However, Molly's decision to become the mistress of this Southern gentleman is blinded by the innocence of youth. As a young girl, she willingly sacrificed herself morally and damned her offspring to a life of hardship so that her "mother [would] nevermore [know] want. Her poor relations could always find a meal in [her] kitchen" (*Cedars*, 371). Molly herself "did not flaunt her prosperity in the world's face, but as her lord had done with her, she hid it discreetly behind the cedar screen" (*Cedars*, 371).

After presenting the relationship between Molly and the white "gentleman," Chesnutt briefly demonstrates to his readers that racial inequality does not discriminate between Southern or Northern whites or even between the races but is a contagion found in all peoples. In *The House Behind the Cedars*, Chesnutt showcases it in the free colored people who had "exercised the right of suffrage as late as 1835," had worked hard, "and dreamed of a still brighter future when the growing tyranny of the slave power crushed their hopes and crowded the free people back upon the black mass just beneath them" (370, 371). As Chesnutt states: Molly "did not sympathize greatly with the new era opened up for the emancipated slaves; she had no ideal love of liberty; she was no broader and no more altruistic than the white people around her, to whom she had always looked up; and she sighed for the old days, because to her they had been the good days," in large measure because "her king" lived (*Cedars*, 373), but also because "Molly's free birth carried with it certain advantages, even in the South before the war.... They were not citizens, yet they were not slave" (370), and this knowledge allowed "Mis Molly [to feel] herself infinitely superior to Peter and his wife,—scarcely less superior than her poor white neighbors felt themselves to Mis' Molly" (382). In Molly, Chesnutt shows us the wide-ranging conflicts in race consciousness felt toward other African Americans, considered of a lower caste.

However, the focus of the narrative is not on Molly's forbidden and questionable relationship with the white Southern "gentleman" or even with her less than magnanimous relationship with Peter and his wife, but rather with her son John and daughter Rena's assimilation into society. Each of these characters in their physical makeup can pass for white people and through them Chesnutt presents the choices available to African Americans as the United States got off the slave exchange. By providing these characters the surname of Walden, Chesnutt wants readers to consider the message that Henry David Thoreau takes up in his long essay, *Walden*, where Thoreau addresses the issues of self-realization, fulfillment, and casting off the chains that bind people to society:

> I learned this, at least, by my experiment; that if one advances confidently in the direction of his dreams, and endeavors to live the life which he has imagined, he will meet with a success unexpected in common hours. He will put some things behind, will pass an invisible boundary; new, universal, and more liberal laws will begin to establish themselves around and within him; or the old laws be expanded, and interpreted in his favor in a more liberal sense, and he will live with the license of a higher order of beings. In proportion as he simplifies his life, the laws of the universe will appear less complex, and solitude will not be solitude, nor poverty poverty, nor weakness weakness. If you have built castles in the air, your work need not be lost; that is where they should be [Thoreau, 214].

Specifically, the main theme of *Walden* centers around the concept of the individual gaining unparalleled happiness by following not in the conventions of society but in the direction of his or her dreams. Although all three characters possess the surname of Walden, Rena alone triumphantly follows her own inner call and suggests through her trials and tribulations the need to remain true to the principles instilled within. Rena, as the meaning of her name suggests, becomes the song or anthem that Chesnutt hopes all will hear.

In John Walden, Chesnutt presents the self-reliant, self-made hero eager to succeed in the world. In order to become somebody in this world, John understands early on that progress will come only when he rejects his roots in the black race. At the age of fifteen, John didn't see himself as a black youth; to him, he was no different than his friends. His outward appearance shows him to be "a tall, slender lad of fifteen, with his father's patrician features and his mother's Indian hair, and no external sign to mark him off from the white boys on the street" (*Cedars*, 373). It's not until a friend informs him that he's black that John has to deny it to the point of being "beaten five or six times" (*Cedars*, 373). Despite the physical beatings that he took from his friends, John "never admitted the charge" since "the mirror proved that God, the Father of all, had made him white; and God, he had been taught, made no mistakes — having made him white, He must have meant him to be white" (*Cedars*, 373). To free himself from being "owned" by this community, John knows that he will have to move away.

Unlike most young African Americans, John has been provided with certain advantages that stem from his racial background. As the offspring of free colored parents, he had been taught how to read by a "faded mulatto teacher, which allowed him the opportunity to tackle the books that his 'distinguished' father kept in the black walnut bookcase"(*Cedars*, 374). These books ranging from the *Collected Works of Walter Scott* to *Don Quixote* allowed John to discover "the portal of a new world, peopled with strange and marvelous beings" that defined the advantages that privileged classes possessed over their counterparts (*Cedars*, 374). These books drive John to seek the aid of Judge Straight in order to become a lawyer. However, Judge Straight reminds John that he is "black" and, according to the "learned Judge Taney" deliverer of "the Dred Scott decision ... 'of an inferior order, and altogether unfit to associate with the white race, either in social or political relations; in fact, so inferior that they have no rights which the white man is bound to respect, and that the negro may justly and lawfully be reduced to slavery for his benefit.' That is the law of this nation, and that is the reason why you cannot be a lawyer" (*Cedars*, 379).

Whereas the explanation of the law by the judge is true, it does not, John feels, apply to him since "a Negro is black; I am white" (*Cedars*, 379). When John realizes that this argument is not leading anywhere, he tells the judge, "I had thought ... that I might pass for white." Because Judge Straight sees "his old friend" in John, he makes the choice to aid him (*Cedars*, 380). The judge informs him, "You need not be black, away from Patesville. You have the somewhat unusual privilege, it seems of choosing between two races, and if you are a lad of spirit, as I think you are, it will not take you long to make your choice. As you have all the features of a white man, you would, at least in South Carolina, have simply to assume the place and exercise the privileges of a white man" (*Cedars*, 381). Before leaving the matter alone, Judge

Straight offered John a job as his servant and allowed him the opportunity to read his law books. After two years of working for the judge, John left Patesville, North Carolina, for South Carolina, leaving, as his mother said, for "the other side" (*Cedars*, 382).

By moving down the river to South Carolina, John continues his dramatic rebirth and transformation from John Walden, illegitimate son of Molly Walden and the never-named white man, to John Warrick, successful white Southern lawyer. By passing as a white man and escaping the paralyzing shackles placed on him as an African American in Patesville, John changes his fortune and climbs the hill of success. The ascent begins with John serving as manager of a large estate. Success in this position during the Civil War and after the war led to marriage with "the orphan daughter of the gentleman who had lost his life upon the battlefield" (*Cedars*, 282). Within two years of the Civil War, John was "admitted to the South Carolina bar" and promptly saw the elevation of his economic and social status. In addition to this elevation in social status, his marriage produces a young son, Albert, who further legitimized his place as a white person in society.

After the death of his beautiful young wife, John found himself cherishing "a tender feeling for his mother" and despite having "shaken the dust of the town from his feet," he returns home again to Patesville (*Cedars*, 286). When present again in his home, John desires to secure the services of his sister Rena for his son, Albert. In the text that follows this request by John, Chesnutt paints the picture of a slave mother, dropping to her knees, hugging her master's legs, and begging him not to sell her child down the river: "'Oh, John,' she cried despairingly, 'don't take her away from me! Don't take her, John, darlin,' for it'd break my heart to lose her!'" (*Cedars*, 283). Despite the pleas from his mother, John is able to procure Rena from her on the grounds that Rena has "no chance here [in Patesville], where our story is known" (*Cedars*, 284). John tells his mother that Rena, who possesses "beauty and brains," has a greater chance with him as he has a place "already made" and that she with "perhaps a little preparation — and ride up the hill which I have had to climb so painfully" will "see her at the top" (*Cedars*, 285). The knowledge that her daughter would only have a "sordid existence" in Patesville removes the last obstacle standing in the way for Molly Walden to consent to her son's wishes for his sister. For Rena, life will never be the same after John (Walden) Warrick enters her life.

In moving down the river to South Carolina and to the world of white society and privilege, Rena is apprised by her brother of all that she must concede to him in exchange for the privilege of stepping into his world and becoming a self-made woman. For starters, she must drop her old surname and identity and "be known as Miss Warwick" (*Cedars*, 296). Then she must attend boarding school. After attending boarding school, Miss "Rowena" Warwick catches the attentions of George Tryon at the annual tournament of the Clarence Social Club. Not only does George become her beloved knight but she is crowned as the "Queen of Love and Beauty." Soon after, the couple is engaged to be married. As marriage preparations develop, Rena, having dreams that her mother is ill, returns to Patesville to check on her mother, thus beginning a series of unfortunate events that clearly show the makeup of each character.

When Tryon discovers Rena inside and then outside the drugstore in Patesville, and, hence, her true background, the intensity of his love quickly fades and, in that moment when the fallen damsel needs her knight so desperately, Tryon fails to give Rena a reassuring "sign of love or sorrow or regret" in exchange for her "appealing glance" (*Cedars*, 360). At this point, all is lost. Tryon sits stunned in the carriage, leaving Rena alone and neglected, and returns home resigned to the fact that he cannot marry a woman with any trace of black blood in her. Tryon dreams of Rena as a "fair young beauty ... by some hellish magic ... slowly transformed into a hideous black hag. With agonized eyes he watched her beautiful tresses become mere wisps of coarse wool, wrapped round with dingy cotton strings; he saw her clear eyes grow bloodshot, her ivory teeth turn to unwholesome fangs. With a shudder he awoke, to find the cold gray dawn of a rainy day stealing through the window" (*Cedars*, 364). Tryon questions how he almost allowed himself to marry outside his race and taint his blood.

Although his mind, clouded by the standards of society, commanded him to dismiss Rena from his thoughts, his heart could not forget her, and when Judge Straight contacts him about business in Patesville, Tryon seizes the opportunity (*Cedars*, 395). In journeying to Patesville, Tryon believes he will find Rena still aching in her heart over him. Thus, when he arrives to the house behind the cedars and sees Rena dancing with a "grinning mulatto, whose face was offensively familiar to Tryon," he immediately questions the decision he made to come (*Cedars*, 414–415). Once more Tryon reveals himself when he sees Rena as nothing more than "the base-born child of the plaything of a gentleman's idle hour, who to this ignoble origin added the blood of a servile race" (*Cedars*, 416). Ironically, Tryon thanks God for opening his eyes once again.

After the demise of her engagement to Tryon and the arrival of Jeff Wain, who is Mary B. Petticoat's second cousin (see Chapter 21) and the man who pitches the idea to Molly Walden of having her daughter come to teach at a black school in his hometown away from Patesville, Rena decides against any return to life as a privileged white person. Instead she will renew her desire to "git a school to teach" (*Cedars*, 285). In taking this step, Rena not only follows in the footsteps of her mother, who sacrificed her life for her family, but also banishes Tryon "from her waking thoughts" (*Cedars*, 430). More importantly, Rena comes to know "the darker people with whose fate her own was bound up so closely" and her new knowledge of them allows her

> to view them at once with the mental eye of an outsider and the sympathy of a sister.... With her quickened intelligence she could perceive how great was their need and how small their opportunity; and with this illumination came the desire to contribute to their help. She had not the breadth or culture to see in all its ramifications the great problem which puzzles statesmen and philosophers; but she was conscious of the wish, and of the power, in a small way, to do something for the advancement of those who had just set their feet upon the ladder of progress" [*Cedars*, 396].

In moving forward with her life, Rena chooses to move upstream from South Carolina, to go against the current of her world, and in so doing, she refuses to be dragooned into going down the same path that her brother forged for himself (Clack). In her own subtle way — learning as she makes her way through life — she chooses to return to her roots and forces people to accept her on her terms, not on theirs.

That Rena did not follow in the same footsteps as her brother is understandable, since, as Chesnutt states, "It had not been difficult for Rena to conform her speech, her manners, and in a measure her modes of thought, to those of the people around her; but when this readjustment went beyond mere externals and concerned the vital issues of life, the secret that oppressed her took on a more serious aspect, with tragic possibilities" (*Cedars*, 317). Rena did not feel right in concealing her identity, and to be damned by Tryon and society for who she was, was a price that she was willing to pay. However, as a woman, Rena faces long odds in escaping the prevailing forces of society or the men who pursue her in order to make her "owned property." When she does flee from both Tryon and Wain and finds "herself penetrating deeper and deeper into the forest" as "the rain fell in torrents," Rena finds relief from her situation in insanity, which delivers her from a world of misunderstanding (*Cedars*, 448).

Although Chesnutt attempts to make John Walden's transformation to John Warrick a noble journey in that his passing cons white society, this passing cannot be seen for anything other than a denial of his blackness and support for all that white society represents. When Rena follows her brother downstream to South Carolina, the sense is that she too has decided to ignore her past in order to become a success in society. But when ties to her mother burn strong, she returns home and begins a series of steps that awaken her from her sleep and push her to understand who she was (imprisoned in the chains of society as a woman and as an African American) and who she is currently. Her awakening, jarred by "a tired body, in sympathy with an over-wrought brain ... brought on an attack of brain fever" that provided her the means to escape the absurdity of the world (*Cedars*, 449).

In crafting the character of Rena, Chesnutt joins other authors who create a truly American figure — one who does not find it in his or her best interests to live by the same rules as the rest of the population. Such characters exist in our history — outlaws or counter-cultural heroes who attempt to be free from the shackles of society and molds made by others, emerging in the long run happier over the decision to escape. Whereas African Americans after the war and during Reconstruction faced the same outlaw conditions that Rena did, her character stands apart from the other characters in the text, most notably her brother John. Through her, Chesnutt demonstrates that white society is not yet ready to accept African Americans on the terms of the Almighty. "If God had meant to rear any impossible barrier between people of contrasting complexions, why did He not express the prohibitions as he had done between other orders of creation?" (*Cedars*, 454–455).

WORKS CITED

Andrews, William. "Charles Chesnutt's 'Magical Realism." In *Fiction, Social Change, and Charles W. Chesnutt's Fayetteville: A Series of Public Lectures Presented at Fayetteville State University*. Fayetteville, N.C.: Fayetteville State University, 1988.

Chesnutt, Charles W. *The House Behind the Cedars*. In *Charles W. Chesnutt: Stories, Novels, and Essays*. New York: Literary Classics of the United States, 2002.

Clack, Randall. Personal Interview. November 14, 2002.

Thoreau, Henry David. *Walden and Civil Disobedience*. Edited by Owen Thomas. New York: W.W. Norton., 1966.

CHAPTER 7

Reading the Transgressive Body: Phenomenology in the Stories of Charles W. Chesnutt

Kim Kirkpatrick

Charles Waddell Chesnutt's short stories, with their double narrative structure, offer texts within texts. Chesnutt provides layers of readings and readers addressing those texts — well beyond his primary reader who holds in hand the pages of the short story. His stories, then, become an analysis of how readers read and lend themselves to a phenomenological, theoretical approach. The Uncle Julius stories of *The Conjure Woman* offer traditional frame stories surrounding the tale told by Julius, as in "The Goophered Grapevine." Chesnutt makes clear from his vocabulary that reading and creating texts to be read are dominant themes in this story. The first-person narrator, John, and his wife, who are contemplating buying a vineyard, listen to the story of the vineyard as told by Julius, who understands that he is creating a misleading story to drive away the prospective vineyard buyers and that he himself is being read as a text by the couple. Julius is centered, both physically and aurally, within John's frame story written by Chesnutt, all three aware of an audience. Before John and Annie hear Julius' story, however, they must read the text of Julius' body: "There was a shrewdness in his eyes ... which, as we afterward learned from experience, was indicative of a corresponding shrewdness in his character" (120). The body represents a character with a story, and that body can tell a story, manipulate a story, or withhold a story, so that the body is a text itself which must be read. Eventually, "from experience," Annie and John will become fluent, repetitive readers of Julius, but for them, this encounter in "The Goophered Grapevine" is a first reading.

Chesnutt cues his own reader to the fact that Julius' story should not be taken as naïve folklore — the storyteller is just too shrewd, a word Chesnutt uses twice in one sentence so that his reader cannot miss it — and there is a purpose in telling this story to the couple. Even as first readers, John and Annie are aware of the depth of motivation propelling the telling of this story to this particular audience so they are aware of their own positioning as audience and the story as an artistic creation. Chesnutt, through the narrator John, emphasizes Julius' storytelling techniques:

> At first the current of his memory — or imagination — seemed somewhat sluggish; but as his embarrassment wore off, his *language flowed more freely*, and the *story acquired perspective and coherence*. As he became more and more absorbed in the *narrative*, his eyes assumed a dreamy expression, and he seemed to lose sight of his auditors, and to be living over again in monologue his life on the old plantation [121; emphasis mine].

Although Julius presents his story as fact, his readers, positioned by Chesnutt as "auditors," question its truthfulness before the first word — is it "his memory — or imagination"? John comments on how Julius starts "somewhat sluggish[ly]," suggesting that he believes Julius, as an artist, is fumbling in creating his story, perhaps because he is uncomfortable telling the story to this audience or perhaps because he is an inexperienced storyteller. The husband and wife think of it as a "story" that is made of "language" which "flows"; the plot needs "perspective and coherence." It is, after all, a "narrative," and they are aware of their role as audience/readers and of Julius as storyteller/artist. But Chesnutt has already identified this storyteller as shrewd — both the "auditors" and Chesnutt's reader know that Julius wants something in telling this story. "The Goophered Grapevine" concludes in analyzing Julius' artistic motivation: "I found, when I bought the vineyard, that Uncle Julius had occupied a cabin on the place for many years, and derived a respectable revenue from the neglected grapevines. This, doubtless, accounted for his advice to me not to buy the vineyard, though whether it inspired the goopher story I am unable to state" (128). John believes Julius has told this story in order to preserve his own material resources. Much has already been written on Julius' artistic motivations in telling his stories (see Andrews, 376–7; Baldwin, 387; Britt, 362); the goal here lies not in the overt telling of the stories but in the multiplicity of readings and readers within Chesnutt's texts. The readings are provided not only by hearing an oral story like Julius' or seeing a written story like John's, but also through reading the bodies of the characters as they perform their stories or participate in their stories, necessarily making their bodies into texts.

Certainly "The Passing of Grandison" is a story about reading bodies as texts. The whole story hinges upon characters reading and misreading other characters, and Chesnutt expects his readers to participate in those multiple readings and misreadings, because the surprise ending is effective only when

Chesnutt's readers have misread Grandison's character. The text of "The Passing of Grandison" opens with an ambiguous sentence: "When it is said that it was done to please a woman, there ought perhaps to be enough said to explain anything; for what a man will not do to please a woman is yet to be discovered" (268). But how is this to be read? What is "it" that was done? What woman is being pleased? Who is the man doing "it"? Chesnutt concludes the paragraph with the focus on Dick Owens, the son and heir to Kentucky plantation owner Colonel Owens, thereby supplying answers as to who the man and woman may be — Dick himself and the woman he is courting, Charity Lomax — and defining the "it" as Dick's endeavor to free a slave. Or is Chesnutt merely providing the first misreading of the text?

Dick and his father, the colonel, pride themselves on reading others, and Chesnutt's audience is provided early in the text with examples of how good these readers are supposed to be. Dick reads his love interest Charity as though she were a text; whereas, Colonel Owens reads his slave Tom. Dick reads Charity in order to ascertain his next step in their courtship. She admires the example of another young man who has done something which she defines as heroic: he freed a slave, but was caught doing so, was tried, and then imprisoned. When Charity calls that man a hero, she says, "I could love a man who would take such chances for the sake of others" (269), which Dick reads to mean that he ought to do something as equally heroic and adventurous, something that would put him in danger while he helped others. Dick has read Charity correctly because when he returns from his trip to Canada and tells Charity how he has provided the opportunity for his slave Grandison to run off, she marries him just three weeks later. The text of Charity was easily read, primarily because Dick was so eager to read this text and felt he had a personal stake in reading it correctly. Wolfgang Iser, in writing about how readers read, points out: "A literary text must therefore be conceived in such a way that it will engage the reader's imagination in the task of working things out for himself, for reading is only a pleasure when it is active and creative" (280). The text presents itself as a type of problem for which the reader cares enough that she must work out the problem for herself. Positing Charity as the literary text, Dick is "active and creative" in his reading; he interprets Charity's admiration of the young man freeing the slave as a quest laid before him — he must become that young man in order to meet Charity's expectations. He reads her text in order to determine what Charity wants from him. The text has led the reader to a response and specific reading, allowing the reader to continue composing his reading along the path suggested by the text, thus fulfilling the expectations of the text.

Chesnutt presents another reader reading when Dick's father, Colonel Owens, reads his slave Tom. Prior to the colonel reading Tom, Chesnutt's third-person narrator provides his audience with an understanding of Tom's text, showing Chesnutt's reader what Tom's state of mind is: "Now, if there was anything that Tom would have liked to make, it was a trip North. It was something he had long contemplated in the abstract, but had never been able to muster up sufficient courage to attempt in the concrete. He was prudent enough, however, to dissemble his feelings" (270). He does not dissemble enough, however, as the colonel is able to read Tom's true feelings after the briefest of interrogations, primarily because the colonel, as described by Chesnutt's narrator, is such an accurate and experienced reader, "having studied [his slaves], as he often said, for a great many years, and, as he asserted oftener still, understanding them perfectly" (271). Although Chesnutt's overemphasis upon the colonel's assessment of his own reading skills — the colonel has "often said" and has "asserted oftener still" — suggests rather that the colonel is not as accurate a reader as he thinks he is, the narrator's previous emphasis upon Tom's desire to go North and Tom's own attempt to "dissemble his feelings" do tell Chesnutt's audience that, in this case, the colonel's reading is accurate. Tom's dissembling shows, however, that Tom is trying to produce a transgressive body, a subversive text with a dissembled meaning so that he can fool the colonel into sending him north. The colonel's public reading of Tom is supposed to expose Tom's transgressive text to the on-looking Dick, just as the narrator has already exposed Tom's transgressive body to Chesnutt's reader. But Dick, too, is an astute reader, and he has read Tom's transgressive text even before his father does, focusing not on what Tom says — "I would n't min' it, Mars Dick, ez long ez you'd take keer er me an' fetch me home all right" — but reading Tom's body. Dick sees that "Tom's eyes belied his words"; Tom's body has told the truth that he will find a way to run away if Dick takes him north (271). This suits Dick's purposes perfectly: he will not have to drive Tom away or actively conspire with Tom; all Dick will need to do is avert his own eyes while Tom leaves and, suddenly, Dick will be Charity's hero.

Dick's ability to read through Tom's text just reinforces his own reading of Charity's text. He believes that his plan of allowing Tom to run away mirrors the previous text of the young man freeing the slave in which the young man is the active hero. Dick is faced with Iser's "virtual dimension of the text":

> The fact that completely different readers can be differently affected by the "reality" of a particular text is ample evidence of the degree to which literary texts transform reading into a creative process that is far above mere perception of what is written. The literary text activates our own faculties, enabling us to recreate the world it presents. The product of this creative activity is what we might call the virtual dimension of the text, which endows it with its reality. This virtual dimension is not the text itself, nor is it the imagination of the reader: it is the coming together of text and imagination [283–4].

But in Dick's case, he brings his imagination to more than just one text: Dick's imagination is confronted with the texts of the transgressive young man, who was tried for freeing a slave; of Charity, who admires the young man and is waiting for a hero; and of Tom, who will run away if only given the chance. His imagination takes these texts and wraps them together, creating a virtual dimension in which he is the action hero winning the damsel. In Dick's virtual dimension, Tom is merely an object acted upon by being freed. In doing this, Dick is following the procedure Georges Poulet has explained as the reading process: "Whatever those ideas may be, however strong the tie which binds them to their source, however transitory may be their sojourn in my own mind, so long as I entertain them I assert myself as subject of these ideas; I am the subjective principle for whom the ideas serve for the time being as the predications.... It is I who think, it is never a *HE* but an *I*" (56). As a reader of the young man's trial, Dick ceases to differentiate between the *HE* of the young man and the *I* of himself. He casts himself in the role of the young man, acting out the virtual dimension he has created for himself. When his father, the colonel, rejects Tom as his traveling companion, Dick never stumbles in his virtual dimension but seeks to find another stand-in for the slave whom the young man freed. In doing so, Dick "assert[s him]self as subject," relegating first Tom and then Grandison as the object which will be freed once the hero Dick acts upon him.

After reading through Tom and rejecting him as a traveling companion for Dick, the colonel reads Grandison's demeanor and pronounces him "abolitionist-proof" (274). At first, Dick is not sure of his father's reading and pronouncement: "[Dick] had no doubt he would eventually lose [Grandison]. For while not exactly skeptical about Grandison's perfervid loyalty, Dick had been a somewhat keen observer of human nature, in his own indolent way, and based his expectations upon the force of the example and argument that his servant could scarcely fail to encounter" (274). In other words, Dick believes Grandison could be persuaded to run away if he were given every opportunity, so during the trip Dick points out the abolitionists who would help the slave, leaves money lying around, and finally takes him to Canada where Grandison was, in fact, legally free already. But Grandison seemingly offers a bland and unimaginative text. He will not run away, even when left alone in Boston with a large amount of money. He apparently lives up to the colonel's reading as "abolitionist-proof." But this is just a performance on the part of Grandison, who endeavors to control his own text and refuses to be acted upon and made into something he is not by his reader, Dick.

Dick has been described as "lazy as the Devil" (268), who likes to make the "least necessary expenditure of effort" (271). He is used to having everything he needs, or even wants, without working to get it. So it is not surprising that he does not work to read the text of Grandison's transgressive body. As Wolfgang Iser states, "If the reader were given the whole story, and there were nothing left for him to do, his imagination would never enter the field, the result would be the boredom which inevitably arises when everything is laid out cut and dried before us. A literary text must therefore be conceived in such a way that it will engage the reader's imagination in the task of working things out for himself" (280). Dick is lazy enough to believe that he has been "given the whole story." Like his father, he believes in his ability to read thoroughly his slaves — so Grandison could not be hiding anything from him. Dick is so bored with his reading of Grandison that he finds it necessary to impose himself upon the text and hires some Canadians to kidnap Grandison. Although Dick is too lazy to put forth any effort or imagination into reading Grandison's text, he is willing to act if in so doing he remains the hero in the story Charity has suggested to him, thereby reinforcing his own identity and his power over his own reading. This corresponds to Norman Holland's thoughts on how readers will create meaning for a text: "All of us, as we read, use the literary work to symbolize and finally to replicate ourselves. We work through the text our own characteristic patterns of desire and adaptation. We interact with the work, making it part of our own psychic economy and making ourselves part of the literary work — as we interpret it" (816). Throughout Chesnutt's story, Dick has fixated on the young man whose trial he attended, the man who won Charity's admiration when he risked his own freedom for a cause. The way Charity reads this young man's text, the man becomes transgressive and therefore heroic when he endeavors to free the slave, an illegal act. Although Dick's motivation in trying to free Grandison is not because of his firm belief in the autonomy of each individual — to the contrary: Dick is willing to free Grandison because his father has so many slaves; one missing will not affect plantation life, he reasons — he does see that he can replicate the young man's transgressive text by driving Grandison to freedom, thereby imitating the illegal action and casting himself in the role of hero which Charity has written for him. In this sense, Charity has suggested a "characteristic [pattern] of desire and adaptation" for a transgressive hero which Dick has embraced. He knowingly has made himself a "part of the literary work" of the hero leading the reluctant slave to freedom. Although Grandison has played a role in this text, it has been minor and Dick's text defines Grandison's role as object acted upon by the hero.

Dick performs a role to win Charity's love and another in order to vacation in the North accompanied by one of his father's slaves; Tom dissembles and performs a role in trying to become that slave; and Grandison performs the role of loyal slave, fooling Dick, Colonel Owens, and Chesnutt's reader. Joel Taxel, in his article "Charles Waddell Chesnutt's Sambo: Myth and Reality," describes how Chesnutt's black characters use a "Sambo mask" or a "Sambo stereotype" (106, 107) to get what they want. "Chesnutt fully explores the notion of Sambo utilized as a deception — a device or 'accommodation' seized upon ... [to] achieve a specific goal" (105). In "The Goophered Grapevine," Julius performs Sambo and "Grandison plays Sambo" (108), but the major difference is that Julius' readers, both Chesnutt's reader and John and Annie, the potential vineyard buyers, know that Julius is performing, whereas Grandison's readers, Dick and the colonel, do not recognize that they witness a performance. The reader of "The Passing of Grandison," too, may be unaware that Grandison is playing the Sambo role and is merely "passing for Black" (Delmar, 374), which is a major point from P. Jay Delmar's Chesnutt study. He suggests that not only are characters like Julius and Grandison wearing masks, but also that Chesnutt's stories are masked and that Chesnutt masks his reader. "The stories themselves tend to be masked. Their ultimate meanings and denouements are often hidden from the reader" (365) and "as soon as Chesnutt has 'masked' the reader into asking these questions, he pulls off the mask with a vengeance" (374), thereby making Chesnutt and his stories transgressive as well. But if the reader is masked, and then unmasked, then Chesnutt is asking her to perform as well, to participate in being duped so as to be delighted and surprised by the conclusion. For Chesnutt's reader, Delmar's "vengeance" is pleasurable surprise, indeed, thankfulness, that Grandison was scheming for freedom all along, although for Grandison's reader, the colonel, a more traditional vengeance is due.

Whereas Delmar credits Chesnutt with this unmasking trick played upon the reader, Wolfgang Iser's definition of text suggests that the text should be credited. Grandison's text retains the power to force an eventual thesis upon Dick and the colonel. Although Dick and the colonel have been following a submissive slave reading of Grandison, all along Grandison has been creating a different text. Iser's use of verbs is indicative of the power exerted by the text: "For the more a text individualizes or confirms an expectation it has initially aroused, the more aware we become of its didactic purpose, so that at best we can only accept or reject the thesis forced upon us" (283). It is the text which has the power to individualize, to confirm, and to force, and Grandison does this when he rejects his object status and voluntarily returns to the Kentucky plantation in a ruse which allows him to emancipate six others of his family. Grandison's two readers, Dick and the colonel, have the colonel's initial "abolitionist-proof" reading at first confirmed upon Grandison's return to Kentucky and then their reader expectations are thwarted when Grandison leaves.

Chesnutt's principal goal in the tales of *The Conjure Woman* is to offer the reader multiple readings. According to David Britt, "The artistry of the tales suggests a studied control of the material that elicits multiple levels of interpretation. One begins with the literal surface meaning suggested by the outside narratives" (369) and "the stories are deliberately structured to allow the reader to be deceived about the more significant levels of meaning if he chooses, or needs, to be deceived. The device that initially permits misunderstanding comes through the double narrative structure: both a black and a white man participate in relating each story" (359). This structure is clearly seen in "The Goophered Grapevine" when the vineyard buyer-narrator controls the frame story and provides a platform for Julius, finally inviting Julius to tell the title story, suggesting that although Julius has the centered story, that story is always controlled by the white, listening narrator, who retells the story or allows it to be told to Chesnutt's audience. This same double narrative structure occurs in "The Passing of Grandison," however. Whereas Julius has been prompted to tell his story, and the narrator and his wife, Annie, are active listeners and comment upon Julius' tale, thereby having the last word, "The Passing of Grandison" allows both Chesnutt's reader and the white characters, Dick and the colonel, to be trumped by Grandison's story of leading his entire family north, a story which Grandison does not verbally relate, as Julius did, but which he sets in motion via his transgressive body. Dick and his father are silenced in reaction to Grandison's powerful story. The colonel now *reacts* to his former slave rather than *leading* him, as he is used to. Neither Dick nor his father is allowed any further speech in the story. Indeed, Chesnutt makes the colonel not only silent but also impotent, as "the latter shook his fist impotently — and the incident was closed" (282). Nevertheless, Grandison's silent story of freedom has been embedded in the frame story of the narrator about how young Dick is able to court and win Charity. In this case both Grandison and Dick achieve their goals — as Dick marries Charity and Grandison marries Betty and achieves freedom.

This double narrative structure allows us to analyze the introduction of "The Passing of Grandison" from the perspective of both narratives, looking for those "multiple levels of interpretation" of which Britt wrote (369). With an eye to "the outside narrative" and "the literal surface meaning" of "The Passing of Grandison," let us return to the opening line of the story: "When it is said that it was done to please a woman, there ought perhaps to be enough said to explain anything; for what a man will not do to please a woman is yet to be discovered" (268). Here, the literal meaning suggests that Dick went to great lengths to free Grandison in order to impress Charity. Certainly this fits the outside narrative with the focus on Dick achieving his goal of marriage. But Grandison, too, has been interested in a woman, Betty. The colonel has used Betty as a means to induce Grandison to stay with Dick on his travels, invoking her name and a potential marriage in his interrogation of Grandison before Dick travels north. "If you please your master Dick, he'll buy you a present, and a string of beads for Betty to wear when you and she get married in the fall" (273). A threat is implied, and Betty is held hostage, so Grandison must perform the submissive slave role and return. From the perspective of this inside narrative of Grandison seeking a wife and freedom for himself and his whole family, that first line can be read with reference to Grandison and Betty, that what Grandison did in returning to the plantation when he had already been freed in Canada was all done for a woman, Betty. Grandison's actions on behalf of Betty are grander and more self-sacrificing than those of Dick for Charity. Especially as Dick is described over and over as lazy and he tries to lead Grandison to freedom primarily by leaving Grandison alone, this first line does not suggest that much was "done" or accomplished by Dick for Charity, thereby indicating a lazy love. Dick loved Charity enough to go on vacation and leave Grandison alone. Grandison, on the other hand, endured much on behalf of Betty: successfully dissembling his true feelings, fooling the colonel and Dick into believing his performance as a grateful slave afraid of the abolitionists, making the journey from Canada to Kentucky, and laying plans with the Underground Railroad to transport his family back to Canada.

Like Julius in the *Conjure* stories, Grandison is the focus and central character of "The Passing of Grandison," despite Dick's role as hero. Julius gets star treatment, with a frame story which highlights him, a narrator who introduces him and a clearly defined audience. His voice is distinctive and heard by the auditors, John and Annie, and by Chesnutt's reader. Grandison's story is silent. Although he has plenty of readers, they have all misread him, and in that way, his text is the most transgressive, because it produces transgressive readings.

WORKS CITED

Andrews, William L. "The Significance of Charles W. Chesnutt's 'Conjure Stories.'" In *Charles W. Chesnutt: Selected Writings*. Edited by SallyAnn H. Ferguson. Boston: Houghton Mifflin, 2001. 370–387.

Baldwin, Richard E. "The Art of *The Conjure Woman*." *American Literature* 43.3 (November 1971): 385–398.

Britt, David D. "Chesnutt's Conjure Tales: What You See Is What You Get." In *Charles W. Chesnutt: Selected Writings*. Edited by SallyAnn H. Ferguson. Boston: Houghton Mifflin, 2001. 358–369.

Chesnutt, Charles W. "The Goophered Grapevine." In *Charles W. Chesnutt: Selected Writings*. Edited by SallyAnn H. Ferguson. Boston: Houghton Mifflin, 2001. 118–128.

_____. "The Passing of Grandison." In *Charles W. Chesnutt: Selected Writings*. Edited by SallyAnn H. Ferguson. Boston: Houghton Mifflin, 2001. 268–282.

Delmar, P. Jay. "The Mask as Theme and Structure: Charles W. Chesnutt's 'The Sheriff's Children' and 'The Passing of Grandison.'" *American Literature* 51.3 (November 1979): 364–375.

Holland, Norman N. "Unity Identity Text Self." *PLMA* 90.5 (October 1975): 813–822.
Iser, Wolfgang. "The Reading Process: A Phenomenological Approach." *New Literary History* 3.2 (Winter 1972): 279–299.
Poulet, Georges. "Phenomenology of Reading." *New Literary History* 1.1 (October 1969): 53–68.
Taxel, Joel. "Charles Waddell Chesnutt's Sambo: Myth and Reality." *Negro American Literature Forum* 9.4 (Winter 1975): 105–108.

CHAPTER 8

"Your people will never rise in the world": Chesnutt's Message to a Black Readership

Tyrie J. Smith

Criticism concerning Charles W. Chesnutt's 1899 framed collection of short stories *The Conjure Woman* has largely centered on Chesnutt's use of folklore to subvert romanticized perceptions of the antebellum South. Many view Chesnutt's character Uncle Julius to be the model for those generations of freed blacks still performing as slaves, using the oral tradition in various forms to subtly undermine the power of their oppressors. For Julius, the tales he tells are devices used to influence and manipulate those in *control*—his new Northern *masters*. Jeannette White notes: "Possessed of great insight gained through years of subservience, the old servant who haunts the tale clearly has come to some understanding of the workings of the minds of his oppressors.... Wearing the veil of ignorance, Uncle Julius weaves a convincing web through which he ensnares his employers" (89). Ultimately, Julius plays the role of the "ole slave," masquerading as the ignorant and simple "darkie," all the while, behind the mask, possessing a folk intellect that he employs to improve his position on the old plantation. This kind of performance is not uncommon in the canon of African American literature. More importantly, it is a common motif in the oral traditions of the African American community, including "master and john tales" (also known as "High John" or "John the Conquerer") and the well-known trickster tales of Brer Rabbit and, earlier, Ananse. The context of the old plantation as the setting for such performance is, again, not uncommon. Considering such contexts as imagined by black and white writers alike, including Mark Twain, Joel Chandler Harris, and, later, Jean Toomer, Zora Neale Hurston, Eudora Welty, and Ralph Ellison, Chesnutt's imagined reconstruction-era plantation is well within the tradition of literary treatment in regard to the pre-civil rights black community of the South. What is distinct, however, is that Chesnutt's plantation in *The Conjure Woman* is in control of a Northern, liberal opportunist as opposed to an antebellum landed master or even a postbellum farm manager, neither of whom would share a Northern perspective on emancipation. John is, in effect, an ambassador of the Northern abolitionist movement, which makes Julius' behavior towards his new *master* all the more interesting.

Julius' ingenuity is viewed by many critics as Chesnutt's appreciation of the "old forms" of African artistic genres including the performance of oral narratives (Redding, 37). Robert Hemenway observes that "Chesnutt's admission to the retelling of folktale in 'The Goophered Grapevine' ... would seem to indicate that he serves primarily as a literary redactor for the tale"(288). Chesnutt himself notes that, "'conjuration' and 'goopher,' [were lifted from] my childish recollections of which I have elsewhere embodied into a number of stories" (quoted in Ferguson, 58). From what we know of Chesnutt's upbringing in North Carolina, it is a fair assumption that the author encountered a variety of African American folkways. Born to free blacks at the beginning of the Civil War, Chesnutt was certainly aware of tales like those he would later use in *The Conjure Woman* and understood how such tales function to reinforce and strengthen a community. No doubt he also observed the ways in which members of the black community applied these oral traditions to their basic survival in a hostile environment. In addition to the oral traditions, Chesnutt would have also observed how these oral forms worked in the context of performance. Like the people of Eatonville, Fla., observed by Hurston a generation later, the people of Fayetteville, N.C., were part of a living, vibrant folk community. And while Chesnutt found inspiration in his experiences in Fayetteville and African American communities in the South for his other works such *as The House Behind the Cedars* or *The Marrow of Tradition*, his use of these experiences in *The Conjure Woman* is unique in that the novel is the only work built almost entirely on African American folkways.

Several critics view Chesnutt's use of folkloric elements as a means to reach a specific white audience. Richard Yarbrough argues that Chesnutt, like many African Americans writing before World War I, "displays not a desire to render black life as accurately and honestly as possible, but a willingness to dissemble, to overemphasize, even to misrepresent — that is, to write with the aim of eliciting sympathy from the white reader" (quoted in Selinger, 666). Chesnutt says as much in his article "An Inside View of the Negro Question," in which he states, "In the united and aggressive public opinion of the North the Negro sees his chief hope for the speedy and peaceful recog-

nition of his public rights in the South" (quoted in McElrath, 64). Further-
ing this argument, Melvin Dixon notes that Chesnutt "is aware that he is writing for a predominately white audience who have a strong nostalgia for the
antebellum Southern tradition.... Just as trickster Julius masked his moral lesson in the fictive world of his folklore to serve his own gains, so too did Chesnutt use the fictive medium of the novel to accomplish his professional goals"
(187–196). It is true that Chesnutt is constructing his work in the tradition
of plantation fiction as seen in the novels of John Pendleton Kennedy, William
Gilmore Simms, Caroline Lee Hentz and others. In regard to a white audience, Chesnutt makes use of a genre in such a way as to gain access to a less-
than-sympathetic readership, subverting anti–Negro sentiment still prevalent
among whites in the South as well as the North. The question that is never
asked is what did Chesnutt hope to accomplish with a black readership
through his use of folklore? What, if anything, did Chesnutt hope to convey
to his own culture, to his own people?

As an educated black man of mixed background in the Reconstruction
South, Chesnutt saw his community through a new set of eyes. His perspective evolved from one of appreciation for the traditions of his community to
frustration, dissatisfied with the seemingly simple, childlike behavior of those
around him. As a light-skinned African American, Chesnutt was granted
access, though limited, to the white perception of blacks in a post-slavery
South. This insight into a point of view outside of his own experience opened
his eyes to how others outside of the black community conceived the Negro's
role in an ever-modernizing United States. From this worldview, Chesnutt
believed that those of his community in Fayetteville and similar African American communities who continued to rely on Old World traditions would be
left behind in the nation's movement towards modernity. In her biography
of her father, Helen M. Chesnutt describes the author's adolescence as one
full of encounters with the "old ways" of his community. She writes of Chesnutt's experiences working in his father's store: "The store was the natural
meeting place for all the people of the neighborhood. Here the more intelligent met and discussed freely the latest political developments. Here the more
ignorant told each other stories of superstition and conjuration, and the boy
Charles took in everything with wide-open ears" (5). As noted by Wiley Cash,
Helen Chesnutt's labeling the storytellers as "ignorant" directly relates to her
father's belief that Southern blacks were "commonplace and vulgar" (Lecture). Like many light-skinned, educated African Americans, Chesnutt had
come to view himself as being superior to his darker-skinned, illiterate counterparts. While Helen Chesnutt's comments may contain the subtle suggestion that her father had been fascinated by, and perhaps even admired, these
folk performances, Chesnutt shows no such appreciation for his community's

folkways later in his life. Early in his adolescence, at age 14, Chesnutt moved to Spartanburg, S.C., to teach at the Peabody School. It is during his time there — boarding with a black family and living amongst a largely rural, illiterate population of blacks — that readers see Chesnutt's disdain for folkways and the apparent lack of education and intelligence such traditions represent:

> Well! Uneducated people, are the most bigoted, superstitious, hardest headed people in the world! Those folk downstairs believe in ghosts, luck, horse shoes, cloud signs and all other kinds of nonsense ... all the eloquence of Demosthenes, the logic of Plato, the demonstrations of the most learned men in this world, couldn't convince them of the falsity, the absurdity, the utter impossibility and unreasonableness of such things [ed. Brodhead, 81].

If we can, from Chesnutt's own words, deduce that the author viewed the African American community's embracing of folkways as problematic for that community's ability to rise up in the post–Civil War south — the new industrialized America — then the majority of criticism on Chesnutt's use of folklore loses some steam. How could someone with so much disdain for his culture's "ignorant" folkways use those same folkways to elicit some kind of positive gain for that community? The answer lies in audience.

As noted earlier, much of the scholarship surrounding Chesnutt's *Conjure Woman* deals with the novel's effectiveness to raise awareness and sympathy for the plight of African Americans within the hearts and minds of a white readership. However, perhaps Chesnutt's masked intention was to reveal to his black readership the need to abandon their old folkways and, instead, work towards joining the ranks of the educated class. The seven tales that make up *The Conjure Woman* do not cast the black community's reliance on superstition, folk belief, and other forms of folklore in a positive light. Instead, Chesnutt shows time and time again how dependence on such things only results in the demise of the African American community. Ultimately, Chesnutt masks his intentions to a white audience and succeeds in gaining the sympathy of that demographic and subverting the power of those wanting to oppress African Americans; however, there is also a deeper, embedded subversion that calls on the black community to abandon the role of the submissive, ignorant slave and gain power in the oppressive South through the opportunities made available through its new-found freedom. While at first glance it appears that Julius gains advantage over his Yankee employer, John, the former slave, a metaphor for the older, largely ignorant population of former slaves, is ultimately forgotten and disappears from the story.

In the opening tale, "The Goophered Grapevine," the reader is introduced to the narrator John, a "carpetbagger" from Ohio, his wife Annie, a caricature of the sickly, delicate woman of the southern romance, and Uncle Julius, the former slave and relic from the antebellum South. John has relocated to the South for his wife's health, which is complicated by the "raw winds, the chill rains, and the violent changes in temperature" of his native Ohio (31). John, as narrator, notes that he hopes to continue his work in "grape-culture" and, after considering the sunny climes of France, Spain, and California, comes to the South believing that "it was a sufficient time after the war for conditions in the South to have become somewhat settled" (31). Moving through a romanticized Southern landscape, John and his wife arrive at the plantation that the Yankee entrepreneur hopes to purchase. Here, he and Annie first encounter Uncle Julius, sitting on a log with a hat full of scuppernongs. Following an awkward introduction in which the two white Northerners take a seat as equals next to Julius, establishing a familiar context for folk performance, John expresses his wish to restore the grape crop on the plantation and Julius meets his interest with a legend about the hexed vineyard.

Julius' intentions are clear long before the narrator's explanation that Julius had set up his own business from the neglected grapevine and had hoped, through his story, to deter John's purchase of the plantation. John, a character manifestation of the growing modern, educated population, is quick to deduce the former slave's intentions. Julius's failure to frighten off the newly-arrived Northerner with his tale of a hoodoo witch and the effects of her charms is the first in a long line of clues to Chesnutt's motivations. John, though a white man, could be read as Chesnutt's recreation of himself in the text. Educated and a man taken with reading philosophy, John is representative of South's future—a South that must catch up with the more industrialized, more educated North. Unlike the antebellum Southern "marster," who, in the oral tradition is just as superstitious as his black counterpart, John's no-nonsense worldview is very much based in logic and reason and not susceptible to the influence of Julius's "tall tales." Through this re-imagining of the trickster character, Chesnutt announces the coming of a new era for blacks in the United States. In his assessment of the black condition, Chesnutt sees the African American community's reliance on deception and subtle subversion to be an outdated and largely inept approach for improving the African American experience in a nation recently released from the disease of slavery. Chesnutt may appreciate the need for such tactics within the context of an oppressive slave system, but views its presence in the emancipated New South as a hindrance to African American progress. To this end, Chesnutt goes so far as to feminize the black folkways, as seen in the relationship between Julius and Annie.

While John sees beyond Julius's subversive tactics, the educated man from the North *is* susceptible to the influence of his wife and Julius is able to manipulate her (and through her subvert John) via his storytelling performances. Readers first encounter Annie's susceptibility to Julius's performances in the second tale, "Po' Sandy." Annie, representative of the largely-feminine abolitionist movement, is sympathetic to the breakup of a pair of lovers, Tenie and Sandy, narrated in the tale, exclaiming "Poor Tenie" at the end of Julius' performance (53). After hearing the story of the unfortunate couple, Annie decides against having her new kitchen built with the lumber from the old schoolhouse — the lumber supposedly cut from Sandy, who was conjured into a tree. The schoolhouse ultimately becomes the new meeting place for a faction of Julius's church that has broken off from the main congregation.

Following the Civil War, the nation as a whole was faced with the challenge of rediscovering the masculine identity of the pre–Civil War, frontier era. The war had cost the country well over 600,000 men, over a quarter of a million on both sides of the conflict. The impact of such losses on communities in the North and South was immense. The majority of those killed were between the ages of 18 and 35. There were entire communities deprived of whole generations. Following the war, these losses were felt in many ways, but one of the more subtle manifestations of this phenomenon, and perhaps one of the most interesting, was a perceived feminization of American society — a trend that began with the largely female-driven abolitionist movement. The country had been de-masculinized and many viewed the situation as dangerous. As a reaction, the U.S. government actively encouraged *masculine* endeavors such as westward migration, construction of a national rail system, the decimation of the western Native American tribes, and the promotion of romantically masculine institutions like the Pony Express. In the context of Chesnutt's time, those institutions viewed as being feminine were characterized as weak, overly-sensitive, and emotional as opposed to reasonable and negative overall. The sensibility of the feminine disposition was counterintuitive to the more masculine ideologies of Manifest Destiny, industrialization, and modernity. By casting Annie as the sympathetic ear to Julius's tales, Chesnutt feminizes and, thus, devalues the pre-emancipation tactics, namely the folkways, employed by slaves to subvert the authority of their white masters. As the reader moves through the narrative, Annie's influence over her husband slowly dissipates until even she cannot dissuade her husband's intentions.

Furthermore, though Julius's telling of "Po' Sandy" works to his advantage in regard to Annie, the tale serves as a treatise on the consequences to those who place too much stock in superstitions. In the tale, Tenie uses her witchcraft to keep Sandy safe after he expresses his weariness with being moved between the plantations of Mars' Maraboo's relatives. Tenie plans to transform Sandy into a pine tree until she can work a stronger charm that will transform them both into foxes so that they "could run away en go some'rs whar dey could be free en lib lak w'ite folks" (49). The plan goes terribly awry and Sandy is cut down and sent to the sawmill. Tenie lives out her remaining days in heartbroken agony. Here, Chesnutt suggests that blacks will never live "lak w'ite folks"—a life of un-oppressed freedom and opportunity—as long as they continue to live lives based in superstition and *hocus pocus*. For Chesnutt, such practices equate to the ignorance that he, in his own words, finds a deplorable characteristic of the uneducated blacks he encountered in African American communities throughout the South.

In the third tale of the collection, "Mars Jeems's Nightmare," Julius once again manages to manipulate John through the sympathies of Annie. Yet what does he gain from preserving his grandson Tom's position on John's plantation? There is no upward movement for Tom in Julius's victory, only the perpetuation of servitude for a young, Southern black male. While this tale ends on a happily-ever-after note, the reality of the situation is grim for the forward-thinking Chesnutt, who wants more for his community. For Chesnutt, Tom is a symbol of potential. He could be a student of one of the newly-created black colleges throughout the South. Instead, young Tom remains a part of an oppressive institution. Later, Julius scores another perceived victory through his telling of "The Conjurer's Revenge," but Julius's ploy only raises John's suspicions of the former slave's intentions. The narrator notes, "For a long time afterwards I took his advice only in small doses and with great discrimination" (81). The breakdown of Julius's tactics speak to Chesnutt's own opinion that such means of subversion, because they are not grounded in reason, lead to troubles for those who rely on them.

In the fourth tale in the series, "Sis' Becky's Pickaninny," the narration appears, more than anywhere else in the novel, to come straight from Chesnutt's own words. Following Julius's description of the rabbit's foot, John makes a statement almost identical in content to Chesnutt's journal entry cited earlier. John says, "Your people will never rise in the world until they throw off these childish superstitions and learn to live by the light of reason and common sense" (83). This quote serves as Chesnutt's thesis and signals the beginning of Julius's eventual disappearance from the novel. Previous to "Sis' Becky's Pickaninny," in "The Conjurer's Revenge," Julius's tale displeases both John and Annie. By losing Annie's enthusiasm and support, Julius's usefulness on the plantation is waning. Finally, in the very next tale, Chesnutt takes an opportunity to explicitly articulate his belief that the African American community's faith in superstitions and other forms of the "fantastic" will only keep the African American community in chains (interestingly, this tale is also the only instance in the collection in which both Julius and the protagonist in his story succeed in their goals). Sis Becky is reunited with her son, Mose, and they all live (seemingly) happily ever after (as happily ever after as one can in slavery), and Julius succeeds in once again winning over the mistress of the house by playing to her feminine sensibility. However, John's insistence in naming Julius's story a "fairy tale" and Annie's observation that the supernatural elements of Julius's tale are "mere ornamental details and not at all essential," take power from the stories and reinforce Chesnutt's thesis (92). Julius's tales are reduced to mere fancies, fairytales, or children's stories. Their function has been devalued to simple entertainments, removing from them the more important elements of folklore, as labeled by William Bascom, to educate, validate, and control.

In the final two tales of the novel, Julius is slowly removed from the narrative — dominated by the more logical, reasoning John. Julius's telling of the "The Grey Wolf's Ha'nt" fails to deter John's desire to clear away an area of land that also happens to be home to a producing beehive. Following the tale of "Hot-Foot Hannibal," Julius is offered a position with John's sister-in-law and her husband, but chooses to remain with John and Annie — though the details of this engagement are glossed over and Julius is little more than an afterthought. In the tale of "The Grey Wolf's Ha'nt," John glosses Julius's tale-telling ability and, by solving the mystery of their telling, takes the narrative power from Julius:

> It was not difficult to induce the old man to tell a story, if he were in a reminiscent mood. Of tales of the old slavery days he seemed indeed to possess an exhaustless store, — some weirdly grotesque, some broadly humorous; some bearing the stamp of truth, faint, perhaps, but still discernible; others palpable inventions, whether his own or not we never knew, though his fancy doubtless embellished them. But even the wildest was not without an element of pathos, — the tragedy, it might be, of the story itself; the shadow, never absent, of slavery and of ignorance; the sadness, always, of life as seen by the fading light of an old man's memory [96].

Here, John shows that the old man's intentions are not unknown to him — that the white readership (in the character of John) sees the masked messages in Julius's tales. However, these tales do nothing to improve Julius's position. He remains, for all intents and purposes, an indentured servant to a white "master." Julius may win some minor battles, but he remains as he was — ignorant, uneducated and a relic in a world moving ever-forward towards modernity.

Critics place a good deal of importance on Chesnutt's use of folklore as a means of eliciting the sympathies of a white audience. White notes that Chesnutt's "strategy was to call attention to the problems [of slavery and race] through the use of folklore, rather than to ignore their existence" (87). However, if Chesnutt's only aim is to educate a white readership about the horrors of slavery, it would appear that he's a bit late. *The Conjure Woman* is not published as a novel until 1899 — 35 years after the Emancipation Proclamation. The more pressing contemporary issues facing the black community included the instituting of Jim Crow, the realignment of labor available to Southern blacks from the peculiar institution of slavery to the equally-oppressive practice of sharecropping, the Klu Klux Klan, lynch mobs, and the other countless atrocities against African Americans carried out in the South and beyond at the turn of the century. In his other novels, Chesnutt addresses these contemporary issues and others, including lynching, race riots, and miscegenation. If his concern was the inaccurate depictions of the slave experience by Southern and Northern whites (as noted by a number of critics), why set *The Conjure Woman* in the postbellum South and why portray Julius in such a poor light? Furthermore, why place Julius in a context far removed from the horrific experience of the majority of slaves working under unsympathetic, Southern plantation owners? The argument put forth by many critics in regard to Chesnutt's writing for a white audience does not hold up to such questions. *The Conjure Woman* does not follow the tradition of the sympathetic appeal as seen in abolitionist literature such as Harriett Beecher Stowe's *Uncle Tom's Cabin*, William Wells Brown's *Clotelle*, or Herman Melville's *Benito Cereno*. Even in regard to the feminine sensibilities of Annie, Julius is unable to maintain relevance. He becomes a nuisance on the periphery of John and Annie's world.

It is not Chesnutt's aim to educate a white readership on the horrors of an outlawed practice. He does not intend to focus on the past when the present is as, if not more, horrific. If one reconsiders audience, his work takes on new meaning. Perhaps Chesnutt was masking, but doing so with a black audience in mind. A white readership would have read Chesnutt's work as sentimental, somewhat romantic "fairytales" of a long-gone era — read in much the same manner as those tales collected and re-told by Joel Chandler Harris. However, a black audience would have seen something different, especially a black audience that had the means and education in 1899 to purchase a work of literature. What this audience would have realized, through the eyes of a white, liberal-minded, educated narrator, is that the success of their people depended on bringing the poorer, underserved members of the black community out of ignorance (an important issue to an African American educator such as Chesnutt) into the light of education as promoted by other educated blacks such as W.E.B. Du Bois and Booker T. Washington. With the increasing number of black colleges and schools such as those at Tuskegee, Howard, Morehouse, and Clark, Chesnutt hopes to encourage his black audience to contribute to the goal of shaking the Old World traditions and taking advantage of the new opportunities available to the black community. Uncle Julius is a relic from the past and he carries the past with him through his stories;

however, he can only maintain the status quo through his limited intellect and knowledge. He can only maintain those most basic of survival needs with his wit and trickster ways. For the next generation, Chesnutt and his soon-to-be contemporaries — Ellison, Hughes, Hurston, Wright, etc.— want something more. In Chesnutt's mind, one of the largest obstacles on the road to black empowerment, second only to racial discrimination in a white-ruled system, is the ignorance that pervades the black community. Yes, there was a place for men like Uncle Julius; however, the success of African Americans in the twentieth century lies in their ability to meet the demands of the times. They must move beyond the silly superstitions and fantastic customs of the past and adapt to the modern world growing up around them.

WORKS CITED

Bascom, William. "Folklore, Verbal Art, and Culture." *The Journal of American Folklore* 86.342 (1973), 374–381.

Cash, Wiley. Lecture on Charles Chesnutt. Given at the University of Louisiana, Lafayette. 17 October 2005.

Chesnutt, Charles W. "An Inside View of the Negro Question." In *Charles W. Chesnutt: Essays and Speeches.* Edited by Joseph R. McElrath, Jr., Robert C Leitz, III, and Jesse S. Crisler. Stanford: Stanford University Press, 2000.

_____. *The Journals of Charles W. Chesnutt.* Edited by Richard M. Brodhead. Durham, N.C.: Duke University Press, 1993.

_____. "Superstitions and Folklore of the South." In *Charles W. Chesnutt: Selected Writings.* Edited by SallyAnn H. Ferguson. Boston: Houghton Mifflin, 2001.

Chesnutt, Helen M. *Charles Waddell Chesnutt: Pioneer of the Color Line.* Chapel Hill: University of North Carolina Press, 1952.

Delmar, Jay P. "The Mask as Theme and Structure: Charles W. Chesnutt's 'The Sheriff's Children' and 'The Passing of Grandison.'" *American Literature* 51.3 (1979): 364–375.

Dixon, Melvin. "The Teller as Folk Trickster in Chesnutt's *The Conjure Woman.*" *CLA Journal* 18.2 (1974): 186–197.

Gordon, Dexter B. "Humor in African American Discourse: Speaking of Oppression." *Journal of Black Studies* 29.2 (1998): 254–76.

Hemenway, Robert. "The Functions of Folklore in Charles Chesnutt's *The Conjure Woman.*" *Journal of the Folklore Institute* 13.3 (1976): 283–305.

Krasner, David. "Parody and Double Consciousness in the Language of Early Black Musical Theatre." *African American Review* 29.2 (1995): 317–323.

Lindroth, James. "Images of Subversion: Ishmael Reed and the Hoodoo Trickster." *African American Review* 30.2 (1996): 185–96.

Redding, Saunders. "Anger and Beyond." *The Negro Writer and American Literature.* Edited by Herbert Hill. New York: Harper and Row, 1965.

Selinger, Eric. "Aunts, Uncles, Audience: Gender and Genre in Charles Chesnutt's *The Conjure Woman.*" *Black American Literature Forum* 25.4 (1991): 665–88.

Sigelman, Lee and Steven A. Tuch. "Metastereotypes: Blacks' Perceptions of Whites' Stereotypes of Blacks." *The Public Opinion Quarterly* 61.1 (1997): 87–101.

White, Jeannette. "Baring Slavery's Darkest Secrets: Charles Chesnutt's *Conjure Tales* as Masks of Truth." *Southern Literary Journal* 27.1 (1994): 85–103.

CHAPTER 9

Vanished Past and Vanishing Point: Charles W. Chesnutt's Short Stories and the Problem of American Historical Memory

Zoe Trodd

"This wayward spirit ... back from the vanished past to haunt him."
— Chesnutt, "The Sheriff's Children" 1899

"The Procrustes, being all margin, merely touches the vanishing point of the perspective."
— Chesnutt, "Baxter's Procrustes" 1899

"'I can't see why you should tell it,'" complains Annie; "'it seems to me like nonsense.'" Baffled, she dismisses Uncle Julius' story of a man turned into a mule. "'I'm tellin' nuffin but de truf,'" responds the pained storyteller, an employee of Annie's husband John. There are so many lies in the world, he figures, that there's no point finding fault with "'tales dat mought des ez well be so ez not.'" He cites the "lie" of the earth going round the sun, and adds: "'dis a quare worl', anyway yer kin fix it'" (*Conjure Tales*, 49). Listening to this exchange and others, John eventually sighs: "'Julius ... your people will never rise in the world until they throw off these childish superstitions and learn to live by the light of reason and common sense'" (52). But, proceeding by this "light of reason," John is immediately made to sigh "for the deceitfulness of appearances" (50); he buys what turns out to be a bad horse — the animal is as blind as John and Annie in dismissing Julius' story. Julius had made a claim for the value of appearances (the sun seeming to go round the earth, the appearance of a man's foot confirming that he was once a mule) and then used "appearances" to his own advantage; pocketing the profit from his secret role in the horse transaction, his own appearance is much improved a few days after the sale.

John, the Northern narrator of Charles W. Chesnutt's *Conjure Tales* (1899), is trying to build a Southern estate after the Civil War. He tries hard to rationalize production, make the plantation more efficient, and impose clock-time on a town with a strange four-faced clock. Yet, while fearing a "conflict of authority in the household" with his wife (39), the real conflict comes with Julius, an ex-slave and now his hired man. Pitting nature and magic against reason and common sense, Chesnutt staged a series of related struggles over time, story and space. Julius wins the time-wars: John and Annie depend on his stories to fill their dull leisure *time*, and so the *timely* stories of a *time* when men and women had no *time* of their own, by one of these previously *time*-starved individuals, dominate the free *time* of two people who have never been dominated by others' *time* sensibilities!

Julius wins the story-wars too: though John is the first-person narrator, Julius is story-teller and plot-maker in the book's embedded conjure tales *and* the ongoing frame story. Far from revolving around John as narrator, John revolves around him, sun around earth, in a backwards solar system. Nature itself is Julius' accompaniment: when he speaks of a man "howlin' en howlin,'" the air around his listeners darkens, and a "rising wind whistled around the eaves ... a long, wailing note, an epitome, as it were, of remorse and hopelessness" (74). If not true to John's "light of reason" and "common sense," Julius' stories are true to nature, at least.

And Julius wins the war for space. Chesnutt's stories of metamorphoses overthrow the mapped space where man controlled nature and occupied a different point in space to other beings. The nature that Western man had seemed to tame wins back some control over him, demonstrating that "'dis a quare worl', anyway yer kin fix it.'" The metamorphoses, that leave animal features on human bodies and human emotions in trees, anticipated the postmodern aesthetic of cross-fertilized worlds, and Chesnutt's narrative structure anticipated postmodern character migrations from embedded stories to framing narratives. The messy metamorphoses and the bleeding of themes across narrative and tales insist upon a shift in understanding from either/or to both, as Michel Foucault might put it. Chesnutt crafted what Foucault would term a *heterotopia*; a space where possible worlds, incommensurable spaces, and multiple voices co-exist.

Chesnutt also used the theme of metamorphosis in his Gothic stories to challenge the argument that slavery had been a civilizing force for African Americans, and highlight the anachronistic irrationalities of the slave system — 70 years before Ishmael Reed asked in *Flight to Canada* (1974): "Why does the perfectly rational, in its own time, often sound like mumbo-jumbo? Where did it leave off for Poe, prophet of a civilization buried alive, where, according to witnesses, people were often whipped for no reason. No reason?" (10). Chesnutt's hauntings evoke this "civilization buried alive," and his conjure tales are a similar challenge to "the perfectly rational" — or John's "reason and common sense." If slavery was "an anachronism" (49), as Reed adds, then Chesnutt's tales of metamorphoses, the sudden clash of one state of being with another (man and tree, man and mule, boy and bird, man and wolf) literalized the anachronism of slavery through cross-fertilized evolutionary moments. So when the Procrustes in Chesnutt's story "Baxter's Procrustes" catches man "to fit him to some preconceived standard, generally to the one for which he was least adapted" (270), we understand the "preconceived standard" of slavery to be as ill a fit for human beings as the standard of wolf, tree or hummingbird.

For Chesnutt was staging yet another war — one that combined the struggles over time, story and space. His characters fight for authority over American historical memory. Prefiguring Reed's historiographic, meta-fictional approach to Western time and history, Chesnutt complicated the national narrative of Reconstruction. The anti-linear framed narratives, along with Julius' stories of sudden metamorphoses and reversals, also prefigured Ralph Ellison's 1964 vision of "American history" as a spiral, "returning at a later point in time to an earlier point in historical space" (567), or Reed's looping chain-letters and alternative to Western history in *Mumbo Jumbo* (1972). Chesnutt's stories move from present to past and back, the frame narrative begins where it ends, and Julius the coach-man takes us on a looping journey.

The layered conjure tales are a veiled exposé of the uncomfortable parallels between the antebellum and postbellum Souths. "Where does fact begin and fiction leave off?" asked Reed in *Flight to Canada*, before questioning the "perfectly rational" (10). At one point Annie and John debate the balance of fiction and fact in Julius' stories. Annie believes a particular story bears "'the stamp of truth, if ever a story did'" (61), and John concedes it might have "'the stamp of truth, faint, perhaps, but still discernible'" (65). The magic and myth are "'mere ornamental details and not at all essential,'" insists Annie, adding: "'the story is true to nature, and might have happened half a hundred times, and no doubt did happen, in those horrid days before the war'" (61). Julius' "true to nature" stories, that "might have happened," were Chesnutt's heavily-sugared pills for his Northern audience. Analogies between the frame-narrative and Julius' stories confirm that the "horrid days before the war" are far from over.

In Chesnutt's post-war America, the past walks hand in hand with the present, the dead with the living. For example, when John attempts to knock down an outhouse and build a new kitchen, Julius explains that the site is haunted and the outhouse timber unusable — it's made from a tree that was once a slave. John foregoes the timber, and it's triumphantly claimed by Julius, who announces that the outhouse is only haunted at certain times of the day. Between these vaguely defined intervals, it can function as a schoolhouse for Julius and the rest of the ex-slave community. Still trying to use symbolically ground-up black humanity as raw material, John embodies a country bound by old power dynamics during its *own* reconstruction. Thaddeus Stevens might have told the House of Representatives in 1866 that "in rebuilding, it is necessary to clear away the rotten and defective portions of the old foundations, and to sink deep and found the repaired edifice upon the firm foundation of eternal justice," and James Garfield might have added in 1867 that America must "remove the rubbish and rebuild from the bottom," but Chesnutt recognized the failure to clear away "rotten and defective portions," and saw the shallow foundations under this "repaired edifice." A clean reconstruction was impossible, Chesnutt knew, because America's national house was haunted by the memory of slavery.

Chesnutt's metamorphoses rendered absurd the idea that Emancipation brought a sudden transformation in the lives of African Americans, and challenged America's relentlessly progressive historical memory. A tree weeps, a man walks on his hoof-foot, and a boy sings like the bird he once was; the transition from slavery to freedom was far from immediate, clean or final, suggests Chesnutt. "You have seen how a man was made a slave; you shall see how a slave was made a man," wrote Frederick Douglass in his famous chiasmus of 1845 (60), but post-reconstruction Chesnutt saw that it was not so easy. The nominal metamorphosis of Emancipation marked no absolute distinction between slavery and freedom. The ghosts of one era haunt the outhouses of the next and, like emancipated slaves, the men morphed in Julius' stories have merely an altered relationship to the same inhospitable world. Sandy remains Sandy though he looks like a tree, and an African American, implies Chesnutt, remained enslaved though he was now called free. Real progress was like Wellington's "day-dreams of an ideal state of social equality," in a story from *The Wife of His Youth and Other Stories of the Color Line* (1899), Chesnutt's second volume of short stories, where the North is a "land flowing with milk and honey ... peopled by noble men and beautiful women, among whom colored men and women moved with the ease and grace of acknowledged right" (208). This "ideal state of social equality" is as unreal as Julius' mythic Southern forest full of human-trees. Wellington "'wuz alluz wishin' fer change, er studyin' 'bout somethin' new'" (236), and the conjure tales are Chesnutt's extended analogy to this fantasy of change. Listening to one of Julius' stories, the endlessly hapless John parses America's false ending to the story of slavery: "'And they all lived happily ever after'" (34).

Chesnutt left two clues that he was challenging this false happy ending, and offering an analogy to the fantasy of social metamorphosis. One is the volume of philosophy that John reads to Annie in "The Gray Wolf's Ha'nt." Though she quickly tires of it, and calls it "'nonsense,'" like Julius' mule-story, in fact the excerpt communicates the broad philosophy of history behind Chesnutt's collection of short stories. John reads:

> "The difficulty of dealing with transformations so many-sided as those which all existences have undergone, or are undergoing, is such as to make a complete and deductive interpretation almost hopeless. So to grasp the total process of redistribution of matter and motion as to see simultaneously its several necessary results in their actual interdependence is scarcely possible. There is, however, a mode of rendering the process as a whole tolerably comprehensible. Though the genesis of the rearrangement of every evolving aggregate is in itself one, it presents to our intelligence —" [63].

He stops reading because Julius appears before them, and so the interrupted last sentence really concludes: "it presents to our intelligence — Julius." Arriving to tell another story, Julius picks up where John's book left off, and grapples with the same process of "transformations." Neither Chesnutt nor Julius renders the process through the "hopeless" mode discussed in John's passage: "a complete and deductive interpretation." Chesnutt offers the process not "as a whole" but as a series of interdependent short stories. The "mode" is an "evolving aggregate" that acknowledges the fragmented, reconstituted but untransformed state of postbellum America. And Julius' messily-conjured men prove America's "transformations" to be "many-sided" and still in process —"undergone ... undergoing," as John's philosophy book puts it.

A second clue came via Chesnutt's journal. In 1879 he copied out a paragraph from Goethe's *Dichtung und Wahrheit*:

> Our desires are the presentiments of the faculties which lie within us — the precursors of those things which we are capable of performing. That which we would be and that which we desire, present themselves to our imagination, about us, and in the future: we prove our aspiration after an object which we secretly already possess. It is thus that an intense anticipation transforms a real possibility into an imaginary reality. When such a tendency is decided in us, at each stage of our development a portion of our primitive desire accomplishes itself, under favorable circumstances by direct means: and in unfavorable circumstances by some more circuitous route, from which, however, we never fail to reach the straight road again [103–4].

Taking up Goethe's line, "we prove our aspiration after an object which we secretly already possess," Chesnutt used the messy metamorphoses of *The*

Conjure Tales to demonstrate that African Americans always possessed freedom; were free human creatures "in fact" if not "in form," as Douglass put it in his *Narrative* (65). Just as no conjure magic turns Dave into a ham, in "Dave's Neckliss," so does no bill of sale or emancipation proclamation add or detract from the real humanity of African Americans. And if African Americans "secretly already possess[ed]" an inherent humanity, then the required shift of perspective is that of Annie in "Hotfoot Hannibal." Echoing Chesnutt's diary excerpt about a "circuitous route," she announces: "'I've changed my mind. I prefer the other route'" (87). She had insisted on taking "'the short road'" (77) and after hearing Julius' story wants to "go by the long road" instead (87). This short road symbolizes the post-war war attempt to simply proclaim the past vanished and embrace what Goethe called an "imaginary reality." The long road is Chesnutt's suggested "other route" for America: a movement forward whilst looking backward — like Julius, sent "'back'" by Annie to look for something while Mabel responds to his story of the past and reaches a "reconciliation" with Malcolm (88, 89).

Chesnutt concluded his meditation on the unreal nature of America's Emancipation transformation in "Dave's Neckliss" and "Hotfoot Hannibal." All magic now vanishes from the stories. Hannibal is transformed from man to woman with merely "'a frock en a sunbonnet'" (86): there is, finally, no change of state, but merely a disguise. And Dave experiences no magical metamorphosis, and doesn't even adopt a disguise. He *literally* becomes a hunk of dead meat, hanging, needing no magic or costume to turn "'ter a ham'" (99). In one sense Dave had *always* been a ham, bearing the Biblical mark of Ham as an African American. Then, still feeling his necklace as a mark, he finds a new one in the rope — though the shackles of slavery were removed from African Americans, Chesnutt implies, slavery continued, via the racism and violence of post–Reconstruction America. If "centuries of repression had borne their legitimate fruit" (91–2), then the fruit was in the tree when Dave hung. Growing, it became the infamous strange fruit hanging from America's lynching trees; according to the Constitutional Rights Foundation, mobs lynched 4,743 people in the United States between 1882 and 1968, over 70 percent of them African American.

Destroyed by his memories, Dave hangs over a fire, but the story has a thread of counter-imagery. Contemplating Julius as the old man begins to tell Dave's story, John sees "a spark ... fed by the memories of the past" which "might become in his children's children a glowing flame of sensibility, alive to every thrill of human happiness or human woe." Memory fuels the cycle of life, the passage of generations, and real change. Beyond short-cuts and unreal transformations, progress might come through an Ellisonian looping cycle: "When the cycle of years has rolled around," writes Chesnutt in his story "The Web of Circumstance," "there is to be another golden age, when all men will dwell together in love and harmony, and when peace and right-eousness shall prevail for a thousand years" (265–6).

Protesting America's historical memory, that vanished the past amid a narrative of reconstruction, reconciliation and progress, Chesnutt positioned himself against poems like Emma Wheeler Wilcox's "Keep Out of the Past," published in *Tanner's* in 1887. "Keep out of the past! for its highways / Are damp with malarial gloom. / Its gardens are sere, and its forests are drear, / And everywhere moulders a tomb," wrote Wilcox. "Keep out of the past! It is haunted. / He who in its avenues gropes / Shall find there the ghost of a joy prized the most, / And a skeleton throng of dead hopes." As a kind of anti–Julius, she concludes: "Keep out of the past! It is lonely / And barren and bleak to the view, / Its fires have grown cold and its stories are old, / Turn, turn to the present, the new!" Initially Julius seems to live in such a past: the "quaint old town" has "a calm that seemed almost sabbatic in its restfulness," and the vineyard suffers from "utter neglect." It's "decayed and broken-down," with a "pair of decayed gateposts" and "rotting rail fence," full of "weeds and briers," "ruined chimneys," and a "shutter ... fallen from its hinges ... rotting in the rank grass" (1, 2, 3, 14). But the landscape of his memory emerges throughout the collection as fertile and cross-fertilized. Far from "drear," the forest rustles with human-trees, and the "dead hopes" of the conjure tale char-acters are actually the vital hopes of the living in the frame narrative. Though there's a "dark and solemn swamp," an "amber-colored stream flowing silently and sluggishly" (79), Chesnutt emphasizes throughout that "the deeper cur-rents of life ... flowed not less steadily than in livelier attitudes" (2). The past *is* "haunted," as Wilcox's poem puts it, but not barren or bleak. And its sto-ries are not stagnant, but rather shifting as required by the storyteller, Julius, who is himself as changeable as the weather. John and Annie moved South because of the "violent changes of temperature" in the Great Lakes region (1), and now confront a "nature ... subject to [variable] moods" (91), and "an authority" on the "subject" of the variable weather (102). So while "at first the current of his memory — or imagination — seemed somewhat sluggish," Julius' language soon flows "more freely" and his stories acquire "perspective" (5).

Chesnutt's past is not that described by Thomas Nelson Page in *The Negro: The Southerner's Problem* (1904) either, a place of happy and familiar plantation slaves. Instead Chesnutt argued for an honest and potentially heal-ing acknowledgment of the past's continual existence in the present. He offered a counter-vision and a usable past. Several characters in the *Conjure Tales* learn to forge vital connections between past and present: Annie sees herself in the character Becky, and so takes the rabbit foot and recovers her own health; Mabel hears that Chloe's Jeff "'ain' neber, neber come back ter her no mo'"" (88) and realizes that her own love might be "neber comin' back," and saves her marriage. A story "true to nature," that "might have happened half a hundred times ... before the war," happens again: from mythical past to recognizable present is less a sudden transformation or metamorphosis than an organic union. Chesnutt heals the breach between past and present, and opens up the future.

In his short stories, Chesnutt suggested that to simply "keep out of the past" would disrupt the natural processes of time as surely as the metamorphoses of the *Conjure Tales,* and ensure the past's return in an unnatural or undesirable state — as hoof-foot or haunted timber. The fantastical elements of the *Conjure Tales* gestured toward a cultural attempt to dismiss the country's slave past as pre-historic myth and/or "half-forgotten dream," as Douglass described his memories of slavery in numerous post-war speeches. In her story "Of One Blood" (1903), Pauline Hopkins observed: "The passing of slavery from the land marked a new era in the life of the nation. The war, too, had passed like a dream of horrors, and over the resumption of normal conditions in business and living, the whole country, as one man, rejoiced and heaved a deep sigh of absolute content" (449–50). But Chesnutt revisited the "dream of horrors," in his surreal world of men sliced up as trees and hung as hams — and the impact of these stories upon characters like John, Annie and Mabel, who are trying to begin what Hopkins called "a new era." He continued this theme in his second volume of stories. Here the vanished past returns as estranged wife, abandoned child or ghostly form, and the disconnect between past and present is the characters' undoing. Unaware of their bloodline and heritage, similarly trying to begin a new era, the characters in *this* collection of stories stumble into incest and tragedy. Without a past, Chesnutt told postbellum America in *The Wife of His Youth* as well as in *The Conjure Tales,* you can't have a future.

For example, the sheriff in "The Sheriff's Children," has "a future to make; the picture of a fair young bride had beckoned him on to happiness" (148). He sells his illegitimate son, disrupts the generational movement, and is eventually forced to ask: "'You would not murder your own father?'" (145). Or, in "The Wife of his Youth," Mr. Ryder's "memory of the past grew more and more indistinct, until at last it was rarely, except in his dreams, that any image of his bygone period rose before his mind" (113). For others in his club the past can be romanticized when not forgotten — "history presented enough romantic circumstances to rob their servile origin of its grosser aspects" (104). But history's shadowy presence remains, initially in the form of those "who had seen, and others who had heard their fathers and grandfathers tell, the wrongs and sufferings of this past generation, and all of them still felt, in their darker moments, the shadow hanging over them" (112). Then Mr. Ryder's wife (the wife of his *youth* rather than *his* wife) is conjured from the past with a verse ("She look'd so lovely"). Like Julius, she looks "like a bit of the old plantation life, summoned up from the past by the wave of a magician's wand, as the poet's fancy had called into being the gracious shapes of which Mr. Ryder had just been reading" (108). Wearing a "blue calico gown" (107), and bearing blue gums, her sudden presence parodies his "Blue Vein Society," and reminds him that his wife and the club, his past and his present, are as inseparable as blood from veins. Faced with this conjured woman, he chooses his past identity.

So, when Clara's search for ancestry, in "Her Virginia Mammy," wins out against her lover's assurances that this search is unnecessary, she is rewarded with a happy ending. Clara's past is "shrouded in mystery" (118), like the mythic past of Julius' conjure tales, and, like those tales, her past needs to be unearthed and relived. But Chesnutt inserts a dark cloud onto her horizon — the couple is perhaps too focused on its "'destiny [which] lies in the future'" (119), and Clara accepts a fictionalized version of the past in order to move forward into her marriage. Mrs. Harper is left with "the unsatisfied yearning of many years" (130) and even Clara wonders if she has "nothing left" (132). Her lover promises he will make the "'future so happy'" that she "'won't have time to think of the past,'" and that "'a lot of musty, mouldy old grandfathers'" are nothing "'compared with life and love and happiness'" (118), but Chesnutt's short stories assert the power of those "musty, mouldy old grandfathers," and the uncertainty of a future where the past is unresolved. "'Those who made [the past] died with it'" (119), insists Clara's lover, while Chesnutt's philosophy of history meant they also lived on as ghosts and disruptive memories.

Clara embodies the post-war cultural amnesia and parallel loss of black identity. She is "'A Miss Nobody, from Nowhere'" (118). As Mrs. Harper explains, "'The war had scattered the people so that I could find no one'" (130). Black communities had fragmented like the bodies of the *Conjure Tales* and the narrative arc of Chesnutt's two volumes, and then, as the narrator of "The Sheriff's Children" explains, the rupture of the war made it "the one historical event that overshadows all others ... the era from which all local chronicles are dated — births, deaths, marriages, storms, freshets" (133). The war began the world over, and Julius' conjure tales — like the haunting presence of past lives in *The Wife of His Youth* — bridge the chasm between now and then.

Chesnutt continued to explore this idea of a new world in "Cicely's Dream." The character John appears just before Sherman, and they call him John, after John the Baptist. He supposedly announces the arrival of this new world and the end of pre-history. Cicely "had not taught him to remember; she would not have wished him to; she would have been jealous of any past to which he might have proved bound by other ties" (178). Like Clara, John embodies the nation's loss of memory after the trauma of war, and also the expectation that a whole people would begin from scratch, in a B.C. / A.D. world. The past mirrors the present as perfectly as the names of Martha and Arthur: "Martha! Martha!" "Arthur! O Arthur!" cry the lovers (187). John's "memory of the past" is a "blank" only until he recognizes Martha and takes up "the thread of his former existence where it had been broken off" (187). Though tragic for Cicely, this, insists Chesnutt, is how the threads of past and present must be: connected, like the threads of the past drawn through the tapestry of the present in the *Conjure Tales*.

As with the *Conjure Tales*, Chesnutt's second series of stories offers a different kind of metamorphosis — the long road of "Hotfoot Hannibal," or Goethe's "circuitous route." The son in the "The Sheriff's Children" has had "until the past few years no possible future, and then one vague and shadowy in its outline, and dependent for form and substance upon the slow solution of a problem in which there were many unknown quantities" (149). Like Annie abandoning the "short road," the son recognizes a "slow solution," and like Julius telling mythic stories, he acknowledges "unknown quantities." Or, for the sheriff, there's the possibility of "clarifying ... the moral faculty" and seeing the "acts of one's life ... in their correct proportions and relations" (148) — abandoning that "preconceived standard" of "Baxter's Procrustes" (270).

Substantive change, rather than an unreal metamorphosis, might come through clarifying moral faculties, finding the "vanishing point of the perspective" (278), and changing minds — as with Annie, who has "*changed [her] mind*" (87) after Julius educates her about the past. The vital change is one of minds, not laws, insists Chesnutt, soon to end his novel *The Marrow of Tradition* (1901) with a similar call to the long road: "'There's time enough, but none to spare'" (329). Without traveling along that "circuitous route" of Goethe's passage, America would continue to encounter characters like Wellington, in Chesnutt's story "Uncle Wellington's Wives," who finds no "time to spare for the waste of adaptation" (230). Wellington takes a short-cut, escapes to the North, breaks with his past, and embraces a new era and white wife. But he's almost conjured back by his wife (so perfect is his timing upon returning home), and dumped right back on Goethe's "direct road" to limp in rags along it. His metamorphosis means that, returning from the North, he's so altered that "few would have recognized in the hungry-looking old brown tramp, clad in rags and limping along with bare feet, the trim-looking middle-aged mulatto who so few months before had taken the train from Patesville" (235). Wellington had "tried to force the current of a sluggish existence into a new and radically different channel" (230) but the "price" of the shortcut is "too great" (234).

Chesnutt's *Conjure Tales* insist that leaving the past *in* the past was impossible, and *The Wife of His Youth and Other Stories of the Color Line* suggest that moving memory-less into the future was undesirable. The collections are two parts of the same meditation upon the legacy of slavery and the long road forward. Chesnutt protested the understanding that emancipation meant a sudden metamorphosis into a brand new era, and the language of self-reliant uplift. His spirits from the "vanished past" arrive to "haunt" the present (148), for America has touched "the vanishing point of the perspective" (278) and found the unbearable blankness of a sheer white page. No longer "vanished," the past writes itself between the lines of the present. And those who would forget, remember.

Works Cited

Chesnutt, Charles W. *Conjure Tales and Stories of the Color Line.* New York: Penguin, 2000.

_____. *The Journals of Charles W. Chesnutt.* Edited by Richard H. Brodhead. Durham, N.C.: Duke University Press, 1993.

_____. *The Marrow of Tradition.* New York: Penguin, 1993.

Douglass, Frederick. *Douglass Autobiographies.* New York: Library of America, 1996.

Ellison, Ralph. *T he Collected Essays of Ralph Ellison.* Edited by John F. Callahan. New York: Modern Library, 2003.

Hopkins, Pauline. "Of One Blood" (1903). In *The Magazine Novels of Pauline Hopkins.* Edited by Hazel Carby. New York: Oxford University Press, 1988.

Reed, Ishmael. *Flight to Canada.* New York: Simon and Schuster, 1974.

CHAPTER 10

All Green with Epic Potential: Chesnutt Goes to the *Marrow of Tradition* to Re-Construct America's Epic Body

Gregory E. Rutledge

Joshua fit de battle of Jericho
Jericho,
Jericho
Joshua fit de battle of Jericho
and the walls come a-tumblin' down.
> —"Joshua Fit de Battle of Jericho,"
> African American Spiritual

So he spoke, and then put glorious Hektor to shameful treatment.
He cut through behind the tendons of both feet from heel to ankle,
and pulled straps of ox-hide through them which he tied fast to his
chariot, so the head would be left to drag. Then he mounted the
chariot and lifted the famous armour into it, and whipped the
horses on, and they flew eagerly on their way. As Hektor was dragged
behind, a cloud of dust arose from him, his dark hair streamed out
round him, and all that once handsome head was sunk in the dust:
but now Zeus had given him to his enemies to defile him in his
own native land.
  So Hektor's head was all sullied in the dust.
> —Homer, *The Iliad* (369)

Introduction: Re-Constructing the Problem

The Marrow of Tradition (1901), Charles W. Chesnutt's meticulous restaging of a horrific event, epitomizes the rise of *de facto* Southern slavery. While Chesnutt does not have to address the problem of slavery, *Marrow* does begin to engage the intersection of race and class in terms of the actual post–Civil War stratification among blacks and the evolution of racism. Even though he writes forty years after Emancipation, the dilemma he confronts may be just as horrific because of the numerous lynchings and pogroms (*mass* lynchings) characterizing the American body politic. Facing not only racism, but the full aesthetic, legal, and cultural rationale supporting it, which is both enlightened and logical even as it was illogical and savage, what strategy could "free" men and women deploy?

Chesnutt's aesthetic response to a problem that must have commanded near-epic dimensions at the period historians call the "nadir" in African American history has been found wanting. His stratagem of pitting an enlightened, cosmopolitan African American against an ethical absolutist whose insistence on racial justice was suicidal was considered by many literary critics to be both a logical and aesthetic failure. Pointing to Chesnutt's deployment of melodrama and sentimentality, his ambivalence toward the heroic "militant," or failings in plot and character development, many scholars ascribe to the opinion that Chesnutt, ultimately, had no solution for his "dilemma" or "moral dilemma." Consistent with this perspective, the consensus favors Dr. William Miller as the protagonists, either because they construe this to be Chesnutt's intention or, when such intentionality is unamenable to scholarly gaze because of Chesnutt's *failed* novel, the protagonist by default because of the parallels between Dr. Miller and Chesnutt.

Notwithstanding the consensus, and in light of more recent inquiry into Chesnutt's *Marrow*, the nature and scale of the "dilemma" he addresses gives cause to revisit this novel and the assessment of Dr. Miller and his foil, Josh Green. While *Marrow* does not grapple with slavery proper, it must be understood as a logical successor to what some abolitionists considered the epic of slavery. Thus, abolitionist and Unitarian minister Ephraim Peabody, in his review of Frederick Douglass's *Narrative* (1845), analogized slavery to "a whole Iliad of woes" and the fugitive slave's position to a "modern Odyssey" (62). Moreover, Chesnutt himself sought to write a novel on the scale of, and in response to, Harriet Beecher Stowe's epic novel, *Uncle Tom's Cabin* (1852) (Andrews, 175).

Not surprisingly, the epic, literary and socio-historical, is at the heart of Chesnutt's aesthetic intentions. What is surprising is Chesnutt's deployment of *classical* European and *traditional* African epics to achieve this aesthetic. Beyond conflating literary and social epics to elevate slavery to epic status, as Peabody does, Chesnutt fashions for himself, and for his largely white and Northern readers more importantly, an African American epic aesthetic. Rooted and routed in the sublimely ironic figure of the African "epic trickster," albeit its diasporic counterpart, Chesnutt has en-fleshed this aesthetic and imbued his protagonists with epic potential valorized by his readers and functioning as the marrow of tradition of the American republic.

Modern invocation of the "epic," either in classical or traditional contexts, is fraught with complications. Indeed, the Western archetypal epic, represented by Homer's *Iliad* and *Odyssey*, has its thematic origins in the objectification of Helen. Hers, as the face that launched a thousand ships, is the ultimate prize-acquisition, and the sacking of Troy a glorious, imperious, comeuppance. Helen symbolizes the commodification of the female body as the lynchpin for the designs of Agamemnon and Achilles at the expense — and the folly — of Hector and his Trojans. Though understandably hailed "as the cornerstone of Western civilisation" (Hammond, 7) since these epics do constitute a grand narrative par excellence, Homer's epics, particularly the *Iliad*, are often associated with modern, post–Enlightenment empire. This owes in large part to the denotation of the epic as grand and magnificent, and the association of classical Athens and Rome with it in the Western imaginary.

Consequently, the epic occupies liminal space in modern Western aesthetics. For example, G.W.F. Hegel and Georg Lukács, in *Aesthetics* (1835–38) and *The Theory of the Novel* (1920), respectively, pined for its return, though both believed it gone with the Heroic Age. Mikhail Bakhtin, in "Epic and Novel" (1941), preferred an "absolute distance" between reality and the epic, which he associated with totalitarianism. In *Anatomy of Criticism: Four Essays* (1957), Northrop Frye sidesteps the socio-political implications — he decries sociology or politics in literary criticism — but posits the encyclopedic (literary) mode as the trait common to classic and modern epics. Still, his recognition of the modern *vis-à-vis* classical epic suggests his agreement with his predecessors' assignment of the traditional epic to a remote socio-historical context. For Frye as for his predecessors, Homer is paradigmatic, and the Greek heroes, Dean A. Miller argues as he speaks of the history of the epic hero, "special and authentic" (xi). Their perspective on the epic is decidedly European.

Although they are diametrically opposed, Hegel's and Bakhtin's epic aesthetics contain an element that leads to a radically different possibility and cultural lens far removed from an Homeric provenance and toward an epic neither countenanced. Hegel's recognition of the epic bard's need to throw off the "yoke" of the dominant culture and write an epic history presenting a nation standing at the "bar of history" (1048, 1061) and Bakhtin's understanding that the role of "patriarchal" distance is creating a "world of the fathers" (13–18) both point to the socio-historical crisis upon which the epic narrative relies. The 1835–38 period in which Hegel made his remarks, and the inter-war interregnum framing Bakhtin's, highlight an epic problem centuries old: Slavery at its antebellum height and, in the 1940s, colonialism filling the gap where slavery previously existed. Clearly, this suggests the need for a paradigm shift, or at least a non–Eurocentric perspective.

In light of the enslavement and colonization of African peoples, the epic, in particular the traditional African epic, provides an important economy useful for understanding this social epic. Among other things, the traditional African epic is literary and performative, ancient and yet a present phenomenon that was still vibrant in the second half of the twentieth century. As such, it challenges the Western epic aesthetic because of what it reveals about the epic as art, politics, identity, and life. However, whatever lessons a study of the African epic may reveal have been ignored, overlooked, or suppressed because it has long faced challenges — slavery/colonialism and powerful contradictions at the core of Westernality — of the highest order. For example, Hegel identified antebellum America as the only European country with epic potential (1062), presumably because it still permitted slavery and, in the mid–1830s, was on the verge of expanding it into South America. Of course, Hegel was not identifying American epic potential with the plight of the slaves and the "other" people most in need of such. Just as disturbing as Hegel's myopia, if not more so, is the Rev. Peabody's invocation of Homer's *Iliad* and *Odyssey*. Although perfectly understandable, Peabody's gesture demonstrates the powerful contradictions confronting the slaves and the traditional African epic: "Democratic" Athens, as classics scholar Page Dubois argues, had many slaves, considered it part of the natural order, and could point to the sacking of Troy in the *Iliad* as an epic that valorized the acquisition of such "prizes" (2004).

The deep ironies of the intersection of the literary and social epics for the enslaved Africans and their descendants evidence the contradictions and the physical, epistemic, and cultural violence done against the traditional African epic. One of the defining premises underlying this study relates to the power of the traditional African epic to reinforce what Pierre Bourdieu calls, in *The Logic of Practice*, the "political mythology." The body is important in this dynamic, for out of it arises the total set of practices and conditions for a given culture, termed the *habitus* by Bourdieu. Thus, just as Bourdieu maintains that in "great ceremonies" the body re-performs the past history (59–76), the epic hero and story are made present and vital once again. They are, in a word, enfleshed through the participant-observers, who vicariously come to embody some of the epic characteristics. In effect, an *epic habitus* results for a given culture with bodies as carriers of the epic tradition. The embodiment of the epic and its actuating potential, which threatens the hegemonic authority, have led to the suppression of traditional epics (Seydou 313, 322).

The attempt to suppress the traditional African epic has not, of course, led to its total erasure, for the enslaved African bodies carried, retained, and passed along heroic traditions scholars have recognized at least as early as Melville J. Herskovitz' pioneering work in *The Myth of the Negro Past* (1941). The heroic Herskovitz excavated has been explored by Americanists such as Eric J. Sundquist in *To Wake the Nations: Race in the Making of American Literature* (1993), and by folklorists such as Roger L. Abrahams and Lawrence W. Levine. However, despite the decades of scholarship, only in the last fifteen years has the traditional African epic figured into the genealogies. None of this is surprising since, even as late as 1970, and years after the first pioneering studies in and translations of the traditional African epic, scholars had to defend its existence against the charge that "epic hardly seems to occur in sub–Saharan Africa" (Finnegan 108). Over the next two decades, scholarship flourished on the traditional African epic. Led by literary scholars such as Isidore K. Okpewho and Daniel Kunene and literary anthropologists like John William Johnson and Stephen Belcher, who demonstrated its wide geographical provenance and occurrence, no one attempted to trace it into the American Diaspora. This began to change in 1989 with the publication of *From Trickster to Badman: The Black Folk Hero in Slavery and Freedom*, John W. Roberts' genealogy of the heroic from the *African trickster proper* into an agonistic New World milieu. Although he was not prepared to fully interpolate the traditional African epic, he appreciated and excavated it enough to argue that it informed the slave spirituals (121–66). Ten years later in 2002, Keith Cartwright completed the first study, *Reading Africa into American Literature: Epics, Fables, and Gothic Tales*, which reads a traditional African epic (Mali's epic of Sunjata) and its *soul* force, *nyama*, into the black vernacular and all of American literature.

Armed with this scholarship, a reading of *Sundiata: An Epic of Old Mali*, the *Ozidi Saga* from Nigeria, and *The Mwindo Epic* of West and West Central Africa, reveals not a monolithic hero, or a closed, ready-made epic figure, but one who evolves and even, on occasion, becomes a transgressive figure opposed to the very people he helped. The early struggles of these figures, who face the overwhelming force of their own epic communities, parallel the trials of the African American trickster-hero studied by Abrahams and Roberts. In this regard, the physical, social, and spatial deformities that forced them to flee suggest similar strategies deployed by the trickster. Though flight for survival defines them, they are not tricksters proper, but "epic tricksters," whose return has its own inimitable style of action and signifying (trash talkin'). As Cartwright notes, the flight into exile entails a fracturing of the self and family, and ultimately a movement into the diaspora, which has to be reintegrated (32). This keen insight makes the allegory at the heart of the traditional African epic powerfully resonant with the experiences of African Americans.

These experiences are full of brutality and epic irony. While the odyssey of racism and slavery suppressed the traditional African epic, it nevertheless nurtured a distinct form of African American epic tradition that, ironically, arises from America's valorization of the epic. The African American story-telling tradition shows, I theorize, the slow return of epic potential to the descendants of the Africans, from the slave heroic to the cosmological poten-tials of black speculative fiction and fantasy protagonists. African American literature and history together constitute a long narrative of a figure to whom the trickster-hero may owe much and who struggles against the limitations of the trickster status. The epic trickster, I argue, struggles even more against the race and *res*— black and chattel — objectification that creates for the West-ern gaze a stereotypical and liminal figure, the *trickster-prop*(erty), easily quantified and controlled because of his or her limited subjectivity. One novel showing the dynamic of the epic trickster as it re-emerges from slavery and cultural suppression to directly confront a hostile, epic American habitus, and the trickster-prop, is Chesnutt's *Marrow*.

In light of the racial massacre of Wilmington, North Carolina, in 1898, and the unstinting and continuous violence around the country, the strategy Chesnutt adapts anticipates black intellectuals' disenchantment with the enlightenment philosophy of racial uplift, that is that racial justice would cease to exist once African Americans proved their intelligence and civility by European standards, thus enlightening white Americans. In light of racial lynchings and pogroms disproving this thesis, the Greco-Roman epic tradi-tion figures significantly. Homer's *Iliad* itself dramatizes a ritualized perform-ance in which the dark-haired, dusky hero, and his ethnic group by extension, become the sport of the victor. Indeed, Chesnutt's United States was a dem-ocratic, Constitution-based civilization that nevertheless engaged in the bru-tal performance of the lynching as continuous re-enactment of the American *Iliad*.

Hence, *Marrow* shows Chesnutt turning away from the "Talented Tenth" approach centered in European culture and deploying the vernacular. The ver-nacular here is not the trickster of indirection and escape, which has the abil-ity to frustrate an oppressive order, but little or no culture-building and transformative power. Rather, Chesnutt uses the African American version of the epic trickster from the traditional African epic to directly and effectively confront the problem of the color line. Hence, reading *Marrow* through the paradigm of the epic trickster reveals reality itself to be twisted into a racially coded mythological hierarchy featuring two epic embodiments, one an ide-alized "white" epic body, the other its "black" antagonist. According to this reading, Chesnutt believed these two figures, as allegorical emblems for two "races," are fated to meet at the racial color line *qua* battle line, with white supremacy the tragic outcome. To confront this, Chesnutt taps into the underclass, appropriates the "epic trickster," and interpolates this ironic figure into the narrative to re-create the African and European American body/politic and imagine two co-equals capable of merging into one. Since "Talented Tenth" figures such as Dr. Miller have too much invested in the system, which has given them some degree of upward mobility, Chesnutt focuses on Josh Green who, as a black stevedore, is at the socio-economic bottom. Green's humble appearance and origins are deceptive, for this humility re-performs the traditional epic strategy of masking "the one's" full epic potential. This strategy unites the epic traditions of Africa, ancient Greece, and Hebrews: Green is deformed like Ozidi, Sundiata, and Mwindo, not to mention Odysseus from the *Odyssey*, but nevertheless is as morally rigorous as his Old Testament namesake, Joshua. Chesnutt utilizes the epic power of Green, one of the earliest representations of the black "bad man" in literature (Sundquist, Introduction xli), to radical effect, at once democratic and epic: the transformation of the most "inferior" black, and hence all blacks, into a co-equal American epic figure his white readers, and all white Americans, could appreciate.

Chesnutt accomplishes this by successfully interpolating the epic trickster into America's Greco-Roman epic aesthetic to foreground the nation's epic qualities and its transgressive contradictions. To get at the prevailing mythologies, show the role of the epic heroic in lynchings and pogroms, demonstrate the dangers this transgressive epic mode poses to all Americans, and transform the black body into an epic figure, Chesnutt creates, *per force*, a complex novel which bears an encyclopedic character. Chesnutt's two-part ("book") structure specifically allows him to make his novel more encyclopedic. He gives readers an anatomy lesson about racial violence as he works his way from a near-lynching to an actual pogrom, a strategy, which leaves a dissected body/politic in its wake. The American legal system, of course, is crucial to Chesnutt's strategy of bringing American democracy and morality into alignment with its epic habitus. Responding in part to the precedent set by *Plessy v. Ferguson* (1896) and the Spanish-American War (1898), Chesnutt anthropomorphizes American jurisprudence to satirize the national and international racial and imperialistic policies of the American epic habitus.

Chesnutt draws upon his expertise in law and literature in a host of ways: the use of legal terms in the chapter titles and legalese throughout the narrative; adoption of a quasi-legal complaint and creation of an extrajudicial forum concerning Sandy Campbell's trial, conviction, and excommunication by his church community (120–21); a strategic use of surnames, which pun on the law and economic exchange — e.g., Letlow, or let/lease low, as in a cheap hire; and, of course, the presence of Mr. Watson, Esq., who is African American.

In contrast to many African Americans of his inter-racial status (he could pass for white) and ideological bent, Chesnutt virulently advocated racial equality. Although initially and widely considered an accommodationist author (Andrews, 174, 200), more recent scholarship presents Chesnutt as a man who, despite his friendship with Booker T. Washington, was largely opposed to his accommodationist ideology and methodology. Still, there was room in Chesnutt's ideology for accommodation as integration or assimilation. Under the near-total presence of white racism, and greater wealth, political, and military strength, not to mention greater numbers, Chesnutt's position is not surprising. As William Andrews remarked:

> The melting pot had served the interests of all other racial and national groups who sought to merge into the American mainstream. Absorption via social intermingling and marriage seemed to Chesnutt the only demonstrable means by which fundamental race prejudice could be wiped out permanently so that the nonwhite population could be free to obtain the rights and opportunities of the American Dream.
>
> Chesnutt did not regard miscegenation as a panacea for America's racial problems. He regarded it as the final outcome of black advancement on a variety of political, economic, and educational fronts. It would be, in his mind, the final proof of Afro-American equality [141–42].

Because of his uncompromising insistence on equality and integrity, Chesnutt's strategy, which his novel allegorizes, requires the elevation of the African American bearers of vernacular culture not just in socio-political terms, but ontologically as well. In short, lower-class blacks, especially the underclass, are more important to this development than the African American bourgeoisie. If the masses of blacks were to be uplifted, then Chesnutt would have to use his fictive platform for social engineering and enlightenment to lift them upon his literary shoulders for his European-American audience to see. But normative, reasonable uplift strategies would perhaps not be enough, for equality benefited the elite and the working class African Americans. If he were to achieve true equality, or at least an equal opportunity environment, then Chesnutt would have to transform the entire black body/politic, which meant making the lower and underclass blacks transcendent en masse. What better way of achieving this than showing, as Richard Yarborough states en route to evaluating this strategy, "that they had the potential to be exemplary men and women, that they could be, in a word, *heroic*" (226). More specifically, it would serve the greatest effect if he particularized this heroic and imbued black men and women with epic moral and physical stature in the epic-oriented society America was and always had been.

Chesnutt's strategy of creating his own transcendent African American epic figure is less radical than one might imagine. At the turn of the century, a *fin de siecle* that was the nadir of black history, and a full generation after the Civil War, not only was the black middle class moving, but the less acculturated and much larger lower class was picking up the momentum that would lead to a strong tradition of folk heroes of the late 1890s and early 1900s. Situated in a vernacular culture where trickster tales, bad men folk heroes, and "conjure" retained much of the vitality of their African origins because they were reinforced by the epic biblical figures and stories, the powerful creative energies associated with the axis of race, class, and modernity were informing culture from blues to jazz. It represents a distinct voice with its own standards and insistence on recognition that many black leaders, intellectuals, and artists dismissed as primitive and inferior. Thus, just as Eric Sundquist identifies him as a manifestation of the folk heroic (*To Wake* 425), Josh Green was already formed and collectively embodied in a body politic associated with the underclass. Chesnutt incorporates Josh Green into his strategy for racial uplift. In other words, he was not, as some scholars have suggested, simply falling sway to the lure of heroic swagger, "caught up in the magnificence of Green's courage" (Yarborough, 235) or expressing his suppressed emotionalism and anger (George and Pressman, 287–98).

The pogrom in Wilmington involved the intersection of white supremacy and Southern "heroism" as an effort to eliminate the social and political gains blacks made during Reconstruction. Wilmington, the largest city in North Carolina, had a majority of black residents, which allowed it to become one of the most prosperous and progressive cities for blacks in North Carolina and the South. Sharing the resentment many Southerners felt toward the North because they believed it imposed inferior, subhuman beings on them as equals and leaders, Wilmington's opinion leaders conspired to reassert their traditional claims of racial superiority. They did this, as Chesnutt correctly indicates, by using the press to invoke heroic, white masculinity to protect their ways and white women from rape, and to restore the natural order, proliferated in the press, pulpit, and political circles. The Republican and Populist government, which had dominated Wilmington since 1894, became even stronger as more blacks made gains leading into 1896. As the gubernatorial election of 1898 approached, the conspirators tapped into poor whites and intensified the sentiment for a quick return to white power. This set the stage for the pre-election violence of November 10, 1898, leading to the death of numerous blacks and the expulsion or exodus of many others from Wilmington.

As bad as a "race riot" is, a "racial massacre" suggests the inability to exercise heroic potential and the subjectivity it signifies. But this violence is only

the sensational dénouement to a political platform amounting to a coup d'é-
tat. Although North Carolina did not disenfranchise African Americans by
reapportioning its voting districts as some southern jurisdictions did repeatedly in the late nineteenth century (Franklin and Moss, 231–32), the white
supremacist regime of Wilmington nevertheless used a host of methods
amounting to a type of gerrymandering. As for Green, the black underclass
he specifically represented, and the future African American body politic Chesnutt made of him, it is better to say he was *Jerry*-mandered: Whites and class-
conscious blacks contained, twisted, deformed, and gerrymandered the
revolutionizing potential he represented as the epic trickster until he seemed
to be a trickster-type even less desirable than Chesnutt's most despicable black
character, Jerry Letlow. True to the socio-historical context, Green is very
much before his time as a stable literary figure, for the African American middle class version of the epic trickster was John Henry, a figure who embodied the African American epic ideal (Levine, 420–27).

Forced to make use of entrenched stereotypes and confronted with a
frightening totality, Chesnutt worked at the conscious level and, through subtle, understated irony, into the psycho-mythical consciousness of his readers
and critics. The totality of the racial massacre, national politics, and the
national consciousness provided him with an abundance of creative and critical space to re-envision the body politics as one. In this endeavor, Chesnutt's
primary challenge was whether he could wield his narrative pivots and irony
subtly enough in the portrayal of the representative characters — the Millers
and Carterets — who would bear the symbolic weight of his effort to erase
inequality. Although often dismissed, Captain McBane and Josh Green are
perhaps the most important individuals to Chesnutt's goal of remaking the
Millers and Carterets into co-equal allegorical embodiments of their respective races. Neither Green nor McBane are compromising in their ideological
positions, or compromised by Chesnutt's studied and steady application of
irony. His treatment of Green and McBane notwithstanding, Chesnutt's irony
functions to erode the reliability of these characters' ethics, perspectives, and
actions. Like the unstable reality created by white supremacy, the integrity of
all of his characters is significantly compromised, if not emptied, over the
course of the novel. For reasons detailed below, Green is the only one of the
protagonists whose integrity is not undercut, or is only marginally so, by the
subtle but incisive erasure operating in Chesnutt's narrative.

A key part of the erasure involves the racial performances central to the
plot, for each character who passes, consciously or not, evidences ethical instability or some significant flaw the text ironizes. Chesnutt's primary concern
is less about the *racial* instability than the total self-deception, the *ethical*
instability, the myth the American racial hierarchy fosters. *Marrow* draws

upon the folk elements of the African American community to obviate racial passing and performances. This involves a strategy of embodying, disembodying, and finally re-embodying the larger mythical matrix. Since the societies in conflict are the actual protagonists, then mythologized bodies (politic) become the real centers, and all the characters function as specific manifestations of these larger literary embodiments. These bodies lurk in the text, gaining momentum toward the racial riot, until they are literally embodied. Thus, from ignominy as a trickster-prop virtually unrecognizable as human, Josh Green quietly moves through the novel as the epic trickster element until he squares off— an equally fated *mêlée* in *Marrow*— against his epic antagonist, Captain McBane, just as the two bodies politic engage in racial battle. The dramatization of this process reflects the ongoing dilemma of the epic trickster, for by re-staging this event, Chesnutt has moved toward creating his own epic that implicitly recognizes the epic trickster and its important role. Indeed, as his meticulous efforts, many asides, overlapping plots, multiple perspectives, and lengthy narrative demonstrate, an encyclopedic array of forces supports the traditional racist framework of Wilmington, North Carolina, and the nation.

By invoking tradition, Chesnutt indicates that one of the key elements sustaining the American body politic is socialization, especially the roles every one performs in reifying the political mythology of racial superiority and inferiority. This phenomenon is similar to the "grand ceremonial displays" Bourdieu references in speaking of the reification of the habitus's political mythology, and the "epic motto" Seydou invokes in describing the function of the traditional African epic reifying the collective identity. *Marrow* demonstrates that at the center of this tradition are an idealized white epic figure and the marginalized black bodies against which the socialization narrative is continuously (re)performed. Ultimately this force, which encompasses the tradition of North Carolina and the South and the national political mythology, is as broad and infinite as the concept of white superiority itself. Because of the mythopoetic dimensions of this dynamic, the idealized white epic bodies would have various names in the American imagination: to wit, Achilles, Odysseus, Aeneas, Arthur, Helen, and Hercules, among others. Even as the body politic idealized these individual figures, and the folk versions such as Davy Crockett and Daniel Boone, the white members of the body politic were their vicarious representatives. In this formulation, each white citizen, especially but not exclusively males, becomes a white hero and warrior who polices and defends the racial mythology. Whether it was Achilles, Odysseus, Crockett or some other figure is irrelevant, for not only are the epic heroes numerous, as are those who identified with them and thus vicariously shared their epic statures, but the ideal epic heroes of the Hellenistic-Hebraic axis are unquantifiable because of their divine origins, support, or transcendence. Ultimately, since they are unquantifiable, the white epic heroic manifestations are unnamable, perhaps unspeakable, creatures of the "higher law," as well as of the imaginary, which collectively represented the "god of racial superiority" (George and Pressman, 297).

Chesnutt is not, it should be noted, necessarily decrying the *truly* ideal and sublime character of the American epic figure. His immediate cultural influences, as an African American, are more European than African, and thus he can lay claim to Homer's epic figures as well as Africa's. Instead, he is exposing another aspect of this epic persona, its excessive and transgressive character that his European-American audience would not see or read about in an editorial, and certainly not in mainstream fiction. At the same time, he introduces them to the epic trickster, Josh Green, whose deformity he reveals to be as heroically and ethically epic as the Hellenistic-Hebraic *ideal* informing the American epic habitus. Although Chesnutt hoped *Marrow* would match the success of Stowe's *Uncle Tom's Cabin*, his method of characterization departed from the creation of virtuous European-American models akin to Stowe's white paragons and black Christian martyrs. Nor did he simply transform blacks and mulattoes into human beings for his audience (Hackenberry, 194), although this was unavoidable and necessary. Part of Chesnutt's strategy involved slowly excavating the excessive, transgressive corollary of the white epic body, and revealing it as a figure far removed from the ideals espoused in the South and nationwide. A twofold strategy of centering whiteness through his characters and their actions and situating his African American characters as individuals struggling against this totality helped to eradicate the significant disparity between European and African Americans. Since the racial hierarchy and the terrorism calculated to perpetuate it existed because of historical, economic, political, theological, scientific, and mythological forces, Chesnutt had to show the organic relationship between European Americans' departure from the ideal and the epic moral struggle of African Americans. Hence, *Marrow* and other novels of the nadir, Robert Nowatzki argues, "signify upon the racist image of black male savagery and appropriate the white supremacist trope of masculine heroism in celebrating and promoting the struggle for racial justice" (61). Informed by the "tradition," Chesnutt's invocation of the metaphorical marrow is the clearest indication of the body troubling society. Encompassing in its girth an entire nation and driving the crisis to which he responds, this body performs its own epic drama in which a racially pure, white male body is opposed by the black male body, a dark and terrible counter-epic. The visual cue, scholar Bryan Wagner maintains in addressing the architectonic and physiological changes of Wilmington, is rhetorically analogous to the rhetoric of "White Supremacy" and

"Negro Domination" repeatedly invoked by the Big Three (Chesnutt, 325–26; Wagner, 312, 325–29).

Although primarily conceptualized and performed as an agonistic contest between male foils, women's bodies are deeply implicated here. Both white and black women's bodies function as the figurative, mythologized contest grounds for the socio-political and territorial hegemony at stake. Though subordinated in the novel, African and European American women's bodies richly inform the complex narrative that motivates the characters. For example, the fate of Josh Green's mother resonated strongly with Dr. Miller, who "had often seen Josh's mother, old Aunt Milly, — 'Silly Milly,' the children called her, — wandering aimlessly about the street, muttering to herself incoherently" (112). Although his father was lynched on the same night, "Silly Milly" functions as the signal emblem of brutality actuating Josh Green and inspiring, however grudgingly, Dr. Miller. Her transformation from *Mrs.* Milly Green, mother and wife, *below* the secondary status symbolized by the epithet *Aunt Milly*, to Silly Milly is significant. She may not have been lynched, but she indirectly experiences it as a witness, the witnessing itself constituting a total assault. Consequently, Milly Green suffers a *deformity* in the form of a psychic shock caused by the trauma. Since she is the mother of Josh Green, Silly Milly's deformity invites comparison to the mother figures of the traditional African epic. The mother-son relationship constitutes a fundamental part of the story in the epics of Mwindo, Ozidi, and Sunjata, for the social deformation of the mother — Nyamwindo, "the preferred one," is demoted to the most despicable; Sogolon, Sunjata's mother is cheated out of her position by her competitor; and, Ozidi's mother, Orea, is widowed — plays a significant role at the outset of the epic narrative. Indeed, each of these cases constitutes a social death, just as Silly Milly's insanity makes her dead to regular and reasoned intercourse with reality. Moreover, the quick return movement of Josh Green to confront his epic enemy maps onto the Malian pattern in which the physical death of Sunjata's mother marks the specific point at which he begins his return to Mali through epic warfare. Next to Josh Green, the epic trickster, and the other major and minor characters, Milly's role seems to be insignificant. Indeed, although scholars have given her little critical attention, Chesnutt uses Milly in a way very crucial to the favorable return of the epic trickster and its acceptance by mainstream readers. Knowing that the emergence of a black epic figure would be a cause for alarm, Chesnutt uses his readers' compassion for Milly's condition and death to circumvent the "bad man" label, while justifying and ennobling the return of the epic trickster.

The "Ochiltree affair," the murder-rape of Olivia Ochiltree for which Sandy Campbell is charged, is the one crime which leads the Big Three to convene at the *Morning Chronicle*. Their initial shock and indignation quickly devolves into preliminary findings of fact. McBane says, "'He has assaulted and murdered a white woman,— an example should be made of him,'" while Carteret agrees, thinking, "The criminal was a negro, the victim a white woman" (181–82). A sentence summarily executed is not enough, for the one crime demands a response of epic proportions:

> "This," said Carteret, "is something more than an ordinary crime, to be dealt with by the ordinary processes of law. It is a murderous and fatal assault upon a woman of our race,— upon our race in the person of its womanhood, its crown and flower. If such crimes are not punished with swift and terrible directness, the whole white womanhood of the South is in danger...."
>
> "Burn the nigger," reiterated McBane. "We seem to have the right nigger, but whether we have or not, burn *a* nigger. It is an assault upon the white race, in the person of old Mrs. Ochiltree, committed by the black race, in the person of some nigger. It would justify the white people in burning *any* nigger...."
>
> "In ancient Rome," said the general, "when a master was killed by a slave, all his slaves were put to the sword" [182–83].

This exchange between the Big Three foregrounds the existence of a black male body, a hyper-subjective threat to the white body politic requiring an epic response, the lynching. Moreover, it demonstrates how the epic trickster gets arrested, for the "bad negro" is literally blackened and burned by white supremacy.

Articulated from this perspective, which implicates bodily purity, genealogy, and the thrill and sport of battle, lynchings function as heroic performances to protect them. The American lynching drama fictionalized in *Marrow* expresses a primal narrative of territorial, mythologized aggression against a perceived threat. In effect, lynching functions as a white supremacist American corollary of the traditional African epic performance. The lynching, as ceremony and festival, reenacts the myth of white origins, for it invokes the marrow of tradition and a sublime white epic hero whose status the participants vicariously embody and experience. The occasion conflates the mythologized body and body politic, which allows all the witnesses, male and female, young and old, to share in this sublime body as principles, agents, and subagents. Chesnutt's narrative approach to Sandy's imminent lynching supports this reading, both in the public and private outrage, and the specific preparations — a T-rail, chains, pine wood — made for the execution to take place, ironically enough, right outside of the jail. Deploying Ellis's frantic witnessing of the unfolding terror to delve more deeply into its dynamic, Chesnutt characterizes it as an *auto-da-fé*, a "ceremony," in which:

> Some enterprising individual had begun the erection of seats from which, for a pecuniary consideration, the spectacle might be the more easily and comfortably viewed.

Ellis was stopped once or twice by persons of his acquaintance. From one he learned that the railroads would run excursions from the neighboring towns in order to bring spectators to the scene; from another that the burning was to take place early in the evening, so that the children might not be kept up beyond their usual bedtime. In one group that he passed he heard several young men discussing the question of which portions of the negro's body they would prefer for souvenirs [219–20].

The ceremony Chesnutt portrays, with organizers inviting thousands of participant-witnesses to join the festive, pro-family atmosphere, has its precedent. As *Marrow* attests through the indiscriminate nature of lynchings, which the aforementioned judgment of the Big Three endorsed, actual culpability is a non-issue. As the center of a social narrative to which so many eyes attest, the victim is the physical and the symbolic embodiment of the epic antagonist. Through such a character, the lynching performance recreates the threat which, because it is perceived as a total challenge, must culminate neither in defeat nor simple humiliation.

For those blacks whose actions were seen as threatening, a grand display had to be made. As a response in kind to the perceived threat, the lynching performance does not stop until it results in a complete dismemberment, which effectively removes the epic potential by stripping the body of its humanity. Chesnutt, *qua* Dr. Miller, argues as much while he ponders the context of and reaction to courageous displays from black men. Instead of drawing "applause from the world," it would be considered "mere desperation," "a mere animal's dislike of self-restraint. Every finer human instinct would be interpreted in terms of savagery" (296). Chesnutt seems to equivocate, or perhaps become philosophical, as the possibility of some absolute parity (direct proportionality) forces itself upon the inverse relationship of epic hero and his complete foil. One might consider this rhetorical rumination, as simple and fleeting as it seems, to nevertheless be a profound insight beyond the vagaries of tradition to a broader humanity. The epiphany leads him to reconsider the paradoxical ironies in behavior characteristically articulated as an absolute mark of savagery. "Or, if forced to admire, they would none the less repress. They would applaud his courage while they stretched his neck, or carried off the fragments of his mangled body as souvenirs, in much the same way that savages preserve the scalps or eat the hearts of their enemies" (296). As this forced admiration suggests, the lynching performers recognize, at the same instance they move to vitiate it, the hyper-subjectivity they have symbolically embodied in their victim. The metaphysical moment is the implicit invocation of the white hero, approximated by the "heroic," communal body, which fashions its own dusty-haired epic antagonist, pulling back the veil on his epic potential, before proceeding to totally dismember such. At its culmination, then, the epic mythos is reified as the narrative is transcribed upon the victim's body through fire, faggot, and disfiguration. This spectacle not only reaffirms the sublime ideology and punishes the symbolic embodiment threatening it, but seeks to suppress any similar hyper-subjectivity.

The isomorphism between epic performances and lynching "performances" suggests the ancient pedigree of both activities. In addition, it implicates an irony which destabilizes the dichotomy between "high" art, the literary classics in particular, and the aesthetics of the mutilation ritual. Rituals are important here, for it is the nature of culture to use these and other practices to generate a self-sustaining and durable habitus which provides a coherent identity and political mythology for the group. This dynamic remains true when a group possesses an actual, organic link to the culture initiating the ritual, and when a group wholly imagines or adopts another's rituals for its traditions. Thus, although tradition may arise from historical or quasi-historical circumstances to which the group organically relates, it is possible for an inorganic bond to arise involving the creation or "invention of tradition" and genealogy where no historical predicate exists. "'Traditions,'" Eric Hobsbawm argues, "which appear or claim to be old are often quite recent in origin and sometimes invented." This "invented tradition," he goes on to say, "is taken to mean a set of practices, normally governed by overtly or tacitly accepted rules and of a ritual or symbolic nature, which seek to inculcate certain values and norms of behavior by repetition, which automatically implies continuity with the past" ("Introduction," 1). Moreover, as Benedict Anderson argues in his widely influential book, *Imagined Communities: Reflections on the Origin and Spread of Nationalism* (1983; 1996), the modern project of nation building results from this very inorganic act of creation (9–65). Since the Greco-Roman epic tradition provided key aesthetic scaffolding for European culture, the same is true of American tradition and nation building. The countries civilized themselves as modern, democratic nations even as they nativized themselves as imperialistic Greco-Roman diasporas. Hence, at the same time as Caroline Winterer argues for the importance of classic Greco-Roman culture as the founding tradition of American culture and the modern intellectual and academic life of the humanities curricula (3–9), the decidedly inhuman(e) aspects of Greco-Roman high aesthetics also structured the polis. From this perspective, the resulting aesthetic tension is one thing, but combined as this tension is with the American political mythology associated with nation building, it becomes a Manichean reality at once beautiful and brutal, democratic and tyrannical, epic and gothic. The adoption of Homer's *Iliad*, particularly its mutilation narrative, is important because it grounds a signature Western archetypal moment, the lynching.

The *Iliad* is one of the most recognized canonical texts in the Western tradition. Its centrality to such, resulting in what one might call supra-canonization, makes it not just a classical text, but a thoroughly American one as well. Its story, the epic conflict between the Greeks and Trojans because of the adulterous relationship between Helen and Alexander/Paris, is one of the most recognizable in the Western canon. The details of the nine-year epic contest are not important here, except for the epic fight between the fair-haired and -eyed Achilles, the Greeks' champion and most favored because he is Zeus's grandson (Homer, *Iliad*, 393–94), and Hektor, the dark-haired and -eyed Trojan epic hero who has no immortal genealogy but is nevertheless favored by the lord of Mt. Olympus.

Though both men are epic heroes, Achilles does not stop with the honorable defeat and death of Hektor. Instead, his battle frenzy is kindled and nothing can satisfy him until Hektor has been completely stripped of his former epic stature. Thus, although Hektor's dead body has all the magnificence of an epic figure, Achilles strips it bare, after which his fellows repeatedly deform it by stabbing the body with their spears. Finally, the last and greatest insult, Achilles straps Hektor's body to a chariot and proceeds to drag, disfigure, and dismember it in his own country as all of Troy looks on in horror:

> Then [Achilles] put glorious Hektor to shameful treatment. He cut through behind the tendons of both feet from heel to ankle, and pulled straps of ox-hide through them which he tied fast to his chariot, so the head would be left to drag. Then he mounted the chariot and lifted the famous armour into it, and whipped the horses on, and they flew eagerly on their way. As Hektor was dragged behind, a cloud of dust arose from him, his dark hair streamed out round him, and all that once handsome head was sunk in the dust: but now Zeus had given him to his enemies to defile him in his own native land.
> So Hektor's head was all sullied in the dust [369].

This desecration takes on a ritualistic economy, for Achilles takes Hektor's body to the camp, unceremoniously throws the body in the dust, "face down," as thousands of Greeks took off their armor and feasted around the body (372). Indeed, for eleven days Achilles engages in the ritualistic abuse of Hektor's body by dragging it at dawn (393, 402). This ritual is Achilles's — or Homer's? — way of making "sport" of Hektor as the Greeks conduct an elaborate burial ceremony and hold funeral Olympics for Patroklos, Achilles's beloved friend whose death he attributed to Hektor (374–77). In sum, "godlike" Achilles has been unleashed in the most inglorious display imaginable, and even though the gods heal and protect his body, Hektor, like his once-epic status, has effectively been blackened ("sullied in the dust"), lynched, dismembered, and dehumanized.

Studying this classical model is insightful, for the paradigm of Achilles unleashed typifies the American expression of violence in general and its relationship with African Americans in particular. When considered in tandem with *Marrow*, the Homeric aesthetic emerges as a significant component of Chesnutt's strategy of re-imagining the American body politic. In this case, the task is immense, for the grandeur of the American epic habitus and "white" body/politic are an extension of the horrors and deformations of the epic at its most grotesque. The latter is perfectly veiled by the former, and moreover complicated by the banalities of every day life. These banalities interweave the epic grandeur into public and private spaces and all the intercourses in between, giving rise to culture and affirming tradition. In this manner, epic and everyday become the same and mutually reinforcing in much the way Bourdieu says everything in the habitus reflects everything else (76–77). The American epic is always already the magnificence of possibilities of whiteness indexed to a necessary deformation of the racial other.

In this archetypal narrative, where the sullied and dusty Hecktor always meets his comeuppance at the hands of his racial and epic superior, Achilles, where is egress possible? Chesnutt's strategy, a brilliant one, is to appropriate the epic narrative by interpolating the epic trickster, a variation of Hektor. However, Chesnutt departs from the customary deformation narrative canonized in the *Iliad*, for his Hektor's death leads to the possibility of a spiritual resurrection. He uses some epic-type irony to interpolate an African American epic trickster into the traditional epic narrative, deposit its ethos and aesthetic, and then kill him off before his white readers decipher Green's significance. Chesnutt's strategy is perfectly sensible here, and *no moral or narrative dilemma*, since, as his title states, the sickness goes to the marrow, and thus encompasses everyone and everything, especially those invested in the traditional mythos, it takes one outside of this rooted totality to see, diagnose, and thus heal it: (re)enter Josh Green, the epic trickster.

All Green with Epic Potential

Of all of the major characters, only Josh Green desires nothing from the system. His only concern is to care for his mother, "Silly" Milly, and get revenge/justice for her and his father when she dies. Although Green has been considered a member of the working class (Wagner, 329), the impression he presents is distinct from that of the other working-class blacks. From the opening description and the questionable status of his employment, Green appears to be a representative of the vast underclass Chesnutt's novel otherwise elides.

Green's underclass status is important in two ways. First, his income is probably a pittance which, since it must support him and his mother, places them *under* class — i.e., Josh has no class — and precariously close to a scramble for survival. This is generally the position of the trickster proper. However, in Green's case it is better to identify him as the trickster-*hero* struggling against a trickster-prop (erty) status, a condition meant to eliminate the subjectivity required for the epic trickster and, ultimately, the epic hero. Second, Green's socioeconomic status is also important for the critical, social distance and insight it gives him. As a member of the underclass who is outside the system, Green is impervious to the rhetoric of democracy, equality, and fusion (party politics) when it is devoid of justice for, as he makes clear, he "'ruther be a dead nigger any day dan a live dog'" (284). More importantly, he is outside of the color-line and the false hierarchy it enshrines. Green sees the total situation clearly, even if he lacks education and rhetorical savvy, and is the only character "who holds to principle without duplicity" (Reilly, 35–36). Hence, unlike the aforementioned nurse, who is figuratively killed off by being fired, Chesnutt *qua* narrator — as distinct from Dr. Miller's thoughts — introduces Green largely unburdened by his narrative critique. He is heroic, as most critics recognize, but Green's exact heroic character and complexity relative to Chesnutt's goal of re-conceptualizing the black and white marrow remain underappreciated or misunderstood.

Indeed, Green's status and stature bear more than a little resemblance to his African epic predecessors. But the African epic trickster's African American counterpart faces the complications of a radically different environment. The American epic habitus "blackened" it in ways — e.g., middle passage, total disconnection from continental Africa, a New World order with its own epic traditions — never countenanced by the epic tricksters of traditional African epics. Whereas the elemental irony confronting the African epic trickster is totally overturned in a matter of years, slavery forced a profound and prolonged irony into its American incarnation until it had been reduced and fragmented into its trickster-proper narratives. But the trickster is the quintessential hero-survivor, the fast-talking, trick-playing, and chaos-creating entity whose very skills of self-preservation ultimately provide the cultural purchase for the epic hero's return. This genealogy, both originating in and refracted through the epic trickster, is also the history of folk heroes, "bad men," and "bad negroes" such as Josh Green.

Green may not have been a slave, but he is surely another Southern product. The deformation which characterizes his first appearance — woolly headed, animalistic, unclean, apparently unemployed — makes of him a distinctly "blackened" figure. The "blackened" self serves as an important convention in the epic narrative, for it functions as a trope which marks the epic figure as a victim of some significant injustice. In the *Iliad*, Homer uses the trope of blackening to externalize his epic hero's internal condition after the trauma of a perceived injustice. When Achilles first hears of Patroklos's death, he pours soot over his head, blackening himself: "And he lay there with his whole body sprawling in the dust, huge and hugely fallen, tearing at his hair and defiling it with his own hands" (310).

Green's dusky and huge body, woolly head, fighting prowess, and biblical significance underscore his epic pedigree as an American figure: he follows the ancient Hellenistic tradition set by Achilles and Odysseus, and the Old and New Testament epics and ethos of Joshua and Jesus, respectfully. Just as important to the Hellenistic-Hebraic tradition is Green's role in foregrounding an African epic tradition as co-equal to the white (American) epic heroes of the Greco-Roman tradition. Although Chesnutt's subtle irony masks Green's later significance, this deformed Green shares the total opprobrium suffered by the fatherless Ozidi, lame Sundiata, and "aborted" Mwindo at the outset of their epic trickster phases. By the time they are forced into exile, they are also relegated to the underclass, or worse. But also better, ironically, since their collective exile and underclass status enable them to see the full corrupt totality.

The same is true of Chesnutt's *Marrow* in that Green's outcast, "outlaw" status gives him the requisite distance to exercise proper ethical sight. Sight or insight into the problem is one thing, piercing and expunging it is another, hence the signal difference between the African and African American epic tricksters. The African American epic trickster represented by Green faces a total barrier created by the absence of the generative habitus and the presence of a totalized system of slavery to suppress his full evolution and return. Although Green is part of and thus can theoretically rely upon the African American community, racism as a legacy of slavery exercises insidious force on this potential constituency. *Marrow* dramatizes how white supremacy impacts the African American community from its elite members to the most low; in effect, it deprives Green of key, fully supportive individuals without whom the epic cycle can have no successful issue.

Even facing a larger, hostile epic community, the protagonists of traditional African epics nevertheless enjoy something Green lacks: a loving, just, and potent microcosm of the epic community. Sundiata, Mwindo, and Ozidi all had strong women — Sundiata's mother and sister; Mwindo's aunt; and, Ozidi's grandmother — supporting them in their formative years. Josh Green, by comparison, has only his mother, and she is the insane "Silly" Green. Moreover, those unrelated African American characters Green does have at his disposal are not even neutral, but directly supportive of the system, as is the case with Jane and Jerry Letlow, or invidiously compromised by it unbeknownst to themselves. Dr. Miller's and Mr. Watson's interactions with Green during Sandy's impending lynching deserve some attention here. Although Miller and Watson profess opposition, because they are so entrenched in the system they work against Green (Reilly, 36), their nominal anti-lynching measures notwithstanding. Thus, while Green embodies direct and immediate action to meet the exigent circumstances, their "professional" command of the situation effectively arrests him, one after another: First Watson to Miller ("'We'd better leave Josh here,'" "'Wait for us here, Josh, until we've seen what we can do'"), then Miller to Watson ("'and you, Josh, learn what the colored folks are saying, and do nothing rash until I return'") (192, 195). Together, Miller and Watson check Green's subjectivity and epic potential until he literally becomes an inanimate object who is, they would prefer, more trickster-prop than trickster proper. This reading shows the character of the Miller-Watson compromise, for they follow the procedures and rules of order pursuant to "democratic," "civilized," and "professional" routes of action when justice commands otherwise. Josh Green is effectively and figuratively exiled, not only by the white supremacist power structure characterized by the Big Three, but by the Big Two of the African American community. Chesnutt sums up the ultimate, decisive failure of their efforts with the chapter title itself: "How Not to Prevent a Lynching."

Heroic, decisive action, not professional compromise with those invested in tradition ultimately takes center stage even as Green is rendered frozen and flat-footed by procedure and Dr. Miller and Mr. Watson engage in their anti-lynching "performance." The Miller-Watson two-step leaves Green without any major support, except for the "small party" of "resolute-looking colored men" he commands in the end (281). These men may be Green's soldiers, a band of heroic fighters for justice his to command, but as Keith Cartwright suggests, male power without female magic, *badenya*, results in an inchoate epic hero. Hence the ironic significance of the death of Silly Milly, which both frees his hand for battle and seals his death. In short, the epic potential Green represents, and the successful issue of the epic journey, are doomed even before he can get started. Still, Chesnutt clearly figures Green as the embodiment of an African American epic figure, although for most of *Marrow*, from his first appearance and quantification by Dr. Miller, he represents the antithesis. Shunted away from socioeconomic stability, political utility, and even the basic terms denoting "full" humanity, Green symbolizes the gerrymandered underclass and Chesnutt's will to transform the entire black body/politic from the bottom up.

Green's demise is far from the end one assumes Chesnutt would give him if he were merely a "militant." Like a general and commander, Chesnutt makes his death nothing less than a sublime blaze of glory. Having survived a hailstorm of bullets that kills all of his comrades, Green stands alone as a

towering "black giant." At this moment, he is an epic figure whose native fore-
runners are Sundiata, Mwindo, or Ozidi:

> Some of the crowd paused in involuntary admiration of this black giant, famed
> on the wharves for his strength, sweeping down upon them, a smile upon his
> face, his eyes lit up with a rapt expression which seemed to take him out of mor-
> tal ken. This impression was heightened by his apparent immunity from the
> shower of lead which less susceptible persons had continued to pour at him.
>   Armed with a huge bowie-knife, a relic of the civil war, which he carried on
> his person for many years for a definite purpose, and which he had kept sharp-
> ened to a razor edge, he reached the line of the crowd. All but the bravest shrank
> back. Like a wedge he dashed through the mob, which parted instinctively
> before him, and all oblivious of the rain of lead which fell upon him, reached
> the point where Captain McBane, the bravest man in the party, stood waiting to
> meet him. A pistol-flame flashed in his face, but he went on, and raising his
> powerful right arm, buried his knife to the hilt in the heart of his enemy [309].

Plucked — or penned — from Chesnutt's imagination, just before the tragic
ending befalls him, Green flings off the veil and shows his resplendent potential as an epic figure at this moment. A simple "militant" he is not, for he
neither kills indiscriminately nor wields the weapons — shotgun or rifle — calculated to do so, and his violence is reasonably tailored for a specific end. He
is armed with the American equivalent of a sword, the bowie-knife, through
which he is fated, and doomed, to mete justice the Civil War only represented. As only an epic or epic-like figure can, Green uses his size, strength
and constitution, speed, and determination to "sweep" through destruction
toward his destiny.

Clearly, Green has been transfigured, but so has Captain McBane. Having once said, "'One white man can chase a hundred of 'em. I've managed
five hundred at a time,'" and called "Mr. White Man" by Green (250, 302),
McBane's confrontation with his lynching victim's survivor brings the bodies Chesnutt places in *Marrow* into their sharpest focus: McBane is the white
epic body to Green's black epic corollary. McBane, as "Mr. White Man," is
the allegorical representative of the unnamable, unspeakable white heroic,
while Green is the allegorical emblem of the "green" potential residing within
the woolly-headed beast implied by white supremacist ideology. Their final
confrontation occurs with all the polarities — white is always Good and
supreme, black always Bad and inferior — reversed, and results in a Pyrrhic
victory: Green defeats McBane, the embodiment of Achilles unleashed, but
he is circumscribed as the "epic trickster," and cannot make concrete and
fully realize his epic potential. His Sundiata/Mwindo/Ozidi resemblance gives
way to his fate as the "black" Hektor, for "the crowd dashed forward to wreak
vengeance on his dead body" (309). Naturally, although it occurs postmortem,
Green's body and his epic potential are lynched in a culminating perform-

ance, and the epic event, a racial riot, peters out once its mission has been accomplished.

Josh Green's and McBane's deaths bring closure to the violence and the epic cycle. In the traditional African epic, when the epic conflict has been resolved, the epic hero washes his face of the violence and rejoins the restored community and land. Traditionally, this means the epic hero undergoes a significant transformation from warrior to regent, and from battlefield to palace. But at the end of *Marrow*, neither of these conditions has been met. Green represents the epic potential, yet he, as "the one," is dead. Then where does this *nyama* go if the task of transforming the black body/politic is unfinished? In yet another ironic twist which resuscitates the Millers, Chesnutt transforms them. He endows them, by virtue of Josh Green, with epic potential.

Conclusion

Chesnutt's rhetorical strategy in situating this battle as the defining moment after which all else pales seems to make the conclusion a footnote. He set out, after all, to rewrite the official record of the machinations leading to what the Southern and Northern press (mis)characterized as a "racial riot." This he had done while critiquing the belief in the "higher law" with meticulous attention to details and the almost encyclopedic range of possibilities. Nonetheless, he included two final chapters devoted to the Millers-Carterets aftermath immediately following the Green-McBane confrontation. Believing these chapters to put things in proper perspective, scholars' oft-asked question has been, how do we read the ending? (De Santis, 92–93; Reilly, 35–37; Wolkomir, 252). The disjunctive proposition presenting Miller or Green as the ideal has been identified by various scholars who have called it a "dilemma" (Reilly, 35–37), "unresolvable moral dilemma" (Delmar, 269), "virtually unresolvable situation" (Hackenberry, 197), and an "ambiguous ending" (Gleason, 39–40), among other things. What these conclusions suggest, some more explicitly than others, is Chesnutt's failure as a novelist, visionary, or both. But careful reconsideration of *Marrow*, in light of Green's and the Millers' coordinate significance to the African American body politic, rescues the novel from these open-ended charges.

Although Chesnutt does not formally divide *Marrow* this way, the story fits into two "phases" or "books" roughly parallel to the two parts of the traditional (African) epic. Book One (Chapter I to XXVII, inclusive) narrates the concretizing of epic tension associated with Sandy Campbell's alleged murder-rape of Polly Ochiltree, whose death quickly sends the white citizens' sentiment from outrage to a lynch fervor just barely averted by the town's opinion leaders. They move quickly to stop the lynching, but clandestinely to close ranks on behalf of Tom Delamere, a white aristocrat from one of the leading families revealed to be the murderer of his own aunt. The "case" is closed as far as Sandy is concerned and, as Chesnutt states to begin Chapter XXVIII, "Wellington soon resumed its wonted calm" (236). What appears to be a clear dénouement actually opens Book Two (Chapter XXVIII to the end), which picks up with the underlying white supremacist political gerrymandering Chesnutt started at the beginning of the novel. As he closely follows the actual historical efforts to divest Wilmington's blacks of their Reconstruction-era political gains, Chesnutt quickly reestablishes the tension and movement leading toward a direct, "epic" conflict that closes the cycle initiated by Book One, eliminates the tension, and ends in peace.

Again, it is easy to overlook Green's potentiality, for when the epic and all the tension ends, the best and last chance to prevent it by force, Josh Green, has been killed and disembodied. According to this traditional line of reasoning, Dr. Miller and his ideals are alive, so Chesnutt must have considered Green's radical, extremist, militant approach a dead end. But Miller's ideal of riding the protestant work ethic into the "twilight" and the "whiteness" of the American Dream, which his son embodies, also meets a dead end. Although he escapes the terrible death of Green and the tragedy that has been his life, tragedy bedevils Dr. Miller, too, since his son dies as a result of a stray bullet. Although he blames Major Carteret, "fiat justitia," Dr. Miller may be substantially at fault as well. His desperate search for his "wife and child," the twilight of his life, and three-time rejection of Green, are symbolic of his constant deferral, equivocation, and inaction in light of a growing crisis. Confronted with the untenable dilemma of selecting between Green's militancy and Dr. Miller's compromises, some scholars turn to Janet Miller.

Janet Miller does show remarkable magnanimity, among other things, but this position is not reached until the Millers, in effect, have been reduced to Josh Green's existential position because they have suffered a loss so tragic it has stripped away their veil of security and set forth the total injustice quite brutally and personally. The death of their son, whose unnamed status brings into sharp focus the tenuous future they were nurturing, awakens their *bodies* to the deeper emotions, urgency, and sense of injustice Green unsuccessfully tried to convey to Dr. Miller. Shocked out of the "twilight," the total reality of "tradition," and their stock in it, impresses itself upon the Millers. This explains why Janet Miller now refuses that which she coveted for so long: a sister's love, legal privileges, and traditions of white bodies.

But the awakening of their bodies and awareness of the insidiousness of the "white" body of tradition suggests how Chesnutt uses Green. Although he is disembodied, his death as a transfigured epic figure opens up the space Chesnutt needed to reshape the marrow of the "black" body implied by tradition. The Millers, in the person of Dr. Miller, who were incapable and unwilling to assume a more heroic stature, assume some of the potential Green created and the death of their son forced upon them. At the same time, the great tragedy threatening the Carterets has diminished their bodies and made them confront the other consequences of their tradition. The "horror of the situation" confronts Major Carteret "at Miller's house, — for a moment the veil of race prejudice was rent in twain, and he saw things as they were, in their correct proportions and relations — saw clearly and convincingly that he had no standing here" (321). The violence and horrors of Achilles unleashed have come full circle and threaten their future in the form of their son, Theodore Felix Carteret. The dimunition of the Carterets-body, concomitant with the ennobling of the Millers-body, is necessary to help reinforce racial equality, per force of justice.

Thus, like the commanding, epic figure Green represented, the Millers now possess some of his moral/personal stature. Major Carteret shrinks from Dr. Miller's censure and gaze, "bowing mechanically, as though to Fate rather than the physician"; Olivia Carteret throws "herself at his feet, — at the feet of a negro, this proud white woman, — and was clasping his knees wildly" (321, 324); but Chesnutt makes explicit the reconfiguration of bodies as the two sisters face one another with Dr. Miller looking upon them:

> The two women stood confronting each other across the body of the dead child, mute witness of this first meeting between two children of the same father. Standing thus face to face, each under the stress of the deepest emotions, the resemblance between them was even more striking than it had seemed to Miller when he had admitted Mrs. Carteret to the house. But Death, the great leveler, striking upon one hand and threatening upon the other, had wrought a marvelous transformation in the bearing of the two women. The sad-eyed Janet towered erect, with menacing aspect, like an avenging goddess. The other, whose pride had been her life, stood in the attitude of a trembling suppliant [325–26].

No longer the aspiring, dusky shadows of the Carterets, the Millers now stand in "marvelous transformation" as equals who can make commands, issue judgments, and rebuff entreaties when morally justified, and yet show leniency for someone whom they recognize as equals, no matter how horrific their behavior.

Although Green is the *other* self that gives dimension to an overly rational, vacillating, and compromised Dr. Miller, both are needed for the new body Chesnutt creates. Green's death makes Miller, and thus the body of African Americans, more commanding and epic in an epic environment; Miller adds the sensibility, intelligence, ambition, and social acceptability

Green lacks in a democratic, civilized one. Thus, the Miller(s) vs. Green dilemma, conflict, and tension is a nonesuch, for if a new African American body is Chesnutt's goal, then the division between them is a red herring. Since Chesnutt seeks to eliminate the entire "black" body politic — middle, lower, and underclass — and uplift it into true American status, neither the Millers nor Green is *the* protagonist, for each is just "one of the novel's protagonists" (Nowatzki, 65). Chesnutt's new African American body replaces them, and even though it has a near-white bourgeoisie face and professional training, it now also has a more heroic, epic character to make it worthy to the larger society as an equal who no longer needs to pass or perform.

WORKS CITED

Anderson, Benedict. *Imagined Communities: Reflections on the Origin and Spread of Nationalism*. London and New York: Verso, 1996.

Andrews, William L. *The Literary Career of Charles W. Chesnutt*. Baton Rouge: Louisiana State University Press, 1980.

Biebuyck, Daniel and Mateene Kahombo. *The Mwindo Epic from the Banyanga (Congo Republic)*. Berkeley: University of California Press, 1969.

Bourdieu, Pierre. *The Logic of Practice*. Translated by Richard Nice. Stanford: Stanford University Press, 1990.

Cartwright, Keith. *Reading Africa into American Literature: Epics, Fables, and Gothic Tales*. Lexington: University Press of Kentucky, 2002.

Chesnutt, Charles W. *The Marrow of Tradition*, 1901. Introduction and notes by Eric J. Sundquist. New York: Penguin, 1993.

Delmar, P. Jay. "The Moral Dilemma in Charles W. Chesnutt's *The Marrow of Tradition*." *American Literary Realism* 14.2 (1981): 269–272.

De Santis, Christopher C. "The Dangerous Marrow of Southern Tradition: Charles W. Chesnutt, Paul Laurence Dunbar, and the Paternalist Ethos at the Turn of the Century." *Southern Quarterly: A Journal of the Arts in the South* 38.2 (2001): 79–97.

DuBois, Page. "Torture, Slavery and Utopia: Ancient Greeks in the 21st Century." Lecture. Center for the Humanities. University of Wisconsin–Madison. 30 September 2004.

Duncan, Charles. "The White and the Black: Charles W. Chesnutt's Narrator-Protagonists and the Limits of Authorship." *Journal of Narrative Technique* 28.2 (1998): 111–33.

Finnegan, Ruth. *Oral Literature in Africa*. London: Clarendon, 1970.

Franklin, John Hope and Alfred A. Moss. *From Slavery to Freedom: A History of Negro Americans*. 1947. New York: McGraw, 1988.

Frye, Northrop. *Anatomy of Criticism: Four Essays*. Princeton: Princeton, University Press, 1973.

George, Marjorie and Richard S. Pressman. "Confronting the Shadow: Psycho-Political Repression in Chesnutt's *The Marrow of Tradition*" *Phylon* 48.4 (1987): 287–298.

Giles, James R. and Thomas P. Lally. "Allegory in Chesnutt's *Marrow of Tradition*." *Journal of General Education* 35.4 (1984): 259–269.

Gleason, William. "Voices at the Nadir: Charles Chesnutt and David Bryant Fulton." *American Literary Realism* 24.3 (1992): 22–41.

Hackenberry, Charles. "Meaning and Models: The Uses of Characterization in Chesnutt's *The Marrow of Tradition* and *Mandy Oxendine*." *American Literary Realism* 17.2 (1984): 193–202.

Hedges, James S. "The Mole on the Neck: Two Instances of a Folk Belief in Fiction." *North Carolina Folklore Journal* 31.1 (1983): 43–45.

Hegel, G.W.F. *Aesthetics: Lectures on Fine Art.* Translated by T.M. Knox. Oxford: Clarendon Press, 1975.

Herskovits, Melville J. *The Myth of the Negro Past.* Boston: Beacon, 1990.

Hobsbawm, Eric and Terence Ranger, eds. *The Invention of Tradition.* Cambridge: Cambridge University Press, 1996.

Homer. *The Iliad: A New Prose Translation.* Translated and introduction by Martin Hammond. London: Penguin, 1988.

_____. *The Odyssey.* Translated and introduction by E.V. Rieu. New York: Penguin, 1959.

Knadler, Stephen P. "Untragic Mulatto: Charles Chesnutt and the Discourse of Whiteness." *American Literary History* 8.3 (1996): 426–48.

Levine, Lawrence W. *Black Culture and Black Consciousness: Afro-American Folk Thought from Slavery to Freedom.* New York: Oxford University Press, 1977.

Lukács, Georg. *The Theory of the Novel.* Translated by Anna Bostock. Cambridge, Mass.: MIT Press, 1971.

McGowan, Todd. "Acting without the Father: Charles Chesnutt's New Aristocrat." *American Literary Realism* 30.1 (1997): 59–74.

Miles, Vernon Garth. "The Politics of Passing: Identity and Community in Charles W. Chesnutt's *The Marrow of Tradition* and James Weldon Johnson's *The Autobiography of an Ex-Colored Man.*" *Kentucky Philological Review* 6 (1991): 27–31.

Miller, Dean A. *The Epic Hero.* Baltimore: Johns Hopkins University Press, 2000.

Niane, D.T. *Sundiata: An Epic of Old Mali.* Translated by G.D. Pickett. London: Longman, 1977.

Nowatzki, Robert. "'Sublime Patriots': Black Masculinity in Three African-American Novels." *Journal of Men's Studies* 8.1 (1999): 59–72.

Ojobolo, Okabou. *The Ozidi Saga.* Translated by J.P. Clark. Ibadan, Nigeria: Ibadan University Press and Oxford University Press, 1977.

Peabody, Ephraim. "Narratives of Fugitive Slaves." *The Christian Examiner.* 4th series 12.1 (1849): 61–93.

Pettis, Joyce. "The Literary Imagination and the Historic Event: Chesnutt's Use of History in *The Marrow of Tradition.*" *South Atlantic Review* 55.4 (1990): 37–48.

Reilly, John M. "The Dilemma in Chesnutt's *The Marrow of Tradition.*" *Phylon* 32 (1971): 31–38.

Roberts, John W. *From Trickster to Badman: The Black Folk Hero in Slavery and Freedom.* Philadelphia: University of Pennsylvania Press, 1989.

Robeson, Paul. "Joshua Fit de Battle of Jericho." *The Power and the Glory.* Columbia, 1991, sound recording.

Roe, Jae H. "Keeping an 'Old Wound' Alive: The Marrow of Tradition and the Legacy of Wilmington." *African American Review* 33.2 (1999): 231–43.

Seydou, Christiane. "A Few Reflections on Narrative Structures of Epic Texts: A Case Example of Bambara and Fulani Epics." Translated by Brunhilde Biebuyck. *Research in African Literatures* 14.3 (1983): 312–31.

Sundquist, Eric J. *To Wake the Nations: Race in the Making of American Literature.* Cambridge, Mass.: Belknap Press, 1993.

Wagner, Bryan. "Charles Chesnutt and the Epistemology of Racial Violence." *American Literature: A Journal of Literary History, Criticism, and Bibliography* 73.2 (2001): 311–37.

Winterer, Caroline. *The Culture of Classicism: Ancient Greece and Rome in American Intellectual Life, 1780–1900.* Baltimore: Johns Hopkins University Press, 2002.

Wolkomir, Michelle J. "Moral Elevation and Egalitarianism: Shades of Gray in Chesnutt's *The Marrow of Tradition.*" *College Language Association Journal* 36.3 (1993): 245–59.

Yarborough, Richard. "The Wilmington Riot in Two Turn-of-the-Century African American Novels." In *Democracy Betrayed: The Wilmington Race Riot of 1898 and Its Legacy*. Edited by David S. Cecelski and Timothy B. Tyson. Chapel Hill: University of North Carolina Press, 1998. 225–251.

CHAPTER 11

"The Wife of His Youth": A Trickster Tale

Cynthia Wachtell

Charles W. Chesnutt's "The Wife of His Youth" is a poignant story of an honorable man's difficult choice between two women: a young, cultivated widow who has captured his heart and an old, uneducated cook to whom he was married during the bygone days of slavery. It is a heart-warming story of a loyal woman's tireless search for her long-lost husband. It is a stirring story of a man's selfless and noble decision to acknowledge and reclaim the wizened, wrinkled wife of his youth. It is, in sum, a "marvelously simple, touching and fascinating" tale (H. Chesnutt, 98).[1] Or is it?

Published in the *Atlantic Monthly* in 1898 and again the following year as the title work in *The Wife of His Youth and Other Stories of the Color Line*, Chesnutt's tale of gentlemanly magnanimity has charmed generations of readers. For more than a century, critics have hailed the work as "both tender and compelling ... a beautifully and significantly conceived story which is structured and developed with great artistic effect" (Heermance, 172). Chesnutt's old story also permits quite a different reading. Whether Charles Chesnutt intended it or not, "The Wife of His Youth" can be read as a wonderful trickster tale.

***

On its surface level, "The Wife of His Youth" explores the social dynamics within an elite, upwardly-mobile, post-war, black community in a fictional, Northern city. A light-skinned, prosperous man with high social aspirations is suddenly brought face to face with the older, blacker, poorer woman he married during the days of slavery. They have not laid eyes upon one another in nearly thirty years, and their marriage, like all slave-marriages not re-affirmed after the war, is not legally binding. Indeed, it has been so long since they last saw one another, and the man has improved his station in life so remarkably, that the woman, who has been faithfully searching for him throughout the intervening years, does not even recognize him. Consequently, it falls to the long-lost husband to decide whether to reclaim the wizened wife of his youth or else to follow the dictates of his heart—not to mention considerations of social advantage—and marry, instead, a young, wealthy, well-educated, and pale-skinned widow.

The rank and file of critics have hailed this story as a sympathetic rendering of a "relatively clearly defined but difficult problem of choice" between "the conflicting claims of love and loyalty" (Andrews, 113, Heermance, 172). They have deemed the hero's course of action, his acknowledgment of his wife of old, as courageous and admirable. "The Wife of His Youth," writes one Chesnutt biographer, "is a sensitive, powerful drama of racial identity and the Socratic commitment to honest self-awareness and self-acceptance" (Heermance, 172). Yet this interpretation, when it stands alone, does not do full justice to Chesnutt's tale. Just as the story can be read as a tale of love, loyalty, and courage, it also can be read as a tale full of wiliness, cunning, and comeuppance.

Before proceeding to the trickster reading, it is essential to understand how the story customarily has been understood, or under-understood. For traditional readers, the plot of "The Wife of His Youth" runs as follows. Mr. Ryder is a learned man and an upstanding member of his community. He has honorable intentions of marrying Mrs. Dixon, a refined, mulatto widow, and has planned an elaborate ball at which to make official their engagement. His plans are unexpectedly altered by the arrival of a little, old, very black woman wearing an absurd bonnet and an ancient looking dress. Her name is 'Liza Jane.

Aloof on his porch, a volume of Tennyson by his side, Mr. Ryder listens patiently, not to mention patronizingly, to 'Liza Jane's story of her long search for her husband. She explains that she last saw her husband before the Civil War, when he had been a fieldworker for her Southern master. She helped him escape being sold down river but then met that same grim fate herself, when her master retaliated against her. Throughout the twenty-five years since the war's end brought freedom, 'Liza Jane has been looking for her lost husband. She has traveled throughout the former slave-states in the hope of finding him. She explains to Mr. Ryder, "'I's be'n ter Noo Orleans, an' Atlanty, an' Charleston, an' Richmond'; an' wen I'd be'n all ober de Souf I come ter de Norf'" (14).[2]

To date, 'Liza Jane has had no luck. Yet she is ever optimistic. "'I knows I'll fin' 'im some er dese days,'" she says, "'er he'll fin' me'" (14). Indeed, she seems confident that her long-lost husband has been faithfully searching for her throughout the intervening years, "'less'n he's be'n sick er sump'n, so he could n' work, er out'n his head, so he could n' member his promise'" (13). Eagerly, she asks Mr. Ryder if he has "'ever heerd of a merlatter man by de name er Sam Taylor 'quirin' round' in de chu'ches ermongs' de people fer his wife 'Liza Jane'" (11).

Mr. Ryder listens silently to 'Liza Jane's story and then presents her with a series of hypothetical scenarios. He suggests that her husband may be dead or "'may have married another woman'" (14). But 'Liza Jane firmly dismisses these possibilities. "'Oh no, he ain' dead,'" she responds, and she confidently asserts, "'He would n' marry no yuther 'ooman 'tel he found' out 'bout me'" (14–15). Mr. Ryder next suggests, "'Perhaps he's outgrown you, and climbed up in the world where he wouldn't care to have you find him'" (15). To this, 'Liza Jane assuredly replies, "'No, indeed, suh, Sam ain' dat kin' er man'" (15). Mr. Ryder finally speculates that 'Liza Jane may have passed her husband "'on the street a hundred times ... and not have known him; time works great changes'" (15). But 'Liza Jane's confidence proves unflagging. "'I'd know 'im 'mongs' a hund'ed men,'" she insists, and to back her claim, she produces an old daguerreotype of her long-lost husband (15–16).

At no point during their conversation does Mr. Ryder acknowledge that he recognizes 'Liza Jane. However, that night at the ball he throws for his fellow Blue Veins (members of an elite club for which eligibility is rumored to depend upon being "white enough to show blue veins"), Mr. Ryder recounts the woman's story (1). He posits a situation in which the woman's long-lost husband, now successful and genteel and "'absolutely safe from recognition or discovery,'" became aware, by accident, that the wife of his youth "'was alive and seeking him'" (22). He requests his friends' advice as to what such a man should have done. "'He should have acknowledged her,'" the Blue Veins uniformly agree (23). Buoyed by his fellow Blue Veins' approval, Mr. Ryder admits that he is the very man. "'Permit to me to introduce to you the wife of my youth,'" he pronounces, and the story ends (24). Or does it?

***

Earl Schenck Miers, who wrote the Introduction to the 1968 and 1972 reprints of *The Wife of His Youth*, describes the "The Wife of His Youth" as a "dignified" tale concerning the "heart-rending conflict of a free Negro's loyalty to the wife he had married while a slave and to the more refined 'blue-veined' Negress he meets later" (Miers, xiii). Yet, even on its surface-level, there is social satire and ironic wit in Chesnutt's tale. The snobbiest of the Blue Veins, the "custodian of [the Society's] standards, and the preserver of its traditions," ends up with the darkest and most unrefined of wives (3).

In being re-joined with his old wife, Mr. Ryder gets his just desserts for being so uppity and pretentious. At the story's start he laments the "growing liberality, almost a laxity, in social matters, even among members of his own set" and rues the fact that he "had several times been forced to meet in a social way persons whose complexions and callings in life were hardly up to the standard which he considered proper for the [Blue Vein] society to maintain" (7). By story's close, he is reunited in matrimony with an unlettered, dark-complexioned woman who has supported herself as a lowly cook. "'I'se a good cook'" 'Liza Jane proudly proclaims (14).

To ignore the social satire implicit even in the surface level reading of Chesnutt's story is to miss the significance of this story of the "color line." Chesnutt clearly intended the story as a strong indictment of the snobbery and prejudice that prevailed among members of the black middle and upper classes in the post-war era. He condemns the black men and women who, like Mr. Ryder, aspired to be absorbed by the "white race" and who lived by the mantra, "Self-preservation is the first law of nature" (7).

In *The Negro Problem*, published in 1903, W.E.B. Du Bois would envision that the "talented tenth" of the black people could help to improve the lot of all black people. These educated and advantaged members of the race could guide the masses. "The Negro race, like all races, is going to be saved by its exceptional men," he proclaimed (Du Bois, 1). But Mr. Ryder and his cohort have no interest in saving the less advantaged members of their race. They do not even wish to be members of their race. Rather, like the prominent Blue Vein in Chesnutt's "A Matter of Principle" who declines to associate with black people, they believe, "People who belong by half or more of their blood to the most virile and progressive race of modern times have as much right to call themselves white as others have to call them negroes" (Chesnutt, *The Wife of His Youth*, 40).

The unabashed goal of Mr. Ryder and his social set is to "do the best we can for ourselves and those who are to follow us" (7). Indeed, Mr. Ryder intends that his ball should serve "by its exclusiveness to counteract leveling tendencies" within the black and mixed-race communities, and his marriage with Mrs. Dixon, who is "whiter than he," will "further the upward process of absorption [by the white race] he had been wishing and waiting for" (7, 5, 8). The underlying irony of Chesnutt's story is that the ball has just the opposite effect.

***

Chesnutt's story, on its surface level, fuses wit with a moral message, but it takes little account of 'Liza Jane's wishes and emotions. She has trekked around the country for twenty-five years motivated by her certainty that, someday, she will find her husband. "'An' den,'" she explains, "'we'll bofe be as happy in freedom as we wuz in de ole days befo' de wah'" (14). But this blissful renewal of her married state is not to be. Mr. Ryder reunites with his wife out of a sense of honor. Duty prompts him, not love. Indeed, "he had set his heart upon another, whom he had hoped to call his own" (22).

'Liza Jane's material circumstances certainly will improve once she moves into Mr. Ryder's well appointed home, but she will lose something even more valuable. Her hope of connubial happiness, a hope that has sustained her for more than a quarter of a century, must die. Her marriage with Mr. Ryder will hold little splendor, little bliss.

'Liza Jane is acted upon rather than acting in the traditional reading of Chesnutt's story. Mr. Ryder consults his blue-veined friends about his decision, but does he consult 'Liza Jane? He leads her "by the hand" before his blue-veined coterie, and she remains speechless as he proclaims, "'Permit me to introduce to you the wife of my youth'" (23–24). Or, more precisely, the story ends before she can say a word by way of a response. The implicit assumption is that 'Liza Jane is only too happy to be reunited with her husband, even if he no longer cares for her and even if he in no way resembles the lazy, loving man for whom she so tirelessly searched.

The conventional reading of the story does not pivot upon 'Liza Jane and her decisions but rather upon Mr. Ryder. Should he choose the wife of his youth or a youthful wife? But this is a very limited and limiting reading of the tale.

***

Carol Pearson and Katherine Pope observe in their co-authored work *The Female Hero*, "Our understanding of the basic spiritual and psychological archetypes of human life has been limited ... by the assumption that the hero and central character of the myth is male. The hero is almost always assumed to be white and upper class as well ... [The] racial minorities, the poor, and women are seen as secondary characters, important only as obstacles, aids, or rewards in his journey" (Pearson and Pope, 4). Pearson and Pope's insights into the racial and gender dynamics at play in myths point to some basic assumptions that inform readers' understanding of Chesnutt's story. Even though the title is "The *Wife* of His Youth," the focus remains very much on the *husband*. Mr. Ryder emerges as the central character, and the resolution of his dilemma, his difficult choice, provides the climax of the story. What of Mr. Ryder's old and all but forgotten wife, 'Liza Jane? What of her feelings? What of her hopes and dreams?

Mr. Ryder is the white (at least white enough to show blue veins), upper-class, male. Consequently, he is the character on whom, according to Pearson and Pope's model, readers have been trained to focus. And 'Liza Jane? She fails to meet the pale standards of the Blue Veins. In fact, she is so "very black" that the gums in her toothless mouth are "not red, but blue" (10). And she is poor. And she is a woman.

'Liza Jane's circumstances seem perfectly to coincide with Pearson and Pope's description of the standard secondary character. Moreover, just as it is the role of secondary characters to stand as "obstacles, aids or rewards" in the hero's journey, 'Liza Jane duly functions as an obstacle. Her sudden reappearance threatens Mr. Ryder's upward spiral to the peaks of blue-veined elitism. Whereas, "his marriage with [the widow] Mrs. Dixon would [have helped] to further the upward process of absorption [Mr. Ryder] had been wishing and waiting for," his past union with 'Liza Jane threatens his standing within his blue-veined social set (7–8).

Pearson and Pope contend that readers are pre-programmed to view a character like 'Liza Jane — a minority, poor, woman — as an ancillary character. Even more alarming, Hazel Carby points out in her work *Reconstructing Womanhood* that, within the works of nineteenth century, white women novelists, "Thinking, articulate, reasoning black women were represented only as those who looked white: mulattoes, quadroons, or octoroons" (Carby, 33). According to these equations, readers have been trained to view characters such as 'Liza Jane not only as of marginal importance but also as unthinking, inarticulate, and lacking the capacity for sound reasoning. True to form, traditional readers of Chesnutt's story seem to view 'Liza Jane as just that. In *Charles W. Chesnutt*, for example, Heermance describes 'Liza Jane as a "dark, ignorant slave girl who has shriveled into a quaint, 'amusing' figure" (Heermance, 172). Is it mere coincidence that the words "dark" and "ignorant" sit side by side?

***

In the conventional reading of the story, 'Liza Jane emerges as a devout but pathetic creature. She is a woman who has trusted blindly and trusted the wrong man. Although she is reunited with her husband at the story's end, their reunion does not fulfill her expectations. 'Liza Jane's long search for her husband has been first, last and foremost a mission of love. For twenty-five years she has roamed the country searching for her husband, all the while keeping his treasured picture pressed tight to her breast. To find Sam Taylor has been, throughout the many years, her single ambition. At last, within the course of Chesnutt's story, her diligence pays off. She finds her man (now calling himself Mr. Ryder), but when she does, it is all too obvious that he does not rejoice in their reunion. He does not reciprocate her love.

The end of the story finds 'Liza Jane safely installed in Mr. Ryder's opulent household. But Mr. Ryder's riches — his good library, piano, choice engravings — are poor recompense for her shattered dreams. She did not search for Sam Taylor in the hope that he would support her. After all, 'Liza Jane admits, "'He wuz good ter me, Sam wuz, but he wuz n' much good ter nobody e'se, fer he wuz one er de triflin'es' han's on de plantation ... I spec's ter haf ter suppo't 'im w'en I fin' im, fer he nebber would work 'less'n he had ter'" (15). 'Liza Jane did not search for Sam hoping to find riches. In fact, she fully expected to find Sam in need of *her* financial assistance.

What 'Liza Jane had hoped to find was a warm, loving relationship with the man who once thought "'a heap er'" her (13). In the course of Chesnutt's story, she does not find anything even approximating that. Here, Homer's *The Odyssey* provides an illuminating point of comparison. In that famous epic, Odysseus returns home after the Trojan War and a journey of many years to find his wife, the ever "circumspect" Penelope, dauntlessly fending off all suitors and loyally awaiting his return. In contrast, 'Liza Jane relocates her spouse after a separation of twenty-five years, marked by the Civil rather than the Trojan War, and discovers that he has turned his romantic attentions and intentions elsewhere. Whereas Penelope unravels her weaving at night in order to keep her would-be suitors at bay, Mr. Ryder lounges on his porch by day and dreams of offering "his heart and hand" to the pale and accomplished widow Dixon (6).

A perceptive reader might well wonder if 'Liza Jane is truly any better off in Mr. Ryder's household than she was as an itinerant cook. Does Mr. Ryder really do her a favor in re-claiming her, in stepping forward to identify himself? Or would 'Liza Jane be better off still cooking for hire with her dream of marital happiness intact?

***

An advertisement for *The Wife of His Youth* which ran in the *Cleveland Ledger* on December 13, 1899, warned perspective buyers that the book merits "something more than careless reading"(Render, 140). What might readers willing to probe beneath the surface of "The Wife of His Youth" discover? Perhaps that 'Liza Jane is not the simple and simple-minded, secondary character that readers have been trained to see.

Mr. Ryder may be a faulty and fickle husband, but 'Liza Jane does not have to be a disappointed wife. Strip away the racist and sexist stereotypes, and her actions can be understood in quite a different way. Indeed, when "The Wife of His Youth" is read as a trickster tale, 'Liza Jane, gets exactly what she wants. In order to understand Chesnutt's story as a trickster tale, readers must bid farewell to their image of Mr. Ryder as a dignified, chivalrous man who magnanimously does the right thing. Instead, they must prepare to see him as a patsy, a pretentious and bigoted man who is thoroughly hoodwinked.

The storyline of this alternative reading of Chesnutt's tale — with some supposition — runs as follows. 'Liza Jane is a woman who has worked hard for many years. She has grown weary. She would like nothing more than an all-expense-ride through old age, and she is not above using her wile and wit to ease her way. After all, as Mr. Ryder himself believes, "Self-preservation is the first law of nature" (7). Although she was married many years ago during the days of slavery to a man named Sam Taylor, 'Liza Jane long since has lost hope, not to mention interest, in locating him. After all, Sam "'wuz one er de triflin'es' han's on de plantation'" (15).

'Liza Jane's life, though not an easy one, is following its course, when she somehow stumbles across a valuable tidbit of information. She discovers that her husband-of-old has done extremely well by himself. He has moved to the Northern town of Groveland, changed his surname from Taylor to Ryder, and grown genteel and prosperous. Most importantly, she realizes, he never has remarried.

'Liza Jane senses a promising opportunity. If she can convince her long-lost husband to reunite with her, she will enjoy an easy life. But she is clever enough to realize that she will have to do more than simply turn up on Mr. Ryder's doorstep, if she wishes to install herself in his home. Slave marriages, as she knows, are not legally binding, and she can guess that a cultured, pretentious man, such as her Sam Taylor has turned out to be, will not rush to reclaim an old, black, uncultured wife. So, 'Liza Jane devises a plan. She realizes that Mr. Ryder will not reunite with her out of love, but she hopes he can be tricked into reuniting with her out of a sense of duty, out of sympathy. How does 'Liza Jane elicit this sympathy? With an old daguerreotype and a sob story.

Cleverly dressed "like a little bit of the old plantation life, summoned up from the past by the wave of a magician's wand," 'Liza Jane arrives at Mr. Ryder's house, gives him a "quaint curtsy," and announces, "'scuse me, suh, I's lookin' for my husban'" (10–11).³ She then proceeds to tell him the most "striking" tale of womanly "fidelity and devotion" that he has ever heard (19). She tells how she was separated from her husband during the final years of slavery. She tells of her futile search for her husband when she "'went back ter de ole home'" after the Civil War. She matter of factly states, "'I's been lookin' fer 'im eber since'" (13). Finally, she pulls the old daguerreotype from beside her bosom and explains that she has been loyally carrying it with her for twenty-five years.

Craftily, 'Liza Jane plays upon Mr. Ryder's sense of guilt. She dwells on the promise Sam made long ago that he would either help her to run away or save up enough money to buy her freedom. She tells how she was whipped and sold downstream when she helped her husband to escape slavery. She asserts that when she visited their old plantation after the war, "'I knowed he'd ben dere to look for me an' hadn' foun' me, an' had gone erway ter hunt fer me.'" She even claims to believe that Sam is still looking for her, unless he is "'sick er sump'n'" ... "'er out'n his head, so he could n' 'member his promise'" (13).

'Liza Jane plays her role of devoted wife to perfection, and Mr. Ryder, with his "air of kindly patronage, "is completely duped (11). He never suspects that her "artless" story is actually a cunning work of invention. When, at his elegant ball, he relates 'Liza Jane's story to his fellow Blue Veins, he remarks, "'There are many who would have searched for a year, some who would have waited five years, a few who might have hoped ten years; but for twenty-five years this woman has retained her affection for and her faith in a man she has not seen or heard of in all that time'" (20). Mr. Ryder pronounces 'Liza Jane's tale the most "'striking'" story of womanly "'fidelity and devotion'" in all of history.

Filled with a fawning reverence for all that is associated with gentility, refinement, and whiteness, Mr. Ryder is not a man to suspect a poor, uncultured, black woman of having the artistic ability to fabricate such a remarkable story. After all, he is a man to be found on an afternoon sitting on his porch with a volume by the estimable Alfred Lord Tennyson, his favorite poet, in hand. Poetry is his passion, and it is to the "great English poets," whose works he has gathered together in his library, that Mr. Ryder turns for romantic inspiration (4).

In fact, Mr. Ryder sits reading some lofty and tidily rhymed lines from "Sir Lancelot and Queen Guinevere," by Tennyson, at the very moment 'Liza Jane appears.

> "She seem'd a part of joyous Spring;
> A gown of green-grass silk she wore,
> Buckled with golden clasps before;
> A light-green tuft of plumes she bore
> Closed in a golden ring ..." [9].

In contrast to elegant Queen Guinevere clad in green and gold, 'Liza Jane wears a calico dress "of ancient cut," an "old-fashioned" brass brooch, and a large bonnet "profusely ornamented with faded red and yellow artificial flowers."

'Liza Jane is the very antithesis of the women "divinely tall" and "divinely fair" with "dainty finger-tips" whom Tennyson and, in turn, Mr. Ryder admire (8–9). Rather than evoking admiration and awe, 'Liza Jane — who is short, dark, and has "withered hands" — elicits smiles "of kindly amusement" (12, 17). But she is wily and secretly powerful.

By story's end, 'Liza Jane's ploy perfectly succeeds. Mr. Ryder, having heard her story of unparalleled devotion and felt the guilty pangs of a delinquent spouse, reclaims her as his wife and introduces her as such to his gathered friends. Though old and grey, shrewd 'Liza Jane wins Mr. Ryder from her rival, the youthful and vivacious Mrs. Molly Dixon. Her days of hard toil as an itinerant cook are officially over.

***

In standard trickster tales, Brer Rabbit or another small, sly animal gains the upper hand over a more powerful foe. For want of superior brawn, the puny trickster uses his superior brains to outsmart his adversary.[44] Beginning in the early 1880s, Joel Chandler Harris popularized trickster tales — and introduced them as a literary genre — through his collections *Uncle Remus: His Songs and His Sayings—The Folklore of the Old Plantation* (1881), *Nights with Uncle Remus: Myths and Legends of the Old Plantation* (1883*)*, *Uncle Remus and His Friends* (1892), and successive volumes. In these collections—which Harris based upon tales told by generations of slaves — an old, former slave named Uncle Remus entertains a little white boy with fables about Brer Rabbit, Brer Fox, and a host of other animals.

Harris well understood the power dynamics implicit in the stories. In the preface to his first volume, *Uncle Remus: His Songs and Sayings,* he acknowledges, "It takes no scientific investigation to show why [the black story-teller] selects as his hero the weakest and most harmless of animals, and brings him out victorious in contests with the bear, the wolf, and the fox. It is not virtue which triumphs but helplessness; it is not malice but mischievousness" (Harris, 57). Eric Sundquist elaborates, "It is plain to every reader, that [Brer Rabbit's] victories over the fox and other stronger animals are motivated by the most transparent aggression and obsequious mocking contempt of the slave for his master" (340). In fact, Brer Rabbit tales are commonly understood as veiled accounts of black slaves triumphing over their white masters. They are protest tales in thin disguise. As Sterling Brown, author of *The Negro in American Fiction,* writes, "Forced to pit his cunning against enemies of greater physical strength, [the trickster] was perhaps a symbol of people who needed craft in order to survive" (Brown, 54). And John W. Roberts further explains in *From Trickster to Badman,* "Like the trickster's dupes who repeatedly fell victim to their own predatory needs and under-estimation of the trickster's ingenuity, the slavemasters often blinded themselves to the potential of enslaved Africans to act in their own best interests by a view of them as grateful partners in the system" (Roberts, 39). Trickster tales, in sum, address an imbalance of power. More specifically, they offer a subversive rebalancing of power.

***

As a trickster, 'Liza Jane is as good as the best of them. She is as wily as dear Brer Rabbit. She devises a cunning fib and succeeds in installing herself in her long-lost husband's plush house, if not exactly in his heart. In one of Joel Chandler Harris's early trickster tales, "Mr. Rabbit Grossly Deceives Mr. Fox," Brer Rabbit fools Brer Fox into giving him a free ride. Likewise, in Chesnutt's story, 'Liza Jane hoodwinks Mr. Ryder into giving her a free ride. She becomes the titular Mrs. Ryder (or "Rider"). But whereas Brer Rabbit's prey usually has sense enough to know when he has been duped, when he has "bin swop off mighty bad," Mr. Ryder is completely unsuspecting (Harris, *Uncle Remus*, 31).

In "The Wife of His Youth," set in the post-slavery era, the pretentious Blue Veins, those men and women "more white than black," have become the darker black men and women's new oppressors (1). The narrator of Chesnutt's story explains, "There were those who had been known to assail [the Blue Vein Society] violently as a glaring example of the very prejudice from which the colored race had suffered most" (2). It is over these new, not-quite-white but proudly blue-veined oppressors that 'Liza Jane triumphs.

The trickster reading of Chesnutt's story is a tale of conquest in which 'Liza Jane bamboozles Mr. Ryder and all his fellow friends of pale skin. "I knew the best way to get around master was to be very humble," wrote the former slave Israel Campbell in his autobiography. "I set my wits to work to find out something that would please him" (Roberts, 40). Similarly, in "The Wife of His Youth" 'Liza Jane draws upon this antebellum tradition of "puttin' on ol' massa." Only in Chesnutt's story, the role of duped master is filled by Mr. Ryder, the "dean of the Blue Veins" (1). 'Liza Jane curtsies to him and addresses him as "'suh,'" and he is "unconsciously flattered by her manner" (11).

If tiny Brer Rabbit, the wily, long-eared prankster, serves as a model of black survival in a hostile white world, 'Liza Jane, a wizened, wrinkled, little woman "not five feet tall," serves as a model for a "very black" woman's survival in the realm of elite mulattoes (9–10). She, like the trickster bunny, is wonderfully devious and single-handedly outwits her adversaries in order to get precisely what she wants. However, it is important to note that, whereas the standard trickster is male, 'Liza Jane is quite obviously female. Thus, in filling the shoes of the wily trickster, she brings a new twist — a new gender — to the role. No "brer" or brother is she.

***

Richard H. Brodhead, the editor of two collections of Chesnutt's writings, wisely cautions, "If Chesnutt's fiction has anything to teach us, it is to beware of one-sided visions of the play of power" (Brodhead, *Conjure Woman*, 18). Indeed, throughout Chesnutt's fiction the "play of power" is intrinsically linked with the dual themes of deviousness and deception. As William L. Andrews, author of *The Literary Career of Charles W. Chesnutt*, notes, "Many of Chesnutt's most memorable heroes are confidence men ... who lead their usually gullible victims 'imperceptibly' and 'unconsciously' to some ironic and unsettling revelation. In the process, the hoaxer's true motives are 'recognized,' while in important ways he is shown to be the equal, often more than a match for his once-superior victim" (Andrews, 15). Clearly, in the trickster reading of "The Wife of His Youth," 'Liza Jane has much in common with these shrewd hoaxers. She successfully bamboozles Mr. Ryder and all of his elitist friends. But did Chesnutt intend for 'The Wife of His Youth" to be read as a trickster tale?

Chesnutt was well familiar with the trickster genre. In fact, he even read Uncle Remus tales to his own children when they were small (Sundquist, 357). Throughout the 1880s and 1890s, Chesnutt worked "against the backdrop of Harris' great popularity," and in 1898 — the same year "The Wife of His Youth" appeared in *The Atlantic*— he completed a collection of his own innovative trickster tales (Sundquist, 357). These stories, published in 1899 as *The Conjure Woman*, feature an old, former slave named Uncle Julius, who bears more than a passing resemblance to Harris's Uncle Remus.

Uncle Julius, like Uncle Remus, is an inveterate storyteller. He entertains the new, Northern owners of the North Carolina plantation on which he once toiled as a slave with "conjure" tales. These tales of the bygone days of slavery are calculated to serve his purposes. He tells the new owners, for example, that certain grapevines are "goophered" because the conjure woman has cast a spell upon them. Then, having convinced the Northern newcomers to steer clear of the hexed vines, he turns a tidy profit on the choice fruit of these old scuppernong vines.

Through the strategic telling of his conjure tales, Uncle Julius guides the new owners to act in accordance with his own interests.[55] His tale-telling serves his ulterior motives. Similarly, in "The Wife of His Youth," 'Liza Jane, who has no legal claim to Mr. Ryder or his property, tells a strategic tale in order to protect her own best interests.

However, Chesnutt nowhere acknowledged his intention that "The Wife of His Youth" could or should be read as a trickster tale. But, then again, he also did not acknowledge that the stories gathered in *The Conjure Woman* could or should be read as trickster tales. Writing for a predominantly white audience, Chesnutt kept mum about the subversive quality of his tales. After all, he wrote at a time when "separate but equal" was the law of the land and when there was blatant prejudice, even within literary circles.[66] As one scholar has noted with regard to *The Conjure Woman*, "Chesnutt faced his vulnerability as a black artist by capitalizing on a popular white literary form [plantation tales], writing within it, and simultaneously subverting and reconstructing the form" (Feinberg, 163). Like his tricksters, Chesnutt was not beyond using a bit of trickery.

***

In the same volume of the *Atlantic Monthly* in which "The Wife of His Youth" first was published, there appeared an unsigned essay titled, "The

Heroine of the Future." It began with an intriguing observation, "The heroine of our choice has always been a more difficult creation than the hero" (139). Heroines, "such as the imagination cherishes," the anonymous essayist lamented, were notably absent from the literature of the day. "Away with the humdrum hackneyed models of the past! Away with the Priscillas of an outworn age!" (141). The essayist called the times "auspicious ... for the maker of heroines" and prophesied that "the development of the heroine will increase the scope of the plot" (140–141).

Ultimately, whether 'Liza Jane is seen as a hindrance or a heroine — a secondary or central character — depends on how readers choose to interpret Chesnutt's tale. 'Liza Jane may be a very dark, very poor woman, but she does not have to be a mere obstacle along the route of a paler, maler character's journey. Rather, the journey can be 'Liza Jane's own. The trickster version of "The Wife of His Youth" provides readers with an opportunity to re-write — or at least re-read — the traditional myth of heroism.

"The Wife of His Youth" can be read as a "marvelously simple" story, but it also can be read as a wonderful, wily, and woman-empowered tale.

NOTES

1. Helen M. Chesnutt, daughter of Charles W. Chesnutt, attributes this quotation to an unidentified reviewer of Chesnutt's work.

2. Charles W. Chesnutt, *The Wife of His Youth and Other Stories of the Color Line* (Michigan: University of Michigan Press, 1972 reprint) xiii. All references to *The Wife of His Youth* are taken from this edition.

3. A certain similarity can be seen between 'Liza Jane's sartorial ruse and Hannibal's in Chesnutt's story "Hot Foot-Hannibal." Hannibal dresses in disguise in that story in order to dupe two other slaves. Afterwards, he explains, "'En den I put on a frock en a sun-bonnet, en fix' myse'f up ter look lack a 'woman'" (Chesnutt, *The Conjure Woman*, 117).

4. Henry Louis Gates, Jr., in *The Signifying Monkey*, and Roger D. Abrahams, in *Deep Down in the Jungle*, both have written about another famous African American trickster figure, the "Signifying Monkey." Of this monkey Abrahams writes, "His existence depends upon his agility, mental and physical.... He is not only a clever hero, smaller and weaker and a diminutive animal but his adventures with the lion qualifies him as a rogue" (143). Abrahams discusses the way in which this "signifying" hero uses words and gestures to create a language of trickery and utilizes a "technique of indirect argument or persuasion" (52).

5. Lorne Fienberg's "Charles W. Chesnutt and Uncle Julius: Black Storytellers at the Crossroads" offers an interesting analysis of the gains Uncle Julius makes by "offering his tales in the verbal marketplace." Fienberg concludes that Julius, as well as Chesnutt, cannot escape "the perils" that go along with the "exhilaration" of having "a dynamic relationship with their white audiences" (172).

6. One reviewer of *The Wife of His Youth*, for example, opined, "To an ordinary thinker the only happy solution of the problem [of the color line] could be a rigid enforcement of the law forbidding miscegenation. The influence of a negro ancestor may be traced to the twelfth generation, but the same is not true of a white ancestor in a negro's family tree. Union must hence mean deterioration of some sort of the white race." "Some of the Latest Publications," *The Bulletin* [San Francisco], 10 Dec 1899: 23. Another critic commented, "These short stories demonstrate the fact that much sorrow and needless suffering has been caused by the withdrawal of the 'Color line,' and the mingling of the races." "New Books," *The Burlington Hawk-Eye*, 1 Dec. 1899, 4.

WORKS CITED

Abrahams, Roger D. *Deep Down in the Jungle: Negro Narrative Folklore from the Streets of Philadelphia*. Chicago: Aldine Publishing Co., 1970.

Andrews, William L. *The Literary Career of Charles W. Chesnutt*. Baton Rouge: Louisiana State University Press, 1980.

_____. *The Journals of Charles W. Chesnutt*. Durham: Duke University Press, 1993.

Brown, Sterling. *The Negro in American Fiction*. New York: Kennikat Press, 1968.

Carby, Hazel V. *Reconstructing Womanhood*. New York: Oxford University Press, 1987.

Chesnutt, Charles W. *The Conjure Woman*. Boston: Houghton, Mifflin & Co., 1899.

_____. *The Conjure Woman and Other Conjure Tales*. Edited by Richard H. Brodhead. Durham: Duke University Press, 1993.

_____. *The Wife of His Youth and Other Stories of the Color Line*. Introduction by Earl Schenck Miers. Ann Arbor: University of Michigan Press, 1972.

Chesnutt, Helen M. *Charles Waddell Chesnutt: Pioneer of the Color Line*. Chapel Hill: University of North Carolina Press, 1952.

Du Bois, W.E.B. "The Talented Tenth." In *The Negro Problem: A Series of Articles by Representative Negroes of To-day*. New York: J. Pott & Co., 1903.

Fienberg, Lorne. "Charles W. Chesnutt and Uncle Julius: Black Storytellers at the Crossroads." *Studies in American Fiction* 15 (1987): 161–173.

_____. "Charles W. Chesnutt's The Wife of His Youth: The Unveiling of the Black Storyteller." *American Transcendental Quarterly* 4 (1990): 219–237.

Gates, Henry Louis Jr. *The Signifying Monkey: A Theory of African-American Literary Criticism*. New York: Oxford University Press, 1989.

Harris, Joel Chandler. *Uncle Remus*. Atlanta: Cherokee Publishing Company, 1981.

_____. *Uncle Remus: His Songs and Sayings*. New York: Penguin Books, 1982.

Heermance, J. Noel. *Charles W. Chesnutt*. Connecticut: Archon Books, 1974.

"The *Heroine of the Future*," Atlantic Monthly, June 1898: 139–141.

"New Books," *The Burlington Hawk-Eye*, 1 December 1899: 4.

Pearson, Carol and Katherine Pope. *The Female Hero*. New York: R.R. Bowker Company, 1981.

Render, Sylvia Lyons. *Charles W. Chesnutt*. Boston: Twayne Publishers, 1980.

Roberts, John W. *From Trickster to Badman*. Philadelphia: University of Pennsylvania Press, 1989.

"Some of the Latest Publications." *The Bulletin* [San Francisco], 10 December 1899: 23.

Sundquist, Eric J. *To Wake the Nations*. Cambridge, Mass.: The Belknap Press, 1993.

CHAPTER 12

With Myriad Subtleties: Recognizing an Africanist Presence in Charles W. Chesnutt's *The Conjure Woman*

Tiel Lundy

"I think," Charles W. Chesnutt wrote in May of 1880, "I must write a book." He would, in fact, go on to publish six books, seven poems, well over a score of short stories, and a number of essays and articles.[1] But it would be his "conjure" stories that would catapult him into the high-culture literary society of William Dean Howells and his ilk. Imbued with tales of voodoo, animism, the exploits of both conjure man and woman, and black resistance to white oppression, *The Conjure Woman* (1899) reveals how the retentions of African folklore and religion continued to shape African American slave culture.

Curiously, though, little of the scholarship has examined the influence of African socio-religious values in the work, a mystifying omission given the collection's title. Viewing the collection through the lens of Western capitalist economics, scholars have focused on the collection's main storyteller, Julius McAdoo, a former slave still residing on the old plantation, who, in a repeated pattern of tricksterism, appears to win certain material advantages over the plantation's new owners.

While this interpretive strategy has been useful in revealing how Chesnutt's text reflects the metastasizing capitalist economy of the post–Reconstruction era, it has blinded critics to an alternative reading, one that acknowledges an Africanist presence at work. The goal of this essay is to complicate the many readings of the collection that have accounted for Julius's motives in primarily self-serving economic terms, suggesting instead that Julius's actions can be better understood as the confluence of both nineteenth-century American capitalism and an ancient African-originated cosmology that stresses community and kinship bonds. To this end, I explore how the collection repeatedly pits communal needs against nineteenth-century property rights. As a corrective to the economic and philosophical ideology that not only failed African Americans but served to subjugate them, Chesnutt subtly integrates Africanist cosmology, thus relocating moral authority and power in communal relations.

***

Toni Morrison and Henry Louis Gates, Jr., among others, have made invaluable contributions to African American literary theory. In *Playing in the Dark* (1992) Morrison explores the "dark, abiding, signing Africanist presence" that is unmistakably present in American literature — in spite of previous generations of literary critics who steadfastly denied such a presence (5). Gates, too, challenged the literary establishment when he claimed, in his work *The Signifying Monkey* (1988), that a black tradition, coming out of African, Caribbean, and African American literatures, is inscribed on our national literature. As a consequence, black literary texts "are double-voiced in the sense that their literary antecedents are both white and black novels, but also modes of figuration lifted from the black vernacular tradition" (Gates, xxiii).

Indeed, this description should sound familiar to readers of *The Conjure Woman*, which is itself about the discursive interplay of black and white voices. Gates, however, is surprisingly laconic on the subject of Chesnutt, dedicating just three pages to the writer. In short, he argues that Chesnutt denied the contributions of his African American literary antecedents so that he could claim the status of being the first legitimate African American novelist.[2] Employing a biting irony, Gates writes that Chesnutt's "great preoccupation" to be the first African American to publish a novel or collection of short stories required him to wipe "the slate of black authors clean so that he could inscribe his name, and inherently the name of the race, upon it" (115, 117).[3]

While Chesnutt may not have consciously acknowledged the black American writers that came before him, he certainly did incorporate black oral culture, reaching as far back as the socio-religious practices of Africans and, later, African Americans. As John W. Roberts convincingly illustrates, Africans enslaved in America held onto their religious beliefs in spite of the hostile conditions slavery imposed upon them; and Albert J. Raboteau suggests that enslaved Africans in America, while hardly homogeneous, shared enough of the social and religious principles deriving from West Africa to allow us to make some generalizations about their religious heritage.[4] More specifically, one can assertion that Chesnutt's collection reflects African religion's emphasis on community, a theme that, while explored in general by a number of scholars, is enriched by a more specific cultural contextualization.

Chesnutt's journals, written from the time he was sixteen years old to twenty-four years old, have led some scholars to focus on his gushing admiration for white writers like Thackeray and Dickens. *Vanity Fair* elicits this response from the twenty-two-year-old Chesnutt: "Every time I read a good novel, I want to write one. It is the dream of my life — to be an author!" (*Journals*, 154). And few authors at the time were more successful than Albion W. Tourgee, whose novel *A Fool's Errand* (1879) was a bestseller for several years and was one of the inspirations for Chesnutt's own writing career.[5] To Chesnutt, Tourgee's novel was inspirational both for its lofty ideals and for the door it opened onto the emerging writer's own imagination and the imagination of the reading public. He writes:

> And if Judge Tourgee, with his necessarily limited intercourse with colored people, and with his limited stay in the South, can write such interesting descriptions, such vivid pictures of Southern life and character as to make himself rich and famous, why could not a colored man, who has lived among colored people all his life —... why could not such a man, if he possessed the same ability, write a far better book about the South than Judge Tourgee or Mrs. Stowe has written? Answer who can! But the man is yet to make his appearance; and if I can't be the man I shall be the first to rejoice at his *debut* and give God speed! to his work [*Journals*, 125–6].

Although the young Chesnutt's journal entries do suggest a desire to distance himself from the working-class African American folk — at eighteen, he derided them as "the most bigoted, superstitious, hardest headed people in the world" (*Journals*, 81) — we know that by the time he saw *The Conjure Woman* published in 1899, he was beginning to recognize African and African American oral cultures as essential spiritual and creative parts of his own authorial identity. "There are many things about the Colored people," he writes in March of 1880, "which are peculiar, to some extent, to them, and which are interesting to any thoughtful observer, and would be doubly interesting to people who know little about them" (*Journals*, 126). In his 1901 essay entitled "Superstitions & Folklore of the South,"[6] Chesnutt explains that the word "goopher" — that is conjure or magic — was in common usage in parts of the American South. "The origin of this curious superstition itself," Chesnutt writes, "probably grew, in the first place, out of African fetishism, which was brought over from the dark continent along with the dark people."[7] Postcolonial critic Ellen J. Goldner also detects in Chesnutt's fiction an Africanist presence; she contends that the stories "forge imaginative links between Chesnutt and colonized peoples, especially in Africa" (41).

What one can demonstrate here is that Africa and its diasporic peoples were very much a part of Chesnutt's thinking, and in time he came to see their influence as an inexpugnable part not only of his own identity but of America's cultural identity as well. While it is beyond the scope of this essay to explore fully the complicated, and often vexed, relationships among personal, authorial, and national identities, we can say with some confidence that Chesnutt's sense of self evolved over time, and he eventually embraced the many artifacts of African and African American religion and storytelling that, by his own account, he had acquired from "old Aunt This or old Uncle That," incorporating them into his fiction ("Superstitions," 372). This is not to ignore the writer's ambivalence concerning his way out of the working-class black community and into the literary community to which he aspired. Richard H. Brodhead writes that Chesnutt's "coming to an appreciation of this local ethos is inseparable from the process by which he strives to secure a life apart from that ethos — a life in the inevitably distant, different world of successful authors" (*Journals*, 25) Similarly, Ralph Ellison's words remind us that revisions to African American literature bring into play "the Negro writer's complicated assertions and denials of identity" (408).[8] In a negotiative, dynamic fashion, Chesnutt's own authorial identity evolved over time to include both black and white storytelling traditions, just as his fiction likewise matured to convey the author's vision of a polyphonous America that recognized its African past.

***

The Conjure Woman opens with the encounter between the new plantation owners, John and Annie, Northerners who have come to the South for the salubrious effects of the southern climate on Annie's fragile health and for the economic opportunities afforded by the post–Reconstruction economy, and Uncle Julius, whose long-time connection to the property has made him the repository of a vast collection of stories about the land. So much an organic part of the plantation is he, by virtue of both his long personal history with it and the custodial regard for its natural resources that Julius appears to be as tied to it as he was before Emancipation. When the couple first encounters him sitting on a fallen log and eating the scuppernong grapes with relish, they learn that he was "'bawn en raise' on dis yer same plantation'" (34).

Signifying on the Joel Chandler Harris "Uncle Remus" stories, each tale begins with what Barbara Herrnstein Smith has called "Storytime," in which John and Annie demand, in childlike fashion, that Julius entertain them with a story.[9] However, Julius's stories are hardly children's fare, and John and Annie learn along the way about the sorrows that continue to haunt the property they have purchased, for with few exceptions, Julius's tales are sad ones. In an important departure from Uncle Remus's jocular beast fables, Uncle Julius's tales have a decidedly morbid pattern, with exploitation, physical and emotional suffering, and death as their central features.

Structured by interactive narrative frames — John's external framing narrative takes place some time after Reconstruction, and Julius's internal framed stories take place during the days of slavery — *The Conjure Woman* delivers an almost undeviating storytelling formula. The two temporal frames interact dynamically throughout the collection as Julius's antebellum tales are usually prompted by some event or topic of conversation that is reminiscent of the time before the war. The implications of this interactive relationship between past and present are twofold. First, by repeatedly going back in time to the days before the war, Julius is able to remind his audience that slavery's past is never far away and continues to make itself felt. One recurring theme in the stories, then, is the persistent presence of slavery, an institution whose effects continue to ripple outward, disrupting the placid surface of the present. Second, by insinuating his own narrative into the discourse, Julius subtly wrests authorial control from John. Though John's narrative may appear to contain Julius's through the structure of the frame, it is the subject of Julius's stories — namely, slavery — that ultimately dictates the larger narrative.

Throughout most of the collection, John and Julius's relationship is characterized by an outward display of *bon ami*, but this politeness belies a subtle power struggle between the plantation owner and former slave. The specific aspect of this relationship that will be focused on is the revelation at the end of the outside narrative that Julius's conjure tale may or may not be totally unmotivated. In a repeated pattern comical for its predictability, nearly every story ends with John's irritable conclusion that he himself has been conjured through Julius's glib storytelling.

Contending that Julius maintains the ulterior motive of procuring various material goods — grapes, honey, a new suit, to name a few — more than one scholar has commented on the pecuniary value of his stories. Brodhead says that "Julius is trying to protect his economic interests through his storytelling" (Introduction, 10), and Lorne Fienberg says that Julius's "words are commodities he can offer in exchange for employment for himself and his relatives and for the continued security of remaining on the land" (166). Houston A. Baker, Jr., in arguing that Chesnutt's depiction of the female conjurer's power pales in comparison to Zora Neal Hurston's depiction in *Mules and Men*, says that Julius's "telling of the 'work' of Aunt Peggy is, like the conjure woman's work itself, designed to influence the economy of *his* situation. His telling of the work is meant to gain ... clearly male material benefits" (78).[10]

If much of the scholarship has focused on Julius's apparent gains, it is because the narrative outcomes of the stories themselves seem to validate John's reading of things. As the narrator of the framed story, John almost always gets the last word, inviting the reader to believe him when he suggests that Julius has finagled some material item out of him. And indeed, our pleasure lies in witnessing Julius, time and again, subvert and revise an economic system that had victimized black Americans for so long. But close examination of precisely what it is Julius gains, and the uses to which he puts these gains, reveals "with myriad subtleties," to use Paul Laurence Dunbar's words, another system at work, one that challenges John's (and the implied reader's) individualistic, capitalistic paradigm.[11]

In "The Goophered Grapevine," when John acknowledges that he is considering purchasing and cultivating the long-abandoned vineyard, Julius warns him off, saying that the vines are cursed, or "goophered." As he (John) doesn't know which ones are safe and which ones are not, any attempt to re-cultivate the vineyard could be dangerous. So as to impress John with the eminent dangers of the vineyard, Julius then tells the story of a plantation master who, tired of having his lucrative crop eaten by his slaves, enlists the help of conjure woman Aun' Peggy to protect the grapes using her magic, a magic so powerful it results in the deaths of two unfortunates who eat the grapes in ignorance of the curse. At the end of story John discovers that Julius's cabin lies not far off from the vineyard and that he has "derived a respectable revenue from the product of the neglected grapevines" (43). As the opening story in the collection, "The Goophered Grapevine" sets up this formula whereby Julius appears to have some profit motive that casts into doubt the innocence of his stories.

Note, however, that such an ulterior motive is ascribed by John, not Chesnutt; since John's reliability as a narrator is suspect and frequently serves to illustrate, ironically, Chesnutt's rhetorical position, his assertions that Julius's motives are necessarily self-serving are at least questionable. In "The Gray Wolf's Ha'nt," John concludes that Julius's repeated attempts to dissuade him from cultivating a particular plot of land are motivated by his desire to maintain his "monopoly" over the honey that comes from a tree on the land. John's suspicions, however, are merely that and are not confirmed in any way through the narrative as the reader never witnesses Julius going to the honey tree. Similarly, in "The Conjurer's Revenge," John believes that Julius has conned him into buying a lame horse and pocketed his share of the profit from a deal he worked out with the horse's owner, the "proof" of which is Julius showing up next day in a new suit that he had earlier admired. But, as the framing narrative underscores, John has based his suspicions on nothing but circumstantial evidence, something that is often misleading. The horse itself illustrates the fallibility of the eyes and their propensity for misjudging appearances, for as fine and strong as it first appears, it turns out to be mostly blind, host to a multitude of diseases, and is dead inside of three months. "But alas for the deceitfulness of appearances!" John laments (80). The reliability of the eyes is again called into question within the story when Julius, taking issue with a young man's claim that the earth orbits the sun, and not, as Julius believes, the other way around, says, "'I sees de yeath stan'in' still all de time, en I sees de sun gwine roun' it, en ef a man can't b'lieve w'at 'e sees, I can't see no use in libbin'—mought's well die en be whar we can't see nuffin'" (79). Julius himself has cast into doubt the reliability of appearances. By extension, then, those circumstances that merely appear to confirm Julius's ulterior motives must be questioned.

Admittedly, Julius does act the trickster, gently manipulating his audience by way of his story and often capitalizing on their sympathies. Worth distinguishing, however, is that between what Julius actually gains and what John *thinks* he gains. Because John himself is always keenly aware of the economic gains to be made, he assumes the same of Julius. In the case of "The Goophered Grapevine," Julius's interest in the grapevines is of a limited, personal nature; that is, he wants the grapes only so that he may continue to enjoy their goodness himself and sell what he needs to make a respectable living—unlike John, whose capitalist instincts are to cultivate and harvest on a much larger commercial scale. And at the conclusion of "Po' Sandy," Julius has secured the use of the schoolhouse for his newly formed temperance church group and obtained a donation for the church from Annie—hardly a windfall as personal gains go. Similarly, through the story of "Mars Jeems's Nightmare," Julius persuades Annie to re-hire his malingering grandson, much to her husband's disapproval. At most, Julius seems to be guilty of an innocuous nepotism here. Thus, the pattern that emerges is one in which we question the extent to which Julius is guilty of perpetrating a scam in order to benefit, a question provoked by John's sour-grapes conviction that he has been taken in by a confidence man.

For most of the stories Julius's intentions remain largely incomprehensible to John because the two men come from vastly different worlds, and they possess entirely different ethoses; thus, their encounters are repeatedly characterized by misunderstood motives. Acknowledging this philosophical gulf, John says that Julius's "way of looking at the past seemed very strange to us; his view of certain sides of life was essentially different from ours" ("Dave's Neckliss," 124). Julius, who is a product of the West African–originated slave culture, knows implicitly what John S. Mbiti says is the source of peace and social order. "Where the sense of corporate life is so deep," Mbiti says, "it is inevitable that the solidarity of the community must be maintained, otherwise there is disintegration and destruction" (200). In such a society that is based on kinship relations "a person cannot be individualistic, but only corporate" (Mbiti, 204). John and Annie's purchase of the plantation, a plot of land far removed from the society of their white urban friends, suggests that they have fled society in search of quiet isolation; what they discover, however, is the long-established society of the plantation culture, one that will slowly pull them in. In contrast to their isolationist proclivities, Julius is a fully integrated part of his community, as evidenced by his peripherally present family relatives, his active role in his Baptist church, and his acquaintance with virtually all the neighbors of the surrounding area. Even his relationship with his employers illustrates Julius's tendency to reach out to others, for in most every situation he has come to them rather than vice versa. Unlike John and Annie, who have been trained to regard individualism as the apex of human values, Julius believes in a community-based cosmology, one that is entirely alien to his Northern white employers.

Once again, we see the collision of two seemingly divergent worldviews — one ostensibly "Western" and the other originating in African socio-religious traditions. A close reading of the stories reveals that Julius, while undoubtedly a participant in the tacit *quid pro quo* relationship with John, ultimately ends up winning a thing of limited or no monetary value, and rather gaining something that will benefit the larger community. Illustrating the importance of the African tradition that informs these tales, a tradition that values the corporate over the individual, Julius's material "wins," if they may be called that, are communal in nature: gainful employment for a relative ("Mars Jeems's Nightmare" and "Lonesome Ben"); a meeting place and support for his church group ("Po' Sandy"); Annie's return to health ("Sis' Becky's Pickaninny"); and the reunion of a feuding couple ("Hot-Foot Hannibal").[12] The more abstract win is the change he is able to effect in his employers' minds (and by extension, the reader's mind), for over time, he will teach them the values of community, forgiveness, and generosity. Thus we see the convergence, if tenuous, of two men and two cultures.

However altruistic Julius's motives may be, though, one can never forget that there is a capitalist system at work in the stories. What Julius and John's tug-of-war most significantly demonstrates is the ever-present tension between a humanistic value system and the capitalist marketplace that had become ascendant in postbellum society. Brodhead illustrates the dominance of the capitalist economy by observing that Julius "is always winning little advantages," but his gains are made "within an order that stays under someone else's control, and his very need to extract concessions repeatedly testifies to the fact that someone else is in charge" (Introduction, 11). Thus, Julius may be the means by which Chesnutt defines an alternative, ideal cosmology in which human relations are privileged over profit-making, but he is still compelled to act within the rules of capitalism, the system of which John is representative.

Often the internal framed stories reflect on the antebellum greed that allowed for the quantification of human life. In "The Goophered Grapevine," plantation owner Dugal McAdoo shrewdly discovers that Henry, his field hand, is worth more to him in terms of resale value than he is working the fields, thanks to Aun' Peggy's goophering, which mirrors in him the annual cycle of the grape vines. So thoroughly immersed in this mindset of the economics of human life is he, that McAdoo, in revenge upon a Yankee carpetbagger whose new agricultural techniques have resulted in the total loss of McAdoo's vines — and, consequently, Henry's slow death — sets off for the war wanting "'ter kill a Yankee for eve'y dollar he los' 'long er dat grape-raisin' Yankee'" (43). Human life is similarly appraised in "Sis Becky's Pickaninny," which begins with the sale of Becky's husband to pay for the dead master's gambling debts. "Po' Sandy" also demonstrates the monetary evaluation of human life and the common practice of breaking up slave families; when Sandy's wife is traded to a speculator for another woman, Mars Marrabo compensates him for his loss with the payment of a dollar. Following Sandy's grisly end in the sawmill — a death made no less disturbing by the fact that he has been transformed into a tree — his body continues to serve the master: as yet another capital resource — in this case, lumber — Sandy is used to build the master's new kitchen, which his ghost will continue to haunt.

Chesnutt will not let his reader forget the human toll of slavery, and its victims' ghosts inhabit several of the stories. In "The Gray Wolf's Ha'nt," Mahaly and Dan's spirits inhabit the plantation's low grounds, "'en eve'body w'at goes 'bout dere has some bad luck er 'nuther'" (105); "Dave's Neckliss" uses the specter of Dave's punishment by embodying it in the Sunday ham. Walter Benn Michaels contends that "haunted-house stories ... usually involve some form of anxiety about ownership" (89). Always present in antebellum America was the question of the legitimacy of the slave owner's right to hold title over another human being.[13] But, as *The Conjure Woman*'s external framing narrative illustrates, anxieties about ownership extended well beyond the antebellum and into the postwar period. Slavery having been outlawed, many freedmen and women saw freedom as commensurate with property ownership. Loren Schweninger poignantly states that "no Americans better understood the meaning of owning property than those who had been considered a 'species of property' themselves" (144). Predictably, though, white landowners responded by erecting various obstacles intended to prevent African American property ownership; they might band together and collectively refuse to sell land to blacks, or they might use physical intimidation and violence to discourage blacks from attempting to purchase land.[14]

Though John hardly reflects this level of hostility, he does betray a hint of protectiveness regarding his real estate: "Toward my tract of land and the things that were on it — the creeks, the swamps, the hills, the meadows, the stones, the trees — [Julius] maintained a peculiar personal attitude that might be called predial rather than proprietary" (55). John's need to assert his ownership of the land, along with a catalogue of its natural attributes, suggests a latent insecurity on his part about the legitimacy of his claim to a property that more truthfully belongs to Julius. While over the course of the stories John and Annie seem to regard Julius as an eccentric inheritance that has come with the property, Julius's experience and knowledge of the plantation's history make it clear that, if anything, they are *his* inheritance.

***

Although John remains cynical and fails to understand what motivates Julius in the absence of profit, by the end of the original collection he has shown some, albeit limited, progress in coming to understand Julius's motives and the latent meanings within his stories. Julia B. Farwell gets to the heart of the tales, explaining that "Julius is forming a community within which the conjure work of the story is both a creative agent and an invitation to the listener to join" (80). By the time we reach the final story in the original collection, she maintains, Julius's stories have begun to serve their integrative purpose, for John and Annie, as well as the reader, appear to be on the way to a more complete understanding of the history of slavery and the worldview that dictates Julius's actions.

Unfortunately, Farwell's essay does not acknowledge the eight so-called "Related Tales" that Chesnutt wrote but Houghton Mifflin refused to include with the collection. Of no little importance, then, is Brodhead's revised edition including the other tales, for these form a more complete whole, demonstrating John's own education and conversion from a strictly self-interested capitalist and skeptic, to one who has come to see a larger sense of community and even perhaps a world beyond his own Enlightenment education. One must underscore the significance of Brodhead's editorial contribution because it allows us to pick up where Farwell left off: that is, the beginning-to-end progression of the complete collection unambiguously demonstrates John and Annie's education about the plantation's ignominious past that necessarily prefigures their eventual integration into the community.

"The Dumb Witness" and "The Victim of Heredity" both provide powerful illustrations of this integration. In an important departure from the formula whereby Julius tells the tale, the story "The Dumb Witness" is the only tale in the collection narrated entirely by John. Of particular relevance is the way in which this authorial swap illustrates John's moral and educational conversion since, as the narrator, he has become a part of Julius's criticism of white oppression and can tell its story.[15] Another of the related conjure stories, "A Victim of Heredity; or, Why the Darkey Loves Chicken," enacts in the space of only two pages part of John's moral evolution as he comes to adopt, if not a spirit of forgiveness, then one of greater leniency. In a comical internal monologue that highlights John's initial reaction as representative of an oppressive white "justice," he gradually amends his proposed punishment for a Negro chicken thief from an absurdly severe five years in the penitentiary to two, then to one, and eventually to six months in the local jail. In spite of the knowledge that the thief has a large family to support and has been subsisting on various odd jobs, John rationalizes his decision to prosecute, saying that "any false sentiment on [his] part would be dangerous to social order; and that property must be protected" (173). For John, then, the preservation of social order is predicated on the protection of one (white) man's property rights rather than the assurance of another (black) man's right to feed and clothe his family.

In the end it is Annie, who, "thinking more or less about the influence of heredity and environment, and the degree of our responsibility for the things we do," asks Julius to free the thief and sends the arresting officer home with the assurance that John will pay for his time lost (182).[16] Annie's thoughtful response to the story of "The Victim of Heredity" illustrates her own moral education by Julius's philosophy, one that points to the immorality of an economy founded on human exploitation.

As the first of the stories render John a cynic and a skeptic, one who can see only charming "fairy tales" in Julius's stories, the later tales in the complete collection illustrate John's gradual appreciation for the stories as both literary assets in their own right as well as truthful accounts of slavery's past. John writes that Julius's tales inspired him "to speculate at times upon how many original minds, which might have added to the world's wealth of literature and art, had been buried in the ocean of slavery" ("Lonesome Ben," 148–9). Moreover, not only does John come to a better understanding of Julius's motives as a storyteller, but perhaps he develops a more complete awareness of his own role in the narrator/narratee relationship, for it is in the simple act of listening that John is responsible for the exhumation of Julius's narrative gifts.

While John and Annie's gradual assimilation into the communal life of the plantation reflects Africanist cosmological values, the issue of property ownership cannot be so easily dispensed with. The stories themselves, through the often competing, sometimes complementary, and always interactive storytelling frames of Julius and John, ask us to consider the tellers' claims to truth and authenticity. Indeed, Julius's conjure stories represent a form of currency in the complicated barter economy he has established with his employers; put another way, they represent his property right. Having told his tales to John and Annie, however, he is turning over to the couple responsibility for the stories. If they are to own the plantation property, then they must also take ownership of the telling of the horrors perpetrated on the plantation, for as Julius sums up, "'It's all in de tale'" (110).

"The Marked Tree," the final story in the complete collection, represents John's ultimate conversion to an alternative belief system. Now a believer in the "'monst'us pow'ful'" goopher that has rendered an old oak tree the site and source of a dark and terrible but just power, John takes the final drastic steps to remove the tree once and for all with the use of explosives. That John has not merely dug up the sinister stump but has blown it to a hundred tiny pieces illustrates the sincerity of his belief in the power of conjure, a power he once scorned. The unsuspecting student of Julius's many tales, John has finally come to believe in the validity of a world beyond his own empirical understanding, one that asserts the primacy of human relations and needs.

Ultimately, John and Annie are integrated into the plantation community, but it must be through the discursive power of the double-voiced conjure stories, stories which require of the couple an acknowledgment of the powers of conjure and community that had previously challenged their Western ideology. As the couple gradually comes to recognize an alternative moral order, so too does Chesnutt himself come to appreciate the value of an African folklore tradition and the African American community that preserved this literary heritage. Thus, as the relationship between the white Northern landowners and black former slave illustrates the collision and eventual convergence of cultural beliefs, likewise Chesnutt's authorial evolution demonstrates the complicated reconciliation of his competing desires to at once distance himself from the African American community and claim his place within it.

NOTES

1. Andrews, *Chesnutt* Bibliography, 279–86.
2. Chesnutt's daughter and biographer, Helen M. Chesnutt, writes, "No great publishing house in the country, as far as he knew, had ever published a volume of stories or a novel written by a colored man, although Paul Laurence Dunbar had published some poems" (quoted in Gates, 115). There was in fact a black novelist who came before Chesnutt, William Wells Brown, whose novel *Clotel; or, The President's Daughter: A Narrative of Slave Life in the United States* (1853) is likely the first African American novel. In 1881 Chesnutt read one of Brown's later novels entitled *The Negro in the American Rebellion, His Heroism and His Fidelity* (1867), but quickly dismissed it on what seem to be aesthetic grounds, saying, "Dr. Brown's books are mere compilations and if they were not written by a colored man, they would not sell for enough to pay for the printing." Helen M. Chesnutt (28).
3. Gates accuses Chesnutt of "determining that no Negro before him could dress language suitably to move the text of himself from the cabin to the Big House of Western literature" (117).
4. See Chapter 3 in Roberts; see also Raboteau, 7.
5. Tourgee went on to play a central role in the drama of *Plessy v. Ferguson*. See Sundquist, 233–49; and Lofgren, *The Plessy Case: A Legal-Historical Interpretation*.
6. Originally published in *Modern Culture* and reprinted in Alan Dundes's collection.
7. For more information on the derivation of the word "goopher," see Dundes's footnote, 371.
8. Quoted in Gates, 117.

9. Smith, 127. Lorne Fienberg examines the power relations in the storytelling relationship: "In requesting a story, the child surrenders authority to a teller who commands the floor, who knows the tale, and who can manipulate its details and its listeners at will.... But the listening child has powers as well: the power to demand a story that is engaging and imaginative; the right to bestow approval or disapproval at the conclusion. Children like stories that contain appropriate morals, but they only occasionally demand that a story be 'true'" (161).

10. While the majority of scholars have focused on Julius's material gains, there are some notable exceptions. Charles Duncan comes closer to articulating what I see as the central feature of John and Julius's tug-of-war-like relationship. "The two narrators," he writes, "do engage in a sort of commerce with one another, but the nature of that engagement seems ... more complicated than matters of mere financial profit and loss." Ultimately, argues Duncan, "as a rubric or motif, economics proves a less-than-consistent key to these works" (86). I also appreciate David D. Britt's perceptive reading of the stories. Noting that Julius is "singularly unsuccessful as a hustler" and gains only "picayune amounts of cash," Britt says that "Julius's tales are not aimed at manipulating John in the way the surface narrative implies. They should be seen as elaborate metaphors, allegories really, in which the supernatural elements point toward those dread realities of the slave's life that lie beyond the comprehension of the ruling class" (362).

11. From Paul Laurence Dunbar's 1895 poem "We Wear the Mask."

12. Richard H. Brodhead comments on the importance of community to middle-class African Americans like Chesnutt, saying that the "incipient black professional class of this time differed from its white social cognate in its inevitably heavy consciousness of its race's social plight and in its linking of individual achievement with duty toward its race" (*Cultures of Letters*, 195).

13. Abolitionist William Goodell wrote that in some states, such as Louisiana, slaves were regarded as "real estate" because they were "attached to the soil they cultivate, partaking therewith all the restraints upon voluntary alienation to which the possessor of the *land* is liable, and they cannot be seized or sold by creditors for the satisfaction of the debts of the owner." Quoted in Michaels, 93–4.

14. Schweninger, 145–6. For a full study of black property ownership in the nineteenth century, see Ch. 5, "Property Ownership Among Southern Blacks, 1860–1915" in Schweninger, 143–84.

15. See Robert B. Stepto's "'The Simple but Intensely Human Inner Life of Slavery': Storytelling and the Revision of History in Charles W. Chesnutt's 'Uncle Julius Stories,'" 29–55. Stepto makes a persuasive argument for the representative value of John's act as narrator, but I believe there is still another way of interpreting this story: I read the story less in terms of John's telling the tale and more in terms of Julius's not telling it. The only story told entirely by John, "The Dumb Witness," illustrates how literacy is the one thing Julius has not managed to acquire. A product of oral culture, Julius tells his stories, many of which have been told to him, in keeping with this oral tradition. Because much of "The Dumb Witness" depends upon the retelling of the lengthy history of the Murchison family, a written history that John traces back to the American Revolution, Julius's illiteracy effectively renders him "dumb" since he cannot tell the stories that come out of the history books or the family journals. The roles of storyteller and audience reversed, Julius must turn over to John the authorial status he has enjoyed and instead be a witness to John's telling. Thus the theme of literacy is made all the more evident as part of both the framing and the framed narratives. While Chesnutt's collection is an homage to the rich oral tradition of the slave culture that inspired it, "The Dumb Witness" plainly asserts its author's belief in the importance of literacy.

16. Turn-of-the-nineteenth-century readers no doubt would have seen the reference to Charles Darwin's 1859 *On the Origin of Species*. Chesnutt is plainly using the idea of heredity here in ironic fashion, suggesting that just as a liking for chicken is hardly a genetic trait of African Americans, neither is a propensity for theft.

WORKS CITED

Andrews, William L. *The Literary Career of Charles W. Chesnutt*. Baton Rouge: Louisiana State University Press, 1980.

Baker, Houston A., Jr. *Workings of the Spirit: The Poetics of Afro-American Women's Writing*. Chicago: The University of Chicago Press, 1991.

Britt, David D. "Chesnutt's Conjure Tales: What You See Is What You Get." In *Charles W. Chesnutt: Selected Writings*. Edited by SallyAnn H. Ferguson. Boston: Houghton Mifflin Company, 2001.

Brodhead, Richard H. *Cultures of Letters: Scenes of Reading and Writing in Nineteenth-Century America*. Chicago: University of Chicago Press, 1993.

Chesnutt, Charles W. *The Conjure Woman, and Other Conjure Tales*. Edited and introduction by Richard H. Brodhead. Durham: Duke University Press, 1993.

_____. *The Journals of Charles W. Chesnutt*. Edited by Richard H. Brodhead. Durham: Duke University Press, 1993.

_____. "Superstitions and Folklore of the South." In *Mother Wit From the Laughing Barrel: Readings in the Interpretation of Afro-American Folklore*. Edited by Alan Dundes. Jackson: University Press of Mississippi, 1990.

Chesnutt, Helen M. *Charles Waddell Chesnutt: Pioneer of the Color Line*. Chapel Hill: University of North Carolina Press, 1952.

Darwin, Charles. *On the Origin of Species*. London: John Murray, 1859.

Dunbar, Paul Laurence. "We Wear the Mask." *The Complete Poems of Paul Laurence Dunbar*. New York: Dodd, Mead, 1917.

Duncan, Charles. *The Absent Man: The Narrative Craft of Charles W. Chesnutt*. Athens, Ohio: Ohio University Press, 1998.

Dundes, Alan. *Mother Wit From the Laughing Barrel: Readings in the Interpretation of Afro-American Folklore*. Jackson: University Press of Mississippi, 1990.

Ellison, Ralph. "Remarks at the American Academy Conference on the Negro American, 1965." *Daedelus* 95.1 (Winter 1966): 408.

Farwell, Julia B. "Goophering Around: Authority and the Trick of Storytelling in Charles W. Chesnutt's *The Conjure Woman*." In *Tricksterism in Turn-of-the-Century American Literature: A Multicultural Perspective*. Edited by Elizabeth Ammons and Annette White-Parks. Hanover, N.H: University Press of New England, 1994.

Fienberg, Lorne. "Charles W. Chesnutt and Uncle Julius: Black Storytellers at the Crossroads." *Studies in American Fiction* 15.2 (Autumn 1987): 161–73.

Gates, Henry Louis, Jr. *The Signifying Monkey: A Theory of Afro-American Literary Criticism*. New York: Oxford University Press, 1988.

Goldner, Ellen J. "(Re) Staging Colonial Encounters: Chesnutt's Critique of Imperialism in *The Conjure Woman*." *Studies in American Fiction* 28:1 (April 2000): 39–64.

Goodell, William. *The American Slave Code*. 1853. Reprint, New York: Arno Press, 1969.

Lofgren, Charles A. *The Plessy Case: A Legal-Historical Interpretation*. New York: Oxford University Press, 1987.

Mbiti, John S. *African Religions and Philosophy*. 2nd ed. Oxford: Heineman Educational Publishers, 1989.

Michaels, Walter Benn. *The Gold Standard and the Logic of Naturalism*. Berkeley: University of California Press, 1987.

Morrison, Toni. *Playing in the Dark: Whiteness and the Literary Imagination*. New York: Vintage Books, 1992.

Raboteau, Albert J. *Slave Religion: The "Invisible Institution" in the Antebellum South*. New York: Oxford University Press, 1978.

Roberts, John W. *From Trickster to Badman: The Black Folk Hero in Slavery and Freedom*. Philadelphia: University of Pennsylvania Press, 1989.

Schweninger, Loren. *Black Property Ownership in the South, 1790–1915*. Urbana, Ill.: University of Illinois Press, 1990.

Smith, Barbara Herrnstein. *On the Margins of Discourse: The Relation of Literature to Language*. Chicago: University of Chicago Press, 1978.

Stepto, Robert B. "'The Simple but Intensely Human Inner Life of Slavery': Storytelling and the Revision of History in Charles W. Chesnutt's 'Uncle Julius Stories.'" In *History and Tradition in Afro-American Culture.* Edited by Gunter H. Lenz. Frankfurt: Campus, 1984.

Sundquist, Eric J. *To Wake the Nations: Race in the Making of American Literature.* Cambridge, Mass.: The Belknap Press, 1993.

Thackeray, William Makepeace. *Vanity Fair.* 1847.

Tourgee, Albion. *A Fool's Errand.* New York: Fords, Howard, & Hulbert, 1880.

CHAPTER 13

Passing for What? *The Marrow of Tradition's* Minstrel Critique of the Unlawfulness of Law

Julie Iromuanya

It is claimed by the plaintiff in error, that, in any mixed community, the reputation of belonging to the dominant race, in this instance the white race, is property, in the same sense that a right of action, or of inheritance, is property.... If he be a colored man and be so assigned, he has been deprived of no property, since he is not lawfully entitled to the reputation of being a white man.
— Henry Billings Brown, *Plessy v. Ferguson*

The problem of the Twentieth Century is the problem of the color-line.
— W.E.B. Du Bois, *The Souls of Black Folk*

Henry Billings Brown's haunting reply to Homer Plessy in the paramount *Plessy v. Ferguson* decision solidified the post–Reconstruction notion that races should be "separate but equal," a notion that lived throughout much of the early twentieth century, and is arguably still in effect. Through inheritance, Brown suggests, one acquires property, and in antebellum and postbellum America, the property of race is the greatest inheritance of all. When Plessy, a man who by all accounts to the naked eye appeared to be white, sat in the streetcar assigned to whites only, his actions challenged the very notion of inheritance, whiteness, reputation — and ultimately privilege.

Brown's choice of words, his linked ideologies of "property," "reputation," and "whiteness" are all predicated on a set of values that Charles Chesnutt critiques in *The Marrow of Tradition*. Published in 1901, *The Marrow of Tradition* is an indirect response to the marrow of the very tradition that Brown references in the landmark Supreme Court decision. According to scholar Bryan Wagner, *The Marrow of Tradition* is also a direct response to the Wilmington, North Carolina massacre, which took place in November of 1898 (312). Much of the novel makes visible the tangled distinction of these two courses, wherein vigilante and institutional constitutions enact unlawful laws and exact punishment for the violation of these laws. Not unlike the Citizens' Committee of African Americans and Creoles, of which Homer Plessy was a member, Chesnutt utilizes the passing trope and minstrelsy to reveal the competing anxieties at the core of political citizenship and racial identification, and advocate assimilation.

Recently, scholars like Angelo Rich Robinson have begun to stress that racial identification is a reactive process. As the black middle class, a burgeoning economic body, rose out of the ashes of the Civil War during Reconstruction, its unquestioned subservience became questionable. Citing Charles W. Mills, Robinson argues that the North Carolina massacre enabled "white" to become a race. Men of different socio-cultural backgrounds trumped their differences and bonded into a group by performing an act of "racial loyalty." Through shared violence and degradation of the black body, "white," coalesced into an identity, an identity which sought to "create and maintain [its] dominance individually and collectively" (97). In doing so, whites attempted to salvage what they believed to be a corruption of their reputations as whites, men, and citizens.

Chesnutt reveals these anxieties in *The Marrow of Tradition*, but in addition to concentrating on the lynching or massacre as a gesture of racial loyalty, he suggests that minstrelsy is equally reactionary:

> Negro citizenship was a grotesque farce — Sambo and Dinah raised from the kitchen to the cabinet were a spectacle to make the gods laugh. The laws by which it had been sought to put the negroes on a level with the whites must be swept away in theory, as they had failed in fact. If it were impossible, without a further education of public opinion, to secure the repeal of the fifteenth amendment, it was at least the solemn duty of the state to endeavor, through its own constitution, to escape from the domination of a weak and incompetent electorate and confine the negro to that inferior condition for which nature had evidently designed him [79].

The language of Chesnutt's white narrator suggests the powerful rhetorical efficacy of humor in response to the lawmaking factions of society and institutions. In this excerpt, Negro citizenship is a "spectacle" and a "grotesque farce." Likewise, stereotypical caricatures of blackness are reenacted by whites in the tradition of minstrelsy, through Sambo and Dinah. "Raising" these dehumanizing white idols from the "cabinet," through minstrelsy, creates a group-forming and norming process similar to the physically violent lynch mob. "As Victor Turner suggests, masks, disguises, and 'other fictions of some kind of play are devices to make visible what has been hidden, even uncon-scious'" (cited in Shinn, 248). Without bloodshed, humor enables the narra-tor of the text to release tensions that have surfaced throughout the community as the dominance of whites is met with daily challenges. Traditionally thought of as an "uncivilized" gesture, humor — psychically and corporeally violent in its own way — is the only aggression short of physical violence for a "civilized" populace which believes that laws have betrayed it. The exaggeration and dis-tortion that each form of humor (farce, spectacle, grotesque, and minstrelsy) denotes characterizes the change that whites *desire* to affect. By representing Negro citizenship as absurd, risky, and perverse they uphold white superior-ity and begin the conditioning that will eventually enable a "civil" popula-tion to react to black mobility with an "uncivil" explosion of physical violence.

Literally and literarily, minstrelsy and the passing trope go hand-in-hand. Both represent the schematics of racial performance and racial anxiety. To that end, initially, when arguing that *The Marrow of Tradition* is a novel about passing and racial hybridity, one may envision Janet Miller. Acting very much like a stock "tragic mulatto," the visibly "white" Janet yearns for the day when she will be acknowledged as a full and equal citizen, lady, and sister to her white half-sister, Olivia Carteret. In the vein of the traditional "tragic mulatto," blackness is a burden. The tragedy of Janet's burdensome race is highlighted through her many feeble attempts to enter doors closed to her, both through her own actions, and extended through her husband, Dr. William Miller.

However, a closer reading suggests that Chesnutt flips the classic "pass-ing" paradigm through Tom Delamere, a character who can pass from white to black. Although commonly interpreted as a white man in blackface con-tinuing the subjugation of African Americans through his minstrel perform-ance, rather, Chesnutt purposefully constructs his aristocratic character as a "black" man in blackface. Using enlightenment notions of "blackness," Ches-nutt's Tom Delamere, even with the "reputation of a white man," is anything but "white." Furthermore, it is this complexity that suggests the indetermi-nacy of racial classification. For, if a "white" man exhibits any and all char-acteristics of the "black" man, then he throws into question the validity of traditional racial classification.

Passing for White/Passing for Black

Tom Delamere is first introduced to readers as he makes his entrance to a christening party arranged for Olivia Carteret, who has labored through a near-fatal delivery to give birth to the next Carteret heir, Theodore "Dodie" Felix Carteret. Dodie is, in fact, the only hope for a Carteret heir as Olivia's delivery leaves her barren. The setting, itself, is also emblematic. An occasion of both tradition and celebration, the christening is Dodie's initiation into whiteness. Through this ritual, his status, and thereby his reputation, are publicly mythologized. From this point on, his individual body will be linked to the bodies of his white forefathers.

Tom Delamere, an aristocratic member of Dodie's class, is also assumed to have gone through the same public ritual of white aristocracy. However, Chesnutt injects doubt into his reader's mind through his narrator's description of Tom:

> Slender and of medium height, with a small head of almost perfect contour, a symmetrical face, dark almost to swarthiness, black eyes, which moved somewhat restlessly, curly hair of raven tint, a slight mustache, small hands and feet, and fashionable attire, Tom Delamere, the grandson of the old gentleman who had already arrived, was easily the handsomest young man in Wellington [15–16].

Tom is "dark almost to swarthiness" with "black eyes" and "curly hair of raven tint." By creating a character who can visibly pass for black — mulatto at the very least — Chesnutt calls into question Tom Delamere's whiteness. It is no coincidence that the young Delamere is introduced only *after* his grandfather's introduction. It is Tom's "reputation" as a white man, and not his appearance, that grants him access to this space. This privilege is only contingent upon his inheritance of the property of whiteness through the elder Delamere. Through this subtle tactic, Chesnutt makes visible the racializing aspect of this space, an aspect even more racial than Major Carteret's lengthy diatribe about the ills of blacks.

Chesnutt evokes dualistic enlightenment notions to buttress the questionability of Delamere's race and undermine his nobility. Tom Delamere is a white man, who is actually "black" in the tradition of enlightenment thought. Roguish, careless, emotional, and uncontrollable, "blackness" is his very nature, as opposed to a careful, rational, and controlling "white." In fact, the narrator's description only indicts Tom further through the emasculating and dehumanizing characterization.

"But," the narrator continues, "no discriminating observer would have characterized his beauty as manly. It conveyed no impression of strength, but did possess a certain element, feline rather than feminine, which subtly made negative the idea of manliness" (16). Here, as Tom Delamere's race is ambiguous, his gender — and ultimately his humanity — fall outside the boundaries of classification. (Furthermore, as the story goes on, even his sexual preference is questionable, with the careless attention he pays to the much-coveted Clara.) "Slender and of medium height, with a small head of almost perfect contour, a symmetrical face" and "small hands and feet," his physical space and masculinity are reduced (15–16). Tom occupies space only through his reputation as a man, and a white man at that.

Tom Delamere is even beyond castration. More accurately, to be feminine would be complimentary. Rather, he is degraded to a beast-like condition through the "feline" characterization. He is the "black cat" which superstition considers a forewarning of danger, tragedy, or bad luck. The premonition is not without merit. Tom Delamere ultimately upsets the presumed balance of racial tolerance. And as scholars like Paul Butler suggest, in the vein of "assaultive retribution," locals coalesce in an attempt to "punish" the alleged criminal, Sandy, and restore justice through the ultimate hate crime, lynching.

The great attention to the physical shape and measurements of Tom Delamere's body align clearly with nineteenth- and early twentieth-century Darwinism. "Slender and of medium height, with a small head of almost perfect contour, a symmetrical face" and "small hands and feet," Tom Delamere's physical description is calculated scientifically, recalling Darwinist attempts at racial classification that justified the supposed superiority of whites through measurements of sculls, feet, and appendages, among other devices (Chesnutt, 15–16). This objectification reduces Tom to a mere object, rather than an agent. In fact, ultimately, Delamere is blackmailed into the control of other whites — a form of bondage and submission — in spite of his presumed privilege. Tom Delamere's "blackness" is his burden. Thorough scrutiny of the tragic mulatto paradigm in *The Marrow of Tradition* indicates that rather than passing for black, Tom Delamere is passing for white.

Chesnutt's classification of Tom Delamere ultimately leads to compelling questions. Rather than attempting to switch the meanings attached to the dichotomous signifiers black/white as later African American writers such as Langston Hughes does with "That Word Black," Chesnutt's use of these racist archetypes begs the question, is he complicit in upholding racist Western notions? Does his own position as a passable African American man betray his own investment in traditional racial hierarchization?

One can argue that although Chesnutt does pay homage to enlightenment notions, he does so in order to subvert them. He argues, "Black is not beautiful," *and* we are not "black," by satirizing anxious early attempts at racial taxonomy. To that end, Delamere, described as dark, animalistic, and emasculated, has won his position as an aristocrat by chance. Chesnutt ultimately argues that race, and the ensuing associations which form the property of reputation, is not scientific or genetic; it is an accident of luck.

Blackface Minstrelsy: A Wage for Whiteness

This accident of luck throws into question every aspect of essentialist racial superiority theory. To further illustrate this point, Chesnutt turns to the familiar ritualized racializing performance: the minstrel act. Tom Delamere can not only "pass" for black unintentionally, he does so in blackface at key moments throughout the novel. Readers first see Tom Delamere engage in minstrelsy in the following scene, but before Tom Delamere is revealed as the minstrel artisan to the reader, the narrator shares the efficacy of minstrel racial violence:

> In order to give the visitors, ere they left Wellington, a pleasing impression of Southern customs, and particularly of the joyous, happy-go-lucky disposition of the Southern darky and his entire contentment with existing conditions, it was decided by the hotel management to treat them, on the last night of their visit, to a little diversion, in the shape of a genuine negro cakewalk [117].

Indeed, as the excerpt implies, minstrel performance was every bit a performance by the minstrel artist and the audience. This "diversion," in the form of a "happy-go-lucky" "Southern darky," was itself a symbolic lynching of blacks, and, like North Carolina's massacre, a ritualized attempt by immigrant whites to gain entrance to "whiteness." In *Turning South Again*, Houston A. Baker, Jr. discusses the white racial politics of minstrelsy:

> Irish workers and other white immigrants in the North were exalting in black-face minstrelsy.... Describing the work of historian George Rawick in his own book titled *The Wages of Whiteness*, Roediger notes: "All of the old habits [sexual promiscuity, quickness to action, agrarianism, immediate gratification of the senses] so recently discarded by whites adopting capitalist values came to be fastened onto Blacks" [95].... Through racialized blackface, a white American artisanate became a white "class" [66–67].

In this paradigm, white immigrants form a sense of racial identity and pride through the "othering" of African Americans. Attempting to mimic the rigid puritanical behavioral codes of the aristocratic upper classes, white immigrants use African Americans as a receptacle for their discarded behaviors. A wage for whiteness, their own nostalgic passions are discarded and fixed to yet another category of "others" in order for these non-whites to eventually assimilate, an assimilation that allows otherwise discriminated against immigrants the reputation of white men and women.

In *The Marrow of Tradition*, this narrative is particularly relevant. Chesnutt carefully delineates intra-racial categories (of both blacks and whites) to display the ever-prevalent racial anxieties encoded through social class and national origin, which eventually evolve into "ethnicity." Captain George McBane, as his name suggests, is descended from Irish immigrant working-class roots. With notorious cruelty and zeal, the young McBane inherits his overseer father's "bane" reputation, the very characteristics the white minstrel artist attempts to cast(e) off through performance. Upon introduction, Captain McBane's appearance is distinguished from the aristocratic Major

Carteret's. Chesnutt suggests that the only true minstrel performer is Captain McBane in his attempts to "pass" for a white gentleman. Captain McBane's

> broad shoulders, burly form, square jaw, and heavy chin betokened strength, energy, and unscrupulousness. With the exception of a small, bristling mustache, his face was clean shaven, with here and there a speck of dried blood due to a carelessly or unskillfully handled razor. A single deep-set gray eye was shadowed by a beetling brow, over which a crop of coarse black hair, slightly streaked with gray, fell almost low enough to mingle with his black, bushy eyebrows. His coat had not been brushed in several days, if one might judge from the accumulation of dandruff upon the collar of his shirt-front, in the middle of which blazed a showy diamond, which was plentifully stained with tobacco juice [32].

Like the young Delamere, Captain McBane's whiteness is omitted. Instead, his dark, furry body connotes a feral quality. Mimesis becomes a signifying act forcing apart the totalizing affect of the racializing signifier, "white." Chesnutt calls attention to this minstrel performance in order to expose the concealed stratifications within whiteness itself. Captain McBane performs whiteness through his attempt to appear clean shaven, well-dressed, and above all, privileged. Yet his "essential" difference betrays him. He is clean shaven — but for the "bristling mustache." His face is speckled with blood, because he "unskillfully" cannot handle a razor in the way a "true" bred gentleman could. And he has not quite mastered rudimentary hygiene as his dandruff and tobacco imply. Most telling of all is the "showy diamond" placed in the middle of his shirt, stained with tobacco juice.

McBane, like the rising black middle class, has gained economic viability in the postbellum South as traditional order and values steadily collapse. Although the elder and younger McBane, in every way, signify the American Dream, a mixture of hard work and (less visible) good luck, McBane is still unable to attain the "reputation" of a gentleman. To the aristocracy, exemplified through the Carterets and Delameres, McBane — himself a white man — is separated by a vast gulf, a gulf that even former slaves recognize and disparage him for. Chesnutt advocates two notions through the naming and actions of McBane. In one sense, Chesnutt implies that McBane's condition is both culturally produced and essentially ingrained in his character. In another sense, Chesnutt suggests that the chaos that issues from the Civil War facilitates white mobility.

Beyond his name acting as a nominal indicator for his position in the narrative, it is shown Chesnutt also critiques patriarchy, which the aptly titled, "marrow of tradition" mockingly insinuates. McBane is "of bane," essentially born with the baseness that his name suggests through the genetic transfer. McBane's father has the reputation of being a needlessly cruel man, a grotesque distortion of white gentlemanliness. Furthermore, this genetic inheritance is culturally reproduced through the conditions that not only allow, but necessitate the elder and younger McBanes's particular form of cruelty to thrive.

As the radically shifting definition of "whiteness" begins to collapse, genteel qualities that men like the elder Delamere possess — calm, reason, control, patience — quickly fall into ruin as well. This is evidenced through the young Delamere, who lacks the composite for the "reputation of a white man," but more specifically, through both Major Carteret and his counterpart, Olivia Carteret, who anxiously oscillate between desires to *be* genteel while expressing unfettered rage at the advancement of African Americans.

It should be no surprise that the major struggles most with how to *appear* as a genteel man, while Olivia later struggles with what to do after destroying her father's marriage license to a black woman. For the major, an act of corporeal aggression would enact the "blackness" to which he believes he is superior. To Olivia, lying, and not the act of burning the marriage license, is the most undignified behavior. Both preoccupations demonstrate the Carterets' rupturing white identities. Because of the chaos caused by war — corporeally and psychically — Chesnutt implies that white identity is fluid, in spite of attempts to bind and fix it.

Mimicking Mimery

While it can be argued that Captain McBane is a minstrel performer, he is the *only* true white minstrel performer in *The Marrow of Tradition*. McBane's minstrel performance is most recognizable as mimicry because of how laughable he is at it. He cannot seem to fool anyone into believing that he is a white southern gentleman. As with Captain McBane, white blackface actors do not fool their audiences into believing they are actually black. Where McBane and the traditional minstrel performance differ is intention. Even with the mobility that the Civil War facilitates, while McBane intends to be white, he cannot attain it fully, because "whiteness" becomes a barely attainable category. Instead, he will come to represent the "ethnic" white. No amount of performance will ever transcend his liminal state; his reputation precedes the performance.

With the traditional minstrel show, the audience not only encourages, but *needs* its actors to give flawed performances of African Americans in order to reaffirm its sense of whiteness. Interdependent acts, viewers of this performance are every bit as important as the blackface character. The "masking" of the white performer's "true" characteristics is essential, but what is even more essential is what is behind the mask. The porosity of this mask enables the "true" white man to seep through in the act. This "trueness" is displayed through a hyperbolic performance and a keen awareness of the audience, creating a reciprocal pantomime between audience and actor.

This is like the reciprocal pantomime to the performance of gender in popular film comedies with men performing in drag. In reality, rather than performing as women, male actors perform *as* "men-in-drag." Audiences engage in the act by pretending to suspend their disbelief. For example, when *Some Like It Hot*'s Jack Lemmon, complete with masculine body — in spite of the makeup, high heels, and high-pitched voice — "accidentally" punches and roughs up a man who attempts to sexually assault him, or when Tony Curtis's voice "accidentally" deepens to a bass as he yells at the young bellboy who accosts him, both play into the audience's shared agreement of what a man and a woman are *supposed* to be. These "accidental" gestures (purposeful errors) are the focus of the audience's vision. This focal point reinforces both the actors' and audience's shared acknowledgement of the performative aspect of cross-dressing.

In no other circumstance would a man be allowed to express the concealed desires that the cross-dressing performance attempts, in a mutated form, to replicate. It is the comedic "stage" which allows the fantasy to be acceptably explored. In truth, the real horror would be if Curtis and Lemmon *convincingly* portray women. For these films to be humorous, these men are *supposed* to be terrible at playing women in order to quell the audience's latent anxiety of homosexuality, on the periphery of both the audience's and actor's vision. Just as audience members are supposed to know that Curtis and Lemmon are really men pretending to be women in *Some Like It Hot*, white minstrel audiences acknowledge that their blackface performers are white and black blackface audiences acknowledge that their performers are not really "black."

While it can be argued that ante and postbellum whites narcissistically projected their own base desires on African Americans, and furthermore played out these desires through the minstrel performance, it is much more complicated. For ante and postbellum whites, it was not that they were replicating what they believed African Americans really were (or even what the whites believed themselves to be). Instead, the fear was that African Americans could truly be human. The feral, sub-human characteristics at the very base of the Great Chain of Being were disturbing and disgusting, ambivalently desirous and contemptuous. By replicating the performance, through white blackface performers (and later black blackface performers) whites quelled their fear that African Americans were like them.

In reality, if African Americans were really "white" like them, then the true horror for whites was realizing that they, like Tom Delamere, were actually "black." Like Tom, not their skin color, but their behaviors, would become racial signifiers. Their horrifying, inhumane treatment of "those like themselves" during slavery and post–Reconstruction would precede the reputation that the brand of their skin color protected. It is, therefore, not that ante and postbellum whites *knew* or even truly *believed* that African Americans were subhuman; it was that they paradoxically *desired* for African Americans to be the subhumans that they so dearly loved to fear and detest.

Chesnutt creates a hyperbolic performance of whiteness through McBane in order to suggest the performativity of race. On the other hand, Tom Delamere's performance is *too* convincing to be minstrel. He performs so convincingly that his white and black audience members believe he is really black, and not only black, but none other than Sandy, a well-known and highly recognizable black manservant. Because of his ability to pass, Tom Delamere can better be read as a "black" blackface performer mimicking mimery:

> The cakewalk was a great success. The most brilliant performer was a late arrival, who made his appearance just as the performance was about to commence. The newcomer was dressed strikingly, the conspicuous features of his attire being a long blue coat with brass buttons and a pair of plaid trousers. He was older, too, than the other participants, which made his agility the more remarkable. His partner was a new chambermaid, who had just come to town, and whom the head waiter introduced to the newcomer upon his arrival. The cake was awarded to this couple by a unanimous vote. The man presented it to his partner with a grandiloquent flourish, and returned thanks in a speech which sent the Northern visitors into spasms of delight at the quaintness of the darky dialect and the darky wit. To cap the climax, the winner danced a buck dance with a skill and agility that brought a shower of complimentary silver, which he gathered up and passed to the head waiter [118].

Rather than viewing Tom Delamere as a white blackface performer, he is an "ultra-darky" to his audience, everything that they love to loathe on display. Instead of the cross-dressing gender performances of Lemmon and Curtis in *Some Like It Hot*, Tom Delamere's performance can be likened more closely to Marilyn Monroe's act. Although many today recognize the performative aspect of Monroe's gender (i.e., the baby voice, hourglass figure, wide-eyed child-like expression and signature walk), more accurately to her audience of men and women, she is viewed as something extraordinary, an "ultra-woman."

A barely attainable category, Marilyn Monroe's "ultra-woman," rather than reinforcing the cohesion of the group through the porosity of the veil in the actor/audience pantomime, in some ways threatens to alienate the audience. Monroe's "true" — or better put, "ordinary" — characteristics are muted under the flashy accoutrements. Unlike the "slip-ups" and flaws that are savored as part of the performance in Curtis and Lemmon's "minstrel" act, Monroe's audience would shirk from the symbol that her ordinary body would imply, disappointed if she were to reveal a frighteningly flawed and average body under the padded undergarments and performance.

Likewise, Tom Delamere's performance of the "ultra-darky" is pleasing to his white viewers who revel in the sheer extraordinariness of the display. Perhaps they would have enjoyed the performance if they believed it to be minstrel. Still, it is most probable that Tom Delamere's audience especially relishes his performance of blackness, because they believe it comes, "naturally" from a real black man. The black cakewalker confirms the white supremacist view that "blackness" is an essential characteristic.

To the African Americans that view Tom Delamere as Sandy, he is a black blackface performer. His acts humiliate and degrade the collective African American race, *because* they believe he is black. If they believed he were a white man, they perhaps would not have been so mortally offended. At best, they may have shared in disgust, but certainly not dismay, at the grotesqueness of the performance. For African Americans, the grotesque aspect is highlighted in the "black" man's ability to willingly subject himself to a sadomasochistic display.

Grotesque humor does more than to fantastically showcase the incongruous, disturbing, or shocking. It unearths the incomprehensible (which paradoxically, is also very comprehensible). In exhibiting disturbing notions, the grotesque alerts society to its hidden horrors. Furthermore, by sharing in the relief of anxiety through laughter, it rewards viewers for not becoming consumed by the horrors. Just as skin conceals blood, the hidden horror that is revealed through shed blood is the frightening sight of mortality. Likewise, for postbellum African Americans, the horror of the minstrel act is the fear that the "darky," sub-human and animal-like, is their "true" nature, a notion whites attempted to convince African Americans of in order to keep them in bondage during slavery.

Tom Delamere (as Sandy) is therefore engaging in explicit and perverted pornographic behavior and is duly punished:

> The cakewalk had results which to Sandy were very serious. The following week he was summoned before the disciplinary committee of his church and charged with unchristian conduct, in the following particulars, to wit: dancing, and participating in a sinful diversion called a cakewalk, which was calculated to bring the church to disrepute and make it the mockery of sinners. Sandy protested his innocence vehemently. But in vain. The proof was overwhelming [120].

Sandy is put on trial by the African American community for allegedly engaging in this illicit performance. And "in the face of positive proof, Sandy's protestations were of no avail; he was found guilty, and suspended from church fellowship until he should have repented and made full confession" (121). The punishment that the community exacts is collectively executed. Once again, vigilante social justice reacts to the unlawfulness of social and institutional law, laws which prevent African Americans from receiving the egalitarian promises of the Constitution. But rather than performing racial loyalty through a lynching or minstrel performance, middle class African Americans in *The Marrow of Tradition* create a makeshift church tribunal, *performing* lawfulness, civility, and morality.

The "uncivil," the "unlawful," and the amoral are notions that the African American middle class collectively desires to eschew, particularly post-emancipation when the distinction between freedmen and Free People of Color was no longer clear. And while these anxieties are replicated through the civil judiciary performance in *The Marrow of Tradition*, they paradoxically hint at an interplay that is both contemptuous and desirous. When Sister 'Manda Patterson witnesses the cakewalk, although horrified, she cannot look away. She must keep her eyes fixed on the hideous image before her.

> He was positively identified by Sister 'Manda Patterson, the hotel cook, who had watched the whole performance from the hotel corridor for the sole, single, solitary, and only purpose, she averred, of seeing how far human wickedness could be carried by a professing Christian. The whole thing had been shocking and offensive to her, and only a stern sense of duty had sustained her in looking on, that she might be qualified to bear witness against the offender. She had recognized his face, his clothes, his voice, his walk — there could be no shadow of doubt that it was Brother Sandy. This testimony was confirmed by one of the deacons, whose son, a waiter at the hotel, had also seen Sandy at the cakewalk [120].

For black audiences of minstrel acts, similar to working class white immigrants, the warning is that each member should dare not act too "black." Black minstrel performers were building on the white minstrel tradition, drawing on two key notions. First, African American performers and audiences were distanced from the image, because they simply did not believe it represented them. They were sharing in a joke, laughing at someone or some-*thing* that did not include them. Second, and particularly in Sister 'Manda Patterson's case, when recognizing familiar behaviors, the performance reinforces social codes by disparaging and ridiculing illicit behaviors. These behaviors reinforce stereotypes that the masses set to distance themselves from. Monetary function aside, for the black audience, the black blackface performance is, in essence, a vernacular assimilationist agent. In the same way, *The Marrow of Tradition*, as a body of text, is Chesnutt's rhetorical assimilationist attempt to circumvent traditional notions of "blackness" and disparage illicit, immoral behaviors.

Chesnutt reinforces these assimilationist notions through Janet and Dr. Miller, who attempt to assimilate, rather than integrate. Inheriting the mobility that Reconstruction affords him, Dr. Miller moves into the Carterets' former home. He is educated, and although he owns his own hospital, he can only be a true doctor when he can finally operate on a white body. Likewise, Janet cannot see herself as a true lady until she is loved and acknowledged by her white half-sister.

A descendent of Quakers, Ellis also attempts to assimilate into whiteness like the Millers. For this reason, he is the only character to at least question Tom Delamere's performance.

> He was invited up to see the cakewalk, which he rather enjoyed, for there was some graceful dancing and posturing. But the grotesque contortions of one participant had struck him as somewhat overdone, even for a comical type of negro. He recognized the fellow, after a few minutes' scrutiny, as the body-servant of old Mr. Delamere. The man's present occupation, or choice of diversion, seemed out of keeping with his employment as attendant upon an invalid old gentleman, and strangely inconsistent with the gravity and decorum which had been so noticeable when this agile cakewalker had served as butler at Major Carteret's table upon the occasion of the christening dinner. There was a vague suggestion of unreality about this performance, too, which Ellis did not attempt to analyze, but which recurred vividly to his memory upon a subsequent occasion [119].

Visibly, the performer looks black. However, unlike both the whites and blacks who witness the minstrel show, to Ellis, Sandy's reputation as a black man precedes the act. The performance seems "strangely inconsistent with the gravity and decorum" for which Sandy is known.

Perhaps what Ellis is most confounded by is the pride in the debasing act. The artisan revels in his inferiority, proudly, rather than simply purporting the "instinctual" behaviors that the whites in the crowd need to confirm their own notions of superiority. This "darky" is a little too eager to share in the "darky dialect" and "darky wit." His performance is a little too neat, succoring the whites' insatiable appetite for the perpetuation of their own superiority and his own inferiority; his performance is a little too well-performed for it to be real.

Once again, Chesnutt uses the minstrel to reveal the inherent stratifications in racial classification, and reveal the rationale behind "class." Ellis "had come of a Quaker family,— the modified Quakers of the South,— and while sharing in a general way the Southern prejudice against the negro, his prejudices had been tempered by the peaceful tenets of his father's sect" (217). This "tempering" enables Ellis to recognize the farcical nature of the performance. Like both McBane and the African American middle class, Ellis attempts to assimilate, but he is separated by a vast gulf: "His father had been a Whig, and a non-slaveholder; and while he had gone with the South in the civil war so far as a man of peace could go, he had not done so for love of slavery" (217). Ellis's inherited reputation binds him.

Ellis's initiation into "whiteness" can only happen through a ritualized performance of whiteness. It is for this key reason that Chesnutt strategically utilizes Ellis as Tom Delamere's counterpoint character. Competing for the affections of Clara, and the ultimate inheritor that her fertility promises, Ellis and Tom must clash before the work of the novel is accomplished. In due form, the two nemeses do clash when Tom commits an act of murder and Ellis, in truth, must symbolically match his "word as a gentlemen" against Tom's. This feat ultimately elevates his reputation to that of a white man, alongside none other than the elder Delamere, who also comes forward to exonerate Sandy. Only in this moment does Chesnutt showcase the true gravity of the subsuming effect of whiteness, through the inheritance of reputation, property, and race.

By engaging in the process of forming a body of law — both socially and institutionally — and being equally recognized under that law, Ellis has transcended his difference. He is finally "white." Although Sandy's clemency is dependent on the kindness of whites, the frightening reaffirmation that his own reputation cannot save him, but instead, the reputation of whites can, only reaffirms the dangerous unlawfulness of law. Chesnutt's utilization of minstrelsy and the passing trope prove that the black man has many more years ahead of him before the egalitarian promises of the Constitution, and all lawmaking bodies — be they social or institutional — will eventually include him. Indeed, it is fair to suggest that Chesnutt would agree with Du Bois's assertion that "the problem of the Twentieth Century is the problem of the color-line" (Du Bois, 7).

WORKS CITED

Baker, Jr. Houston A. *Turning South Again: Re-Thinking Modernism/Re-Reading Booker T.* Durham: Duke University Press, 2001.

Butler, Paul. "Much Respect: Toward a Hip-Hop Theory of Punishment." Stanford Law Review Symposium, *Punishment and its Purposes*, 2004.

Chesnutt, Charles W. *The Marrow of Tradition.* Ann Arbor: University of Michigan Press, 1969.

Du Bois, W.E.B. *The Souls of Black Folk.* 1903. New York: Paperview Group, 2005.

Hughes, Langston. "That Word Black." *The Writer's Presence: A Pool of Readings.* Edited by Donald McQuade and Robert Atwan. 5th ed. Boston: Bedford/St. Martins, 2006. 709–715.

Plessy v. Ferguson. 210, U.S. Supreme Court, 18 May 1896.

Robinson, Angelo Rich. "Race, Place, and Space: Remaking Whiteness in the Post-Reconstruction South." *Southern Literary Journal* (September 2002): 97–107.

Shinn, Christopher A. "Masquerade, Magic, and Carnival in Ralph Ellison's *Invisible Man.*" *African American Review* 36.2 (2002): 243–261.

Wagner, Bryan. "Charles Chesnutt and the Epistemology of Racial Violence." *American Literature* 73.2 (June 2001): 311–337.

Wilder, Billy. *Some Like it Hot.* Metro Goldwyn Mayer, 1959. DVD.

CHAPTER 14

Geographies of Freedom: Race, Mobility, and Uplift in Charles W. Chesnutt's Northern Writing

Michelle Taylor

In the late nineteenth century, novelist and race man[1] Charles W. Chesnutt delivered a series of speeches in which he heralded a new dawn in the lives of African Americans. In speeches with titles such as "The Future of the Negro," "On the Future of His People," and "The Future American: What Race is Likely to Become in the Process of Time," Chesnutt laid out his vision of what life would look like for African Americans in the twentieth century. In these speeches, Chesnutt discussed the importance of the memories of the slave past, but he was careful to point out that African American citizens should not become beholden to the past, but instead ready themselves for a future that was dependent upon their ability to exert the intellectual and psychical effort necessary to achieve equality and citizenship. Consider, for example, his statements in "The Future of the Negro," delivered in 1882 in Fayetteville, N.C.:

> It is not my intention to paint you the horrors of slavery. More eloquent tongues have discoursed upon them, and better men in former years have spent their lives, aye, have even laid down their lives in the endeavor to show to the world this American Institution in its true colors. I represent a new element, another generation. I never saw a slave. Half of the faces that surround me are the faces of those who never felt the weight of the lash — who never bowed under the yoke of bondage" [*Speeches*, 25].

The remainder of Chesnutt's speech is devoted to counting the many ways in which African Americans can secure their place in the future of the nation and enhance their standings as productive citizens and like many race men before him, he cites education and economic responsibility as the means through which African Americans can create a lasting foundation for economic, political, and social uplift. "We need money, for in common but suggestive language, 'Money makes the man go.' And education will teach us how to make money. It will teach us how to save and to invest money" (*Speeches*, 25). He underscores the relationship between newness, education, and economic responsibility. In this speech, delivered a few years before Chesnutt began one of the most prolific phases of his writing career, Chesnutt establishes the foundation for much of his fiction. The rhetoric of the new and the future that he uses throughout these pieces is familiar rhetorical territory to many African American elites. Just as Chesnutt was calling for a new era in the lives of African Americans, the African American national body was itself preparing for a new era. In voicing the need for a concerted political change, Chesnutt pointed out that there was an obvious lack. Because he was writing in the period known as the "nadir," there was no way for him to disregard the institutionalized terror that was sweeping the South. His most famous treatment of this type of violence in *The Marrow of Tradition* speaks to his investment in shedding light on the realities of Jim Crow laws and racial terror. But despite his focus on the rhetoric of the new, Chesnutt is often absent from critical discussions about the New Negro Movement, or the Harlem Renaissance. Interestingly, despite the rhetoric of the new that Chesnutt deploys in his speeches, why is he often left out of discussions related to the Harlem Renaissance and the New Negro Movement?[2] Renaissance writers and the critics who analyze them all associate Chesnutt's oeuvre with a past that is not in keeping with the work of the emergent scholars and writers who descended on Harlem in the early twentieth century. Many critics have suggested that the years leading to the Harlem Renaissance signaled a downward spiral in his career, one in which his novels were deemed outdated and removed from the style and ideology of the Renaissance era. As Charles Duncan states in *The Northern Stories of Charles Chesnutt*, Chesnutt's career had certainly stalled, due in large part to his decision in 1902 to return to his stenography business. Duncan argues, "Although he published one of his novels and a handful of stories after his return to business, he could never again generate the sort of focused authorial energy that had enabled him to publish five books between 1899 and 1901. By the 1920s, Chesnutt had apparently been consigned to the back bench of the American literary establishment, in part because of the ascendancy of the black writers associated with the Harlem Renaissance, whose works seemed spectacularly more 'modern' than his" (Duncan, xv).

Although the prose of his later writings did indeed reflect awkwardness uncharacteristic of his early fiction, this is a return to the economy of the short story as the forum through which to represent the stories of the New Negro.

It is precisely through the "handful of short stories" to which Duncan refers that Chesnutt expresses his modern sensibility. Therefore, stories such as "The Doll" allow him to articulate the holy trinity of African American needs at the turn of the century: physical freedom and mobility, economic mobility, and sociopolitical equality. In doing so, Chesnutt participates in a tradition of black male writers seeking to renegotiate the black male image in the American public sphere.[3] Chesnutt's efforts place him squarely among the likes of Harlem Renaissance thinkers such as W.E.B. Du Bois and Alain Locke.

The stories themselves emerge as a new entity — hybrid texts that combine elements of the migration narrative and the uplift novel to create texts that speak specifically to an upwardly mobile African American citizenry. More specifically, these stories of upwardly mobile, civically responsible African Americans revolve around a very stylized model of the respectable, representative African American male. Thus in creating his own model of modern black manhood, Chesnutt restores the race man for a new generation of readers; and in locating this idealized black male in the North, more specifically Ohio, Chesnutt highlights the historical significance of Ohio in the African American migratory experience. Chesnutt's short stories take on an added significance when examined within the context of the migration narrative. African American migration narratives typically chronicle the migrant's movements from the South to a hopefully freer, but often unforgiving Northern space. As Farah Griffin suggests in *Who Set You Flowin'?: The African American Migration Narrative*, the migrant is often traumatized by the initial confrontation with the urban landscape and that there is "no evidence of their characters' membership in a black horde. Instead, fear and confusion consume the migrant psyche" (51). However, Chesnutt's Ohio is constructed as an affirmative space and one in which African Americans can not only survive, but thrive; because Ohio was both a literal and figurative border in the antebellum era, Chesnutt is asking readers to once again acknowledge the significance of the state as a site for black power and progress.

(Re)Birth of the Race Man

In his treatment of Chesnutt's short stories, Charles Duncan argues that Chesnutt achieves a revolutionary vision that had yet to be seen in African American literature. Duncan suggests that: "Chesnutt stands virtually alone as a turn-of-the-century African American chronicler of Northern culture, anticipating such figures as James Weldon Johnson, Langston Hughes, Richard Wright, Ralph Ellison, James Baldwin, and Toni Morrison. For Chesnutt was fascinated by the ways the North went about its business ... as the country struggled to enact, in the post–Reconstruction era, the ideals of freedom and economic opportunity intrinsic to America as he conceived of it" (Duncan, xx). Duncan is correct in pointing to Chesnutt's pioneering treatments of African Americans in the postbellum North; however, suggesting that Chesnutt was solitary in his efforts to depict the allure of the North reaffirms the distance between Chesnutt and Harlem Renaissance writers. Chesnutt was far from the only writer to envision the power of the North, but he was one of the first to do so in the postbellum moment and establishes a model for Harlem Renaissance writers. Critics would be wise to stress the continuity between Chesnutt and Renaissance writers, not the disparity.

At the center of the movement northward and hopefully away from social and economic marginalization is the representative black male, through whom Chesnutt challenges the emasculating restrictions of the Jim Crow South. The figure of the black race man has been a mainstay in the African American literary imagination since the publication of Frederick Douglass's *The Narrative of the Life of Frederick Douglass*. In this self-representation of the heroic search for freedom and self-hood, as well as in the two autobiographies that followed, Douglass set the standard for what African American men should do for themselves and their people. Critics have since held Douglass and his contemporaries such as Martin Delaney and Prince Hall as the exemplars of nineteenth-century black masculinity.[4] Chesnutt's own contemporary W.E.B. Du Bois, himself a self-appointed race man, continued this focus on exemplary masculinity in *The Souls of Black Folk*. As Hazel Carby points out in *Race Men*, these nineteenth-century leaders were valuable models: "These revolutionary figures appear in Du Bois's narrative both as 'true' black men and genuine leaders of black men" (Carby, 40). Thus, twentieth-century scholars and writers like Du Bois and Chesnutt were the descendents of this genealogy of black masculine self-determination, as well as the torch carriers for the future of this philosophy.

The idea of an exemplary black male was certainly problematized by the extra-legal machinations of the racial terror at work in the Jim Crow South. The racialized violence of lynching and the myth of the black male rapist made it virtually impossible for black men to enact the traditional masculine narrative of adequately defending one's family and property. Marlon Ross's study of black masculinity in the Jim Crow South underscores the particular troubles facing Southern men: "The Jim Crow regime poses an impossible paradox for those endeavoring to build an efficacious black manhood. On the one hand, the Jim Crow system insists that men of African descent are not fully men — in effect, that they are not capable of being normal men — as a justification for excluding them from those rights, rites, networks, and entitlements that endow middle-class white men with their proper claims as proprietors and entrepreneurs within the economy, fathers and defenders of the state, heads of households ... [and] empowered citizens of the nation and the world" (Ross 2).

Chesnutt was well aware of the difficulties inherent in living in the Jim Crow South and made his thoughts on the subject quite clear in a letter to his colleague Robert Anderson dated September 1904:

> The Negro question in the South as it is at present in its most acute form, is how can the White people be induced to do justly by the Negro; how can lynching be suppressed? By a strict and impartial enforcement of law. How can crime be suppressed? Certainly not by cruel and unusual punishments inflicted by mobs, but by the fostering of education and the general spread of enlightenment.... There can be but one citizenship in a free country [Chesnutt, 217].

Chesnutt's searing critique of the nature of equality in a nation known for its notion of freedom is fundamental to an understanding of his mission. Chesnutt's insistence on viewing the issue as a political one that underscores African American citizenship and correctly assume black equality, positions the "Negro question" on the national agenda. In doing so, Chesnutt argues that African American equality and citizenship are national priorities, not merely sectional concerns.

Although Chesnutt's endorsement of the North may be too optimistic because it does not give voice to the type of racial violence common to urban spaces, it does anticipate the rhetoric expressed by the thousands of African Americans heading to New York and Chicago during the Great Migration. Alain Locke's "The New Negro" is perhaps the most well-known treatise on the era and is particularly important for present purposes because of the similarities between Chesnutt's and Locke's ideas. The similarities highlight Chesnutt's importance to the postbellum, pre–Harlem era, as well as his connection to the defining rhetoric of the Harlem Renaissance.

It was only a few years later that Locke wrote the manifesto for the movement, "The New Negro." In "The New Negro," Locke elaborates on the ideas that Chesnutt introduced a few years before. In the essay Locke prioritizes not only a sea change in the way African Americans think of themselves, but also a psychical shift to accompany the move northward. Locke argues: "A main change has been, of course, that shifting of the Negro population which has made the Negro problem no longer exclusively or even predominantly Southern. Why should our minds remain sectionalized when the problem itself no longer is? Then the trend of migration has not only been toward the North and the Central Midwest, but city-ward and to great centers of industry.... And finally with the Negro rapidly in progress of class differentiation, if it ever was warrantable to regard the Negro en masse it is becoming with every day less possible" (Locke, 14). Like Chesnutt, Locke also placed race relations at the top of the national agenda. Locke argues for a move to cities that would serve as sites for industry and uplift, which not only echoes Chesnutt's comments to his colleague Robert Anderson, but also echoes Chesnutt's statements quoted at the beginning of this essay. Chesnutt and Locke believed in personal industry and economic responsibility and felt that these twin goals, made possible only by a move to the North, were the essential tools for the future of the race.

The notions of economic responsibility, respectability, and uplift are aligned in the publication of *The Crisis*, the official journalistic organ of the National Association for the Advancement of Colored People (NAACP). First published in 1910, *The Crisis* was founded and edited by Du Bois, with whom Chesnutt often corresponded. *The Crisis* was one of the most important journals of the Renaissance era and as Du Bois wrote in his autobiography published posthumously in 1968, "Most of the young writers who began what was called the renaissance in the '20s saw their first publication in *The Crisis* magazine." (*Oxford*, 185) Chesnutt submitted a number of stories and often advised Du Bois on the quality of the literary pieces submitted to the journal. In one letter to Du Bois, Chesnutt reveals his own preference for a more traditional type of African American literature:

> I have read the manuscripts submitted several times.... Mr. Fisher's sketches and Mr. van Vechten's powerful and vivid delineation of certain tawdry if not sordid aspects of Harlem Negro life are Sunday school stuff compared with the scenes and subjects which these budding realists have selected. If they are writing about the things they know, as a writer ought to, they must have a wide knowledge of the more unsavory aspects of life among the colored people [Chesnutt, 221].

Although Chesnutt has always been thought to be on the sidelines of the Renaissance, his correspondences with Du Bois suggest otherwise. But even more telling is Chesnutt's assertion that writers should write about "things they know," which is exactly what he did in the pieces that he published in *The Crisis* during the early years of the magazine's tenure. Just as Fisher and van Vechten chose to write about the "underside" of urban life in Harlem in an effort to show the range of black life in the early decades of the twentieth century, Chesnutt chose to write about a different rendering of black life in the twentieth century. Nevertheless, the writers shared a commitment to representing the diversity of the African American migratory experience.

We can best understand Chesnutt's contributions to the intellectual and creative spirit of the era through a reading of his short fiction. Chesnutt was no stranger to the genre of the short story; indeed, the genre was the source of much of his early success. However, the lesser-known stories, often referred to as the "Northern writings," give a different perspective on Chesnutt insofar as the stories reflect a modern, urban sensibility. Chesnutt centers the action of his migration narratives in Groveland, a fictionalized version of

Cleveland, Ohio. And it is with good reason that Cleveland would serve as a model for Groveland because Chesnutt's Cleveland was a site for African American economic and social mobility. When Chesnutt returned to Cleveland in 1883, there were only 2,500 blacks living in the city. However, by 1920, there were 35,451 African Americans living in the city. And as Marlon Ross points out, "Given the relatively progressive and integrated conditions of black migrants in cities like Cleveland, Chesnutt has some reason to hope that this trickle of African American migrants will, over a long period of time, become scattered and absorbed within the larger population, rather than concentrated and huddled in consolidated, segregated ghettoes" (Ross, 32).

At the heart of many of these stories is the New Negro masculine ideal. This twentieth-century representative black male allows Chesnutt to create a character that reflects his own sense of economic responsibility, Locke's urban sensibility, and Du Bois's intellectualism. These stories, "The Doll" in particular, perform both the anxieties and aspirations inherent in the African American male migratory experience. As Ross points out in his reading of Chesnutt's short story, "Uncle Wellington's Wives," there is a very specific agenda at work in these texts: "his speech enlists a specific intended audience, the aspiring colored men of the lodge in a specific social agenda: the remaking of the manhood of the race" (Ross, 26). The notion of remaking the manhood is certainly key in understanding the motivation behind Chesnutt's Northern writing and he does so by instilling his vision of and for the future of the race in the solitary figure of the race man, made new by a move to the North and the concomitant opportunities that accompany such a geographic shift.

Honor Thy Father

Published in *The Crisis* in 1912, "The Doll" explores the inner psyche of an upwardly mobile African American businessman. In this particular story, the protagonist has a chance encounter with his father's murderer, a plot twist that bears striking resemblance to the plot line involving Josh Green in *The Marrow of Tradition*. Chesnutt uses the patrilineal relationship between father and son to underscore the sense of masculine responsibility and respectability that he believes to be at the core of African American uplift. The story takes place in the thriving barbershop owned by Tom Taylor. The barbershop, typically thought of as an affirmative, urban black male space, is potentially transformed by this encounter and can become either a site of redemption or revenge. Taylor's decision to spare his enemy's life is important, but what is of even greater significance is the range of choices and opportunities that Chesnutt gives to the protagonist. In structuring a story that revolves around black male space and opportunity, Chesnutt dramatizes the possibilities available to black men who are willing to forego the tragedies of a Southern Jim Crow past in exchange for a Northern identity made new by freedom and opportunity.

The story opens with a relatively benign domestic scene that has Taylor promising to have his daughter's doll repaired before the end of the business day. The scenery quickly shifts to a conversation between two white men — each representing the all important sectional divide — who engage in a discussion about the "Negro question." The conversation between the Southern colonel and the Northern judge sets the stage for the action of the story insofar as the colonel seeks to disprove the judge's sentiment that "Northern Negroes are different" (203). The men then enter Taylor's well-appointed barbershop, a bastion of good taste that spatially and physically symbolizes all of Taylor's hard work and personal commitment to responsibility and respectability.

The importance of the physical surroundings is crucial in understanding the complex relationship between racialized histories, Northern spaces, and black masculine agency. Consider, for example, the detail Chesnutt uses to represent the interior of the barbershop:

> The shop was the handsomest barber shop in the city. It was in the basement, and the paneled ceiling glowed with electric lights. The floor was of white tile, the walls lined with large mirrors. Behind ten chairs, of the latest and most comfortable design, stood as many colored barbers, in immaculate white jackets, each at work upon a white patron. An air of discipline and good order pervaded the establishment. There was no loud talking by patrons, no unseemly garrulity on the part of the barbers. It was very obviously a well-conducted barber shop, frequented by gentlemen who could afford to pay liberally for superior service. As the judge and colonel entered a customer vacated the chair served by the proprietor [Chesnutt, 204].

This detailed description of Taylor's shop and the interior of the shop offer important clues about the interior mind/psyche of the barber who will soon be forced to make a life-altering decision. The interior of the shop also reflects the extent to which the proprietor has gained dominion over an urban space that can sometimes be unforgiving.

As Farah Griffin points out in her study of migration and urban spaces, the sites of urban subjectivity are generally contested spaces: "urban spaces — kitchenettes, workplaces, street corners, prisons and theaters — are some of the sites where migrants, white powerholders, and the Northern black middle class vie for control" (Griffin, 102). Griffin also suggests, "All of these spaces are created by a sophisticated urban power, yet this very power is engaged in a constant struggle to maintain control over them. The contest over space is symbolic of the larger contest over black bodies. Within these spaces, a struggle ensues in which the migrant tries to resist efforts to dominate him" (Griffin, 102). Griffin's assertion is significant because it is a contest between wills and competing historical narratives that drive the action between Taylor and the colonel.

After the colonel recounts his own story in which he killed Taylor's father in the post–Civil War south, Chesnutt probes Taylor's interior psyche with the same intense detail that he had previously given to the interior of the shop itself. Whereas the colonel remembers the killing as being indicative of a "bumptious nigger," Taylor remembers the story as one in which his father fought heroically on behalf of his daughter. Taylor's memories reflect the histories of the population of recently freed slaves, of whom his father had been a member. He remembered a father who desired to provide for his children and who "had sent his children regularly to school" (206). He then reflects on the chaos that ensued in his own life after his father's death: "Poverty, disease and death had followed them, until he alone was left. Many years had passed. The brown boy who had wept beside his father's bier, and who had never forgotten, nor forgiven, was now the grave-faced, keen-eyed, deft-handed barber, who held a deadly weapon at the throat of his father's slayer" (207). But despite the fact that "in his dreams he had killed this man a hundred times," (207), Taylor spares the colonel's life and does so through a process that allows him to survey his accomplishments and his responsibilities. Consider, for example, the passage through which Chesnutt reverses the tragedies of the Jim Crow South by making them affirmative markers of Northern opportunity:

> So strong, for the moment, was the homicidal impulse that it would have prevailed already had not the noisy opening of the door to admit a patron diverted the barber's attention and set in motion a current of ideas which fought for the colonel's life.... It was a handsome shop, and had been to the barber a matter of more than merely personal pride. Prominent among a struggling people, as yet scarcely beyond the threshold of citizenship, he had been looked upon, and had become accustomed to regard himself, as a representative man, by failure or success his race would be tested ... he knew full well that should he lose the shop no colored man would succeed him ... a center of industry ... would be lost to his people.... Their fates were all, in a measure, dependent upon the proprietor of the shop [209].

His decision to choose his own self-made identity and the future of his people indicate the extent to which this migrant has been able to negotiate and conquer the Northern center of industry. He does so by upholding both the nineteenth-century rhetoric of uplift and Du Bois's notion of the Talented Tenth. Thus, in envisioning himself as a representative man, a member of the Talented Tenth, he is endowed with a responsibility to act in the best interest of his people. He is perhaps the epitome of the image Chesnutt spoke about in his 1882 speech, "The Future of the Negro." He could also be thought of as the model for the New Negro that Alain Locke envisions for the Renaissance era, a man who is aware of the best, but one who is not conquered by the past.

Taylor's restraint and refusal to avenge his father's death further distances him from the emasculating effects of the Jim Crow South. The story suggests that this model of psychic and economic success can divest Jim Crow if its traumatizing hold on those African Americans who are willing to migrate northward and uphold the rhetoric of hard work and racial responsibility is released. Chesnutt trades the negative masculine narrative of violence for the traditional patriarchal narrative of family protection and civic responsibility because it is ultimately the memory of his daughter that saves the colonel's life and releases Taylor from his Jim Crow memories: "If the razor went to its foal he would not be able to fulfill his promise to Daisy!... The jointed doll had saved the colonel's life. Whether society had conquered self or not may be an open question, but it had stayed the barber's hand until love could triumph over hate!" (210). The narrative deployment of female influence is particularly important at this point in the narrative. The role of women, both Taylor's deceased sister and his young daughter allow Chesnutt to avoid troped ideas about black masculinity. Importantly, it is the reverence for his father and the women in his life that drive him to avoid violence. The daughter's centrality in Taylor's deliberations identifies her as a site of deliberation for the complexities of masculinity, migration and the black family. Her role is also in keeping with a very distinct Du Bosian model of uplift. The idea of the Talented Tenth extended itself to the progeny of the elite as indicated by Du Bois's interest in African American children. As Daylanne English argues in *Unnatural Selections*, Du Bois recognized the role of children as the future purveyors of his rhetoric: "from 1910 to 1934, *Crisis* advocated a kind of intraracial family planning. During his editorship, Du Bois helped construct a fully illustrated narrative of a successfully eugenicizing facial family.... *The Crisis* documented ... the expansion of modern black middle-class urbanity" (English, 45). Indeed it was in a 1915 editorial, published only three years after "The Doll" but well within the timeframe of Chesnutt's association with *The Crisis*, that Du Bois made clear his sentiments about the necessity of well-bred African American children: "the immediate program" of the "American Negro" is to "seek out colored children of ability and genius to open up to them broader, industrial opportunity and ... to find that Talented tenth and encourage it" (Du Bois).

Taylor's decision therefore places him in an elite new corps of African American men, the newness of whom we can best understand if we compare him to Josh and Dr. Miller, the two protagonists of Chesnutt's 1901 novel, *The Marrow of Tradition*. Like Taylor, the folk hero in *Marrow*, Josh Green was also faced with an important decision — to avenge his father's death or seek to revise the image of black masculinity through restraint and responsibility. However, Green, who was nominally literate and clearly representative of a Southern man marked by Jim Crow, avenged his father's death by killing his father's murderer. Though Josh is marginally cast as a hero, his ultimate death and Dr. Miller's survival suggest a very specific genealogy of black masculinity. While Josh's death is prefigured by his folk status, Dr. Miller's life in the midst of a race riot is anticipated by his intellect and responsibility to his family. And a few years after the publication of the novel, Chesnutt creates yet another marker in the genealogy of representative male identity.[5]

This type of representative elite thinking was the catalyst for Du Bois's creation of *The Crisis*. Further, Chesnutt's adoption of this rhetoric further signifies his response to the social climate of the nadir, as well as his critical intervention in Harlem Renaissance–era social and political discourses. Chesnutt's use of the Taylor family history not only asserts his interest in the legacies of black families, but also indicates the extent to which he is invested in constitution of the black family as a conduit for political change and social equality.

Calming the Crisis of Black Masculinity in *The Crisis*

The Crisis was an important forum for the distribution of African American literary art, and it also proved to be an important venue for the dissemination of the rhetoric of black respectability and uplift. The idealized black man that developed in the minds of Chesnutt, Du Bois, and Locke and later manifested in the pages of the journal was clearly a response to and cure for the racial terror that gripped much of black America. And as English points out, during the first two decades of the new century, "*Crisis* repeatedly represents such men as paradigmatic New Negroes within an ever-improving racial family" (English, 47). To be clear, Chesnutt's use of the representative man is not without out its ideological complexities. Indeed, the elitism and somewhat troubling uses of women are certainly provocative sites for further critical investigation. But complexities of class and gender notwithstanding, this reading and others that give voice to Chesnutt's role in the Renaissance era will hopefully usher in a new chapter in the ever-growing body of criticism on the work of Charles W. Chesnutt.

NOTES

1. "The term Race Man (a term not much in use today) applies to an Afrikan man totally dedicated and completely devoted to the uplift of his people (the Race). A Race Man places the interests of his people above all else. A Race Man embodies the words of that great nineteenth century champion of Afrika and the rights of Black people — Dr. Edward Wilmot Blyden. In application to himself, Dr. Blyden emphatically stated that: 'Let me forever be discarded by the Black race, and let me be condemned by the White, if I strive not with all my powers, if I put not forth all my energies to bring respect and dignity to the Negro race.'" 1998 Runoko Rashidi. "Words Of A Race Man: Afrikan Theology, Cosmogony and Philosophy: An Introduction." The Global African Presence: *http://www.cwo.com/~lucumi/theology.html*

2. In one of his most famous essays, "Post-Bellum-Pre-Harlem," Chesnutt discusses the extent to which his work was ignored as a result of the rush to Harlem and the literature of urban America. In many ways, this essay set the tone for the ways in which Chesnutt's oeuvre has been remembered in African American literary history. However, this discussion along with the publication of a collection of essays on the era known as "Post-Bellum, Pre-Harlem" all show the extent to which critics are re-examining Chesnutt's relationship to early twentieth century African American literature. See *Post-Bellum, Pre-Harlem: African American Literature and Culture, 1877–1919*, Barbara McCaskill and Caroline Gebhard, eds., New York: New York University Press, 2006.

3. Chesnutt participates in a very important tradition of African American male writers who use literacy and uplift as the mechanisms through which they attempt to reconstruct the image of black masculinity. See Maurice Wallace's *Constructing the Black Masculine: Identity and Ideality in African American Men's Literature and Culture, 1775–1995*, Durham: Duke University Press, 2002, and Marlon Ross's *Manning the Race: Reforming Black Men in the Jim Crow Era*, New York: New York University Press, 2004 for more on this discussion.

4. See Wallace's *Constructing the Black Masculine*.

5. See Eric Sundquist's *To Wake the Nation* for an intriguing discussion of Chesnutt's use of masculinity and genealogy in *The Marrow of Tradition*.

WORKS CITED

Carby, Hazel. *Race Men*. Cambridge: Harvard University Press, 2000.

Chesnutt, Charles, "The Doll" in *The Northern Stories of Charles Chesnutt*, Duncan, ed. Athens: Ohio University Press, 2004.

_____. *Charles Chesnutt: Essays and Speeches*, Joseph McElrath, Robert C. Leitz, Jesse Crier, eds. Palo Alto: Stanford University Press, 2001.

Duncan, Charles. *Absent Man: Narrative Craft of Charles W. Chesnutt*, Athens: Ohio University Press, 1999.

English, Daylanne. *Unnatural Selections: Eugenics in American Modernism and the Harlem Renaissance*. Chapel Hill: University of North Carolina Press, 2004.

Griffin, Farah. *Who Set You Flowin?: The African American Migration Narrative*. New York: Oxford University Press, 1996.

Locke, Alain. "The New Negro" in *Norton Anthology of African American Literature*. Cambridge: Harvard University Press, 2004.

Ross, Marlon. *Manning the Race: Reforming Black in the Jim Crow Era*. New York: New York University Press, 2004.

Sundquist, Eric. *To Wake the Nations: Race in the Making of American Literature*. Cambridge: Harvard University Press, 1993.

Wallace, Maurice. *Construction the Black Masculine: Identity and Ideality in African American Men's Literature and Culture, 1775–1999*, Raleigh-Durham: Duke University Press, 2002.

CHAPTER 15

Motherhood, Martyrdom and Cultural Dichotomy in Charles W. Chesnutt's *The House Behind the Cedars*

B. Omega Moore

A theory with which many of us may agree is one based on the belief that our interpretations of works of art, including literary analyses, vary according to the mindsets we carry with us into the act of interpretation. From a personal perspective, my first reading of Charles W. Chesnutt's *The House Behind the Cedars* was when I was an undergraduate student in an American literature class. At that time, a perfunctory reading of the novel sufficed in order for me to write a paper on the characterization of "Rena" and get a respectable grade on it. A second reading, which occurred while I was a graduate student, found me eager to place this 1900 novel in the American literary canon, and to accept the compartmentalization of Chesnutt as a minor American author and as a major African American author.

At this present juncture of over a century after the centennial mark of the publication of *The House Behind the Cedars*, my interpretations of this book (which Chesnutt spent nearly a decade writing) are those of someone who no longer has a mother, a reality of the human condition in the lives of many others. Most importantly, however, is the fact that my earlier readings of the novel did not allow me this particular vantage point to analyze what is arguably the most complex of all human relationships — the one between a mother and her children. Just as Michelangelo depicted the quintessence of human sorrow and suffering when he sculpted the slain Christ lying lifeless in the arms of his mother in the Pietà, Chesnutt, in *The House Behind the*

Cedars, portrays Molly Walden as a long-suffering matriarch attempting to carry the sorrows of her biracial children.

Their most disturbing sorrows in life are brought on by the racially intolerant community in Patesville and beyond. Chesnutt's choice to name this character "Molly," a diminutive of "Mary," underscores the character's position in the narrative. Molly Walden's children, John and Rena, are cast in a world generally hostile to those who have what W.E.B. Du Bois calls "the red stain of bastardy" (218). The suffering of a martyr, consequently, is easily recognized in Molly Walden's character, as the third-person narrator relates early in the novel that John, who has chosen the name "Warwick," encounters a "coffin-maker not at all impressed by the melancholy suggestiveness of his task, whistling a lively air with gusto" (Chesnutt, 5). This image of John, the son of Molly, juxtaposed to the coffin-maker may be said to parallel the two worlds of the "Walden" children, who long to exit one world, of limitations and bigotry, to enter another world of privilege and power which they will "pass" into. As readers, we are drawn into a narrative dichotomy, or a separation of different or contradictory things, from that point onward in *The House Behind the Cedars.* We need not discuss any further the fixed image of the coffin itself, but surely we cannot ignore its foreshadowing the pall to be placed on the "house behind the cedars" when Rena dies upon being rejected by the same world she believed would grant her unlimited and unbiased opportunity.

One of the first images of Molly Walden is that of a distraught mother, emotionally overwhelmed by her fears for her children. She is, on the other hand, naturally compelled to protect them. When John returns to Patesville after a ten-year absence, Molly's thoughts are revealed. "She would have given all the world to warm her son's child upon her bosom, but she knew this could not be" (24). As his visibly black and secluded mother, Molly Walden was forbidden entry into the world her son had entered ten years earlier. Such contradictions continue and become more intense when Molly must part with Rena, who will serve as surrogate mother for John's child, who has lost his own mother. While it may come across as melodramatic to contemporary readers, Molly's reaction to John's request to have Rena join him is again characteristic of the long-suffering matriarch. Chesnutt's narrative voice states: "The mother looked from son to daughter with a dawning apprehension and a sudden pallor. When she saw the yearning in Rena's eyes, she threw herself at her son's feet" (24). Molly makes what may be considered the ultimate maternal sacrifice when she agrees that Rena should cross over into the world devoid of the caste system of color. By joining her brother, Rena will automatically sever ties with her mother. Sylvia Render points out that "Chesnutt must have known that going over to the other side demanded sacrifice" (90).

The story of John and Rena's departure from the black world into the white world is said to be one lifted from the Chesnutt family history. Although that history may have morphed into fiction as *The House Behind the Cedars,* it is almost tantamount to another historical record. There is a similarity between the two mothers, Mary and Molly, whose offspring are rejected and betrayed by those closest to them. George Tryon initially rejects Rowena Warwick/Rena Walden after an ill-fated meeting when he learns of her true ethnicity by happenstance: "Custom was tyranny. Love was the only law. Would God have made hearts to so yearn for one another if He had meant them to stay apart forever?" (292).

Another illustration of Molly Walden as the epitome of the suffering matriarch is evident in the series of letters she dictates to both John and Rena through Frank Fowler. The letter to Rena is a testament to the mystical connection between mother and child, a point made more salient by the recurrent dream Rena had had for three days that her mother had not been well. The letter reads in part, "'I should like to see you, but if it is the Lord's will that I shouldn't, I shall be thankful anyway that you have done what was best for yourselves and your children, and that I have given you up for your own good'" (94). Her letter to John also includes a reference to the Deity and a willingness to submit to that Deity. It reads as follows: "'Rena has had a heap of trouble on account of me and my sickness. If I could have dreamed that I was going to do so much harm, I would have died and gone to meet my God ... but I didn't know what was going to happen'" (149). Both letters include the closing, "'Your affectionate mother, Mary Walden'" (94, 152). Undoubtedly, Charles Chesnutt, master of name symbolism and creator of characters who are literally "the noise of their names," intended for readers to recall the name of another mother named Mary, arguably among the most esteemed mothers in human history.

Interestingly, it is another mother, Elizabeth Tryon, mother of George Tryon, Rena's white lover, who contributes to a meteoric rise of tension in the novel. It is Elizabeth who suggests that George go to Patesville to tend to some family legal matters. Because of this errand for his mother, George meets Rena in Patesville, an epiphanic event brought on unwittingly by his mother, completely oblivious to the fact that the errand would catapult her son into a downward spiral. The discovery of Rena's genealogy leaves George despondent and obviously crestfallen in the eyes of his mother.

Through an interior monologue, Mrs. Tryon's feelings are made clear: "It was Mrs. Tryon's turn to sigh and shed a clandestine tear. Until her son had gone away on this trip, he had kept no secrets from her: his heart had been an open book, of which she knew every page; now, some painful story was inscribed therein which he meant she should not read" (191). The connection between a mother and her child is again central to the flow of events in the narrative. The Waldens/Warwicks and the Tryons, despite their racial difference, are classic reminders of the universal dynamics in mother/child relationships.

While it is evident that Mrs. Tryon knew intuitively that George had suffered some type of emotional shock, she was unaware of its severity:

> His emotions were varied and stormy. At first, he could see nothing but the fraud of which he had been made a victim. A negro girl had been foisted upon him for a white woman, and he had almost committed the unpardonable sin against his race of marrying her ... the clock struck two ... he fell into an unquiet slumber and dreamed again of Rena. He dreamed of her sweet smile, her soft touch, her gentle voice. In all her fair young beauty, she stood before him, and then by some hellish magic, she was slowly transformed into a hideous black hag [146–47].

One instantly connects the significance of dreams in the lives of the main characters: Rena's dreams of her mother's ill health led her back to Patesville. Similarly, the nightmarish dream described above would lead George to Patesville, only under the most surreptitious plans. The unknowing mother, Elizabeth Tryon, tries to comfort her son. "She stroked his hot brow with her small, cool hand as he sat moodily nursing his grief" (190). The probing heart of a caring mother continues to lead her: "If she could have abdicated her empire to Blanche Leary [her choice of a wife for George] she would have yielded gracefully, but very palpably some other influence had driven joy from her son's countenance and lightness from his heart" (191).

The root causes of suffering in the two mothers are elucidated through a narrative commentary: "He was still fighting a battle in which a susceptible heart and a reasonable mind had locked horns in a well-nigh hopeless conflict ... the deep-rooted prejudices of race and caste commanded him to dismiss Rena from his thoughts. His stubborn heart simply would not let go" (192).

The House Behind the Cedars indeed mirrors the culture of its era, and befitting its postbellum setting, it still maintains an allegiance to antebellum customs. We are reminded by William Andrews in the introduction to the 1988 edition of *House* that Chesnutt thought that this novel should cause "some commotion" (vii). Though early critics generally believed there was little worthy of serious criticism in Chesnutt's novels, it should be noted that Chesnutt was aligned with the Victorian ideal of womanhood and motherhood when he wrote *The House Behind the Cedars*. Victorian ideals aside, Chesnutt also wrote during the period of American Realism. As such, the novel is typically critical of the blatant racial injustices of the day. In an article titled "Rena Walden: Chesnutt's Failed 'Future American,'" Sally Ann Ferguson

sums it up best: "The protagonist's white looks and boarding-school education are consistently undermined by stereotypical feminine and racial traits
that inhibit her progress" (quoted in McElrath, 204).

In *The Chesnutt Grapevine*, the newsletter of the Charles W. Chesnutt
Association, Thomas Cassidy writes in his review of *Mandy Oxendine*, "Charles
Chesnutt is experiencing a string of posthumous successes" (6). One is forced
to concur with the reviewer because the "commotion" of *House* continues, and
quite probably it will continue.

Molly Walden is given a heartache unparalleled in human grief when
Rena dies. Natural law usually follows a pattern in which parents precede their
children in death; however, natural law is disturbed as Molly is changed into
the mother of a martyred daughter by the conclusion. Rena's death was
brought on by her own fragile state, both physical and emotional after the
break from George Tryon. *The House Behind the Cedars* is a multi-faceted
example of social realism. The complex relationship between mothers and
their children in this novel is fractured by the dichotomy of the racial groups
in which those children are placed by the social order of the late nineteenth
century.

WORKS CITED

Cassidy, Thomas. Review of *Mandy Oxendine*. *The Chesnutt Grapevine: Newsletter of the
        Charles W. Chesnutt Association* 1.4 (Spring 2000).
Chesnutt, Charles W. *The House Behind the Cedars*, 1900. Introduction by William
        Andrews. Athens: University of Georgia Press, 1988.
Du Bois, W.E.B. *The Souls of Black Folk*, 1903. In *The Negro Classics*. Edited by Julius Lester.
        New York: Random House, 1971.
Ferguson, SallyAnn. "Rena Walden: Chesnutt's Failed 'Future American.'" In *Critical Essays
        on Charles W. Chesnutt*. Edited by Joseph L. McElrath, Jr. New York: G. K. Hall,
        1999. 198–205.
McElrath, Joseph L. Jr. *Critical Essays on Charles W. Chesnutt*. New York: G.K. Hall, 1999.
Render, Sylvia L. *Charles W. Chesnutt*. Boston: Twayne Publishers, 1980.

Epilogue: The Gifts of Ambiguity

Michelle Taylor

The Library of America is committed to publishing and preserving some of the nation's most important writings. The New York Times Book Review considers the Library of America as the "quasi-official national canon" of American literature. Each year, the Library of America adds new volumes to the list by collecting essential novels, stories, poetry, plays, and other writing. In February 2001, the organization published a volume of Chesnutt's work. *Charles W. Chesnutt: Stories, Novels, and Essays* is hailed as the largest and most comprehensive edition ever published, presenting for the first time the full range of his achievements as a writer and social critic. Included in this edition are "Po Sandy" and "The Goophered Grapevine," as well as the complete texts of *The House Behind the Cedars* and perhaps his most important novel, *The Marrow of Tradition*. As promised, this collection does indeed represent the very best of Chesnutt's work.

Seven years after Chesnutt's publication by the Library of America, the United States Postal Service honored Chesnutt with the 31st stamp in the Black Heritage Series. The postal service introduced the Black Heritage Series in 1978 to recognize the achievements of prominent African Americans. Past honorees have included Sojourner Truth, W.E.B. Du Bois, and Jackie Robinson. Literary honorees have included Zora Neale Hurston and Langston Hughes. Even in an era of electronic communication, the issuance of a new Black Heritage Stamp is an important moment for philatelists and scholars alike.

The image of Chesnutt that appears on the stamp is that of the concerned scholar, an image that many of us find both familiar and provocative. On the one hand, the image reminds us of the Chesnutt that we have read, studied, and taught. On the other hand, this image invites speculation about the quiet frustration of a man disturbed by a world stubbornly resistant to

219

change. And importantly, the image forces us to consider the meaning of Chesnutt's work and legacy. How does his work relate to the world in which we live? And how do we understand and interpret Chesnutt's literary and cultural gifts?

One way to begin to answer that question is to suggest that Chesnutt was far ahead of his time and that his acute attention to the vexed relationship among race, class, and progress is instructive for the sociopolitical atmosphere of the era in which we live. Indeed, his writings during the postbellum, pre–Harlem phase of his career indicate his growing impatience with an unjust world. In a letter to Booker T. Washington dated June 3, 1903, Chesnutt foregoes his usual dignified reserve and offers a forthright and "frank" analysis of black citizenship. Chesnutt writes, "Pardon my frankness; your letter invited it. I feel deeply on this subject. I want my rights and all of them, and I ask no more for myself than I would demand for every Negro in the South. If the white South will continue to ignore the Constitution and violate the laws, it must be with no consent of mine, and with no word that can be twisted into the approval or condonation of their unjust and unlawful course."[1] Ironically, many believed that Chesnutt disappeared during the years preceding the Harlem Renaissance; however, to the contrary, Chesnutt remained a crucial figure in the battle for equality and refashioned himself as an even more vocal advocate for justice and progress. The attentions generated by the Library of America publication, the postal service stamp, and this collection of essays will hopefully mark the beginning of a new era in Chesnutt studies.

In many ways, Chesnutt's moment is similar to the moment in which we live. When Chesnutt wrote *The Marrow of Tradition*, he reflected on what he believed to be a world gone mad. A world in which hatred, misunderstanding, and violence replaced honor, understanding, and peace. Dr. Miller's final words, "There's time enough, but none to spare," have special meaning if we fast forward to 2008, to a time when we are still haunted by the ghosts of slavery and the dark shadow of Jim Crow. My point is not to suggest that we run roughshod over centuries of progress and decades of change, but I do want to think about the extent to which Chesnutt's work in general, and *The Marrow of Tradition* in particular, intersect with some of the issues that impact this particular history-making moment in which we now find ourselves.

As many of the essays in this collection have argued, power, knowledge, class, and progress were key factors in Chesnutt's intellectual projects. And it is in *The Marrow of Tradition* that he brilliantly portrays the class issues at work in the black community through folk hero Josh Green and the learned Dr. Miller. It is through this relationship that we begin to see the need for the merger of action and intellect. Scholars have long debated the meanings of Josh's death and Dr. Miller's conciliatory efforts at the end of the novel and admittedly, there are no easy answers. Indeed, one might argue that the conclusion of *The Marrow of Tradition* is one of the most ambiguous in early African American literature. But one way in which we might make sense of the ending is to think about the ways in which this ambiguity is actually a blessing in disguise. The novel's end allows the reader, perhaps even forces the reader, to think, which is always the mark of a "powerful" novel and the goal of many writers. Readers have the opportunity to think about the relationship between action and intellect. We have the opportunity to think about protest and redemption. And finally, and perhaps most importantly, we as readers have the space to think about our individual and collective quests for progress and honor in a troubled world. This opportunity for introspective analysis is only one of the many gifts that Chesnutt has given us, and let us hope that our own interests will allow his gift to continue for generations of new readers.

NOTES

1. Charles Chesnutt, to Booker T. Washington, 27 June 1903 in *"To Be an Author": Letters of Charles Chesnutt, 1889–1905,* Joseph R. McElrath, Jr. and Robert C. Leitz, III, eds. Princeton: Princeton University Press: 181-2.

About the Contributors

Linda Belau is associate professor of English at the University of Texas-Pan American. She is the author of a number of articles on literary theory, particularly psychoanalytical theory and deconstruction and is co-editor of *Topologies of Trauma: Essays on the Limit of Knowledge and Experience*. She is currently completing a book entitled *Encountering Jouissance: Trauma, Psychosis, Psychoanalysis*.

Christopher Bundrick completed his doctorate in 2006. He is an instructional assistant professor at the University of Mississippi in Oxford, Mississippi.

Ed Cameron is assistant professor of English at the University of Texas-Pan American. He has written numerous articles on topics ranging from Gothic literature and psychoanalysis to serial homicide and religious cults. He is currently finishing a book on sublimation in the Gothic novel.

Wiley Cash is an assistant professor of American literature and fiction writing at Bethany College in West Virginia. His short fiction and essays have appeared in *Crab Orchard Review, American Literary Realism, Thomas Wolfe Review, Roanoke Review, South Carolina Review*, and other publications. He is co-editor of the forthcoming book *"This Louisiana Thing That Drives Me": The Legacy of Ernest J. Gaines*. He is at work on two projects: a novel set in Madison County, North Carolina, and a book on the portrayal of North Carolina in the literature of Charles W. Chesnutt and Thomas Wolfe. A native of western North Carolina, he received his Ph.D. in English at the University of Louisiana at Lafayette in 2008.

Willie J. Harrell, Jr. is assistant professor of English at Kent State University, where he teaches graduate and undergraduate courses in African American literature. His most recent work has appeared in *CLA Journal, Canadian Review of American Studies* and *The Encyclopedia of African-American Folklore*. He is editor of *We Wear the Mask: Paul Laurence Dunbar and the Politics of Representative Reality*, forthcoming from Kent State University Press.

Julie Iromuanya is a Ph.D. student in English at the University of Nebraska-Lincoln. She specializes in creative writing and ethnic literature. Her research interests include ethnic humor, cinema, and immigration and diaspora studies. She is currently working on a novel and short story collection.

David Garrett Izzo is a writer of fiction and drama as well as a scholar of modern British and American literature, with numerous books and articles of literary criticism, literary philosophy, literary biography, and literary history. (See www.davidgarrettizzo.com.)

Kim Kirkpatrick is assistant professor of English at Fayetteville State University in North Carolina where she teaches literature, writing, and women's and gender studies. She attended Washington University in St. Louis, the University of Cincinnati, and Saint Louis University. Her interests include feminist science fiction literature, film, and television. She has written on Golden Age science fiction, cyperpunk, and Buffy the Vampire Slayer.

Tiel Lundy is an instructor of English at the University of Colorado Denver, where she teaches American literature with a special emphasis on ethnic literatures. Her work also includes film studies.

B. Omega Moore is a professor at Savannah State University in Georgia.

Coleman C. Myron has a Ph.D. in English literature from Duquesne University. His interests include British and African American literature, distance education, and creative writing. His current project is an electronic Old English dictionary.

Maria Orban is assistant professor of English at Fayetteville State University in North Carolina.

Gregory E. Rutledge teaches African-American literature at the University of Nebraska–Lincoln. He earned his Ph.D. in English literature from the University of Madison–Wisconsin (2005), where he also earned an M.A. from the Afro-American Studies Department (1999). His present projects include *The Epic Trickster: From Sunjata to So(u)l*, a study of the trans–Atlantic (dis)continuity of the traditional African epic, and an historical novel, *Whispers of a Fire in the Forest*. He has published literary criticism, law review articles, fiction, review essays, and photography in various legal and literary journals. This essay, from *The Epic Trickster*, draws upon Dr. Rutledge's legal training; in 1992 he received his J.D./M.A.M.C. from the University of Florida.

Tyrie J. Smith is a folklorist and an assistant professor of the humanities at Abraham Baldwin Agricultural College in Tifton, Georgia. He received his Ph.D. in folklore from the University of Louisiana in Lafayette. Smith's research interests focus on the relationship between folk tradition and literature. Smith is also active as a public folklorist, coordinating the Georgia Folklife Festival and working with traditional artists throughout the state.

Michelle Taylor is a professor at Miami University (Ohio).

Zoe Trodd is on the Tutorial Board in the History and Literature Department at Harvard University, where she lectures on American protest literature. Her books include *Meteor of War: The John Brown Story* (Blackwell, 2004), *American Protest Literature* (Harvard University Press, 2006), *To Plead Our Own Cause: Narratives of Modern Slavery* (Cornell University Press, 2007), and *The Long Civil Rights Movement* (Bruccoli Clark Layman, 2007). She has also published numerous articles on American literature, history and visual culture.

Cynthia Wachtell, assistant professor of English at Stern College of Yeshiva University and director of the S. Daniel Abraham Honors Program, holds a Ph.D. in the history of American civilization from Harvard University. She is completing a study, *War No More: American War Literature from the Civil War through World War I*, and has published essays on subjects ranging from Herman Melville to *Four Lights*, a publication of the Women's Peace Party of New York.

Index